SEXUAL DREAMS

OTHER BOOKS BY GAYLE DELANEY

LIVING YOUR DREAMS

BREAKTHROUGH DREAMING: HOW TO TAP THE POWER OF
YOUR 24-HOUR MIND

NEW DIRECTIONS IN DREAM INTERPRETATION (EDITOR)

SEXUAL DREAMS

Why We Have Them, What They Mean

DR. GAYLE DELANEY

FAWCETT COLUMBINE
New York

A Fawcett Columbine Book
Published by Ballantine Books
Copyright © 1994 by Gayle Delaney

Grateful acknowledgment is made to Bantam Books, a division of Bantam
Doubleday Dell Publishing Group, Inc., for permission to reprint excerpts
from Breakthrough Dreaming by Gayle Delaney.

Library of Congress Catalog Card Number: 93-90452
ISBN: 0-449-90901-8

Text design by Ruth Kolbert

Manufactured in the United States of America
First Edition: March 1994
10 9 8 7 6 5 4 3 2

To Jan M. Edelstein,
faithful friend, lawyer, leader, and advocate
for cleaning up our country's environment.
Thank you for all you have done
for me and for all of us.

CONTENTS

ACKNOWLEDGMENTS

Thank you, Dr. Bill Domhoff, for sharing with me your survey on the sexual dreams of students at the University of California at Santa Cruz. Drs. Johanna King and Jacqueline Sheenan, your comments on the chapter about the dreams of the sexually abused are gratefully acknowledged. Thank you, Dr. Joe Natterson, for your thoughtful comments, references, and comments. Dr. Donato Dino Cafaro, director of the European School of Training in Psychosexology and of the Association for the Study of Psychoanalysis and Research in Sexology in Rome, our association has enriched this book and delighted my Italophile heart. Bruce Flath, librarian of the California Institute of Integral Studies, your help in locating obscure articles was invaluable. Thank you, Korje Guttormsen and Mary Hall of The Depot, our fairy-tale bookstore and café in Mill Valley, for your support of local writers like myself. Cara Bechenstein, your suggestions have not been forgotten. Linda Mihaly, having you as a neighbor and as a dauntless first draft editor is a double blessing.

Dr. Steve Walsh, thank you for your understanding of this writer's needs and for all the spaghetti vongole and tiramisu. Thank you again, Virginia Allison, for your support, enthusiasm and wisdom, and for your hospitality that allowed me to once again mix writing with ice skating in Sun Valley. Dr. Loma Flowers, my colleague and precious friend, your careful commentary, suggestions, exasperations, and witticisms were wonderful, really wonderful. And thank you again, Bill Delaney, for being a father of such good cheer whose love and support brighten the foggiest days in San Francisco.

My thanks to all of you who have shared your dreams with me. Whether or not you find your dreams in this book, know that they are in my heart and that they continue to teach me as I review them over the years. Each one is important and I wish I could tell them all.

SEXUAL DREAMS

Introduction

THIS IS A PRACTICAL BOOK ABOUT SEXUAL DREAMS. IT IS about those exhilarating, tantalizing, puzzling, embarrassing, and troubling sexual dreams we all have and rarely talk about to anyone. This book is about how you can understand your erotic dreams and use them to create a healthier, more fulfilling sexual life. Your dreams can help you do this because you are much more honest with yourself when you dream than when you are awake. When you dream, you look at your life from a wiser, less defensive, more mature perspective. The picture language you think in while you sleep can tell you exactly what you need to know about yourself and your relationships when you most need to know it; that is, now, rather than later, after so much time has passed that hindsight is your only comfort. As you work with your dreams you will find that they are usually several steps ahead of your waking self in the degree and quality of insight they offer. The greater openness of your mind in sleep can give you access to clearer perceptions and understanding months and even years before you might arrive at them through waking life experience alone.

To demonstrate the insightfulness of your mind in sleep I will not be taking your dreams and force-fitting them into an elaborate psychosexual theory. Sexual dreams too often have been subject to arbitrary interpretations that do more to bolster an analyst's authority than to assist dreamers in better understanding their sexuality. Stereotypical notions about the nature of males and females that define women as more passive and receptive and men as more aggressive and creative, and so on, have held dream interpretation hostage to patriarchal prejudices that, sometimes blatantly, sometimes almost invisibly, severely limit our understanding. As some contemporary scholars such as Carol Gilligan, Jessica Benjamin, and Louise Kaplan have argued, our societies have developed beliefs about the natures of maleness and femaleness that rob both men and women of a great deal of their sexual and relational potential.

Translated into dream interpretations, these beliefs frequently have led analysts to interpret a dream according to a set of a priori beliefs about what certain images mean for male or female dreamers, and to value certain qualities such as tenderness or assertiveness as more natural to one sex than the other. If we suspend at least some of our personal or theoretical prejudices about just what constitutes a sexual dream image, about just what constitutes maleness or femaleness, and about how the male and female psyches are constructed, we can far more effectively listen to what a specific dreamer or our own dream is telling us today in our own time and microculture. By learning to look into the dream itself, rather than to traditional formulations, we will be less likely arbitrarily to read sex into a dream, to miss the direct sexual information revealed in some manifestly sexual dreams, and to undervalue the rich metaphoric nature of much sexual imagery that portrays how a dreamer feels in other areas of his or her life.

I have developed a practical method of dream interpretation called Dream Interviewing, which will help you connect directly to your private dream language without sending you out of your way for a theoretical indoctrination. This method will enable you to see how the images in your dreams are metaphors that shed new light on the things that are important to you in your daily life. By learning to interview yourself about your dream experiences, you will learn to explore and use your sexual dreams to recognize and work through misconceptions, fears, and inhibitions that limit your freedom to live passionately your sexual, interpersonal, and creative lives. You will learn to grasp the insights and take advantage of the new ideas you present to yourself in your sleep.

Our sexual dreams fascinate us. Sometimes they embarrass and sometimes they delight us. They can even be very frightening.

Dream lovers can evoke sensuous, sexual euphorias that remind us of the best sexual experiences of our past or that strikingly inform us of what we are missing and of what we are capable. Such dreams do not come to us out of the blue. We dream them at particular times in our lives and they can serve us very well indeed if we can learn to understand them. A number of our apparently nonsexual dreams do, in fact, deal with sexual issues. We needn't assume that such dreams are trying to hide their sexual themes. If instead we look at them as presenting sexual themes from new perspectives, we can better appreciate and take advantage of the enriching and meaningful metaphoric language of dreaming.

For example, Michael dreamt of taking a piano lesson in which he was instructed by his teacher not to "storm" the keys but to caress them and to treat the piano as an exquisitely sensitive instrument that would then produce beautiful music. After describing the imagery and feelings in this dream, Michael was reminded that his wife had recently said she felt more like a strategic military site that he stormed during sex than like the sensual but delicate sexual being she felt herself to be. Michael knew consciously that his wife longed for and had asked for a slower, more sensitive touch, but, for a variety of reasons, he had resisted giving this to her.

The wonderful thing about dreams is their ability to furnish us with a moving firsthand experience. Michael's dream gave him the *experience* of wanting to emulate the master by learning to touch the piano with more sophistication and finesse. At last Michael felt his own desire to touch his wife like a maestro rather than like a charging soldier conquering a hill.

Our dreams can show us how to live fuller sexual lives by showing us graphically our restricting attitudes, our conflicts, and our potential. Ilena had been troubled for years by her boyfriend's requests that she engage in fellatio. Putting a penis in her mouth turned her off and made her gag. She felt obliged and coerced and, of course, very resistant, even though she often acquiesced to his demands. Yet she was curious to know how any woman could enjoy such a thing. Since she really wanted to explore this problem, I taught her how to ask for, or "incubate," a series of dreams.

Incubating a dream, or suggesting to yourself that you will have a dream about a particular topic on a given night, is quite easy to do. Briefly, I instructed Ilena to write down on a piece of paper a one-line request for insight on her "problem" and then to go to sleep repeating her incubation question over and over as she fell asleep.

Before sleep one night, Ilena wrote the following question in her dream journal: "Is there any way I could actually enjoy fellatio?" Ilena dreamt that she was naked with a man in a beautiful satin-and-lace bedroom. He lay on his back and asked, "Would you do this for me?" She knew what he meant, but for the first time she felt no obligation. She knew beyond any doubt that her lover would still care for her even if she refused. Gone were her old feelings of resentment at such a demand. Instead she felt playful and desirous of giving her lover this pleasure. Very slowly she began to lick his penis as if it were a sweet lollipop! After tracing every ridge and curve with her tongue, she decided to put just the head of her dream lover's penis in her mouth. His sighs of pleasure delighted her. She felt no need to gag. On the contrary, she basked in the pleasure of being able to give pleasure. From that dream on, Ilena began to savor what had once been so distasteful to her.

Typical of good dream work, Ilena's dreams helped her understand the conflict (that is, her fear of loosing affection if she said no) that lay behind some of her feelings of coercion and distaste for fellatio. Then her dreams gave her a firsthand experience of enjoying fellatio and offered her the chance to improve her relationship both by better defining her boundaries and by developing and trying out a new set of attitudes and behaviors. Your dreaming mind is not content just to treat a symptom, but consistently will lead you to explore the reasons behind the apparent problem. Once you understand the origin of a symptom or conflict, you are in the best position to design a fundamentally sound strategy for finding a satisfying solution.

While dreaming, we seem to enter a metaphorical mode of perception and expression that is less defensive, more open, and more synthetic than our waking mode. In our dreams we employ these enhanced abilities to review the concerns of the preceding day from a perspective that draws upon our entire life history. Our sexual dreams offer us the opportunity to look directly at our innermost sexual feelings with a maturity and immediacy seldom equaled when we are awake.

Our sexual dreams are generally quite different from our sexual fantasies in several ways. Our sexual fantasies are usually erotically exciting, they unfold in a predictable manner, and they follow a fairly uncomplicated story line. Our sexual dreams, on the other hand, are sometimes not at all erotically exciting; there are usually all sorts of surprises, interruptions, and twists in the plots; and the story lines can be very complex indeed. Most of us call up sexual fantasies to turn us on, whereas our dreams come unbidden and sometimes shock the daylights out of us. We can identify some of our sexual conflicts by asking ourselves if a given fantasy relieves us of some inhibiting guilt or shame. Thus, one of my clients' fantasy of being forced to have sex in front of a group of handsome firemen served to relieve her of her guilt at being desirous of sexual satisfaction since she couldn't help herself. It also gave her a sense of expanded time in which she could work up to orgasm since she imagined that each handsome fireman would have sex with her until she climaxed so she did not feel rushed as she often does in waking life. Such a fantasy can be highly pleasurable, but a dream of being forced to have sex is rarely, if ever, pleasurable. In most cases, sexual dreams are more complex than fantasies in that they explore, and assess the existence and causes of, sexual or emotional conflict. As you will see in later chapters, dreams of being coerced to have sex often signal deep conflict, guilt, and sometimes sexual abuse. Our dreams tell a story in pictures about how we feel about our sexuality and about our sexual relationships. They go much further than fantasies; they show us when we are in trouble, how we got there, and they give us the understanding to work our way out of our difficulties.

Because the students at our dream center and the clients in my dream consultation practice are largely heterosexual, I have not worked with enough sexual dreams of lesbians and homosexuals to say very much about them with much confidence. Therefore I have decided to organize this book around the sexual dreams of heterosexuals, with which I have a good deal of experience. I would like to note, however, that the dreams of homosexuals with whom I have worked do not seem to differ markedly from those of heterosexuals except in the predictably greater frequency of the appearance of a partner of the same sex. Both heterosexuals and homosexuals dream of having sex with same and opposite sex partners, both groups dream of being naked in public, of being interrupted while having sex, of having sex with surprising and famous lovers, and of being terribly in love in romantic sexual dreams. Both groups use sexual dreams to explore sexual and nonsexual conflicts, and both tend to be upset if they dream about sex with someone who is not of their sexual orientation.

In part one of this book we shall look at sexual passions as they manifest themselves in women's and men's sexual dreams. We shall discuss what each sex can learn from understanding the erotic dreams of the opposite sex. You will see that from the beginning I have used a sexual vocabulary that includes many levels: the polite, the clinical, the graphic, the vulgar, and the everyday. When I tell a client's dream, or quote a client, I use the words he or she used. In discussing various issues in the text, I use whatever level seems the most appropriate. If you take note of your responses to the words used to describe sexual organs and acts, you may learn something about your own levels of comfort or discomfort in thinking, reading, and talking about the nitty-gritty of sex. Most of my clients, my friends and I, and most of my professional colleagues, feel awkward talking graphically about sex. Some words seem too clinical, some too vulgar. I hope this book will encourage you to work out your own sexual vocabulary and to use it to write out your sexual dreams and to talk about sexual issues with your friends as well as with your lover.

One simple reason most of us lead constricted sexual lives is that we don't know how to talk about what we want and need, so we don't learn much from more experienced friends and we don't communicate well with our lovers.

In this section we will look at what research studies have revealed about how men's and women's dreams differed thirty years ago and how they compare today after so many developments in the women's movement and the sexual revolution.

Next, we shall explore common sexual dreams and how to interpret them so that you will learn how to tell when your symbolic dreams concern sexual issues and when they are dealing with other aspects of your life. I will show you how to use the Dream Interview method of dream interpretation, and illustrate it with dreams from clients in my private practice and from students at the Delaney & Flowers Dream Center. [1]

In this section, we will also consider those surprisingly practical and welcome dreams that actually teach us a new or improved sexual technique. In the last part of this section, you will learn how to incubate or target your dream problem-solving abilities to better understand and resolve the uncomfortable, problematic, or undeveloped parts of your sexuality.

Part two, "Intimate Passions," will explore how your sexual dreams can help you recognize and take action to remove your blocks to intimacy with your partner. Just as in waking sex, dream sex usually reflects how we feel inside and how we are really (not ideally) connected to our partners. If you dream that your wife scorns your penis, it is probably time for you to look at your dawning awareness that she scorns you in important ways you have not fully recognized. You wouldn't have such a dream if you had already successfully worked out the issue between you. It is almost impossible to have consistently good sex without establishing a trusting intimacy and working communication.

In an important chapter on the dreams of adults who were sexually abused as children we shall explore typical patterns in these disturbing dreams that many of us (including therapists) often fail to recognize as warning signals of childhood abuse and sometimes of more recent abuse from unethical therapists.

We will then focus on how you can turn your dreams and

nightmares into powerful allies in breaking out of limiting patterns of belief and behavior, and thus freeing you to enjoy a less conflicted sexual life and a richer intimacy with your lover.

Part three, "Creative Passions," will explore the connection between sexuality and creativity. Does the quality of your sex life have anything to do with your creativity? Some people can often be more productive during periods of abstinence or quiescence. Others insist that their creativity is enhanced when they are having satisfying sexual relations. Since the importance of sexuality varies greatly between individuals and fluctuates over the span of an individual lifetime, this connection is not always a strong one. In fact, a number of people see no relation between their sexual and creative activities. Yet some people who have underestimated the importance of their sexuality have been delightfully surprised to discover that their dreams can help them to tap unsuspected reservoirs of creativity as well as of sexuality. We will consider the possibility that unblocking ourselves in one area could unleash new, happier, and less pressured energy in the other.

In the appendix I shall invite you to participate in a study on sexual dreams that my colleague, Dr. Loma Flowers, and I are conducting at the Delaney & Flowers Dream and Consultation Center. Whether or not you choose to participate, filling out this questionnaire will assist you in appreciating and studying your own sexual dream life.

The resources section will provide you with information on videos, books, and organizations that I have found especially helpful. There you will also find a description of the dream study center that Loma Flowers, M.D., and I direct in San Francisco.

PART ONE

SEXUAL PASSIONS

CHAPTER

1

Women's Sexual Dreams and What Men Need to Know About Them

I am in bed in my own room. I know my eyes are closed. Up and down my body I feel an electrical sort of sensation. I say to myself, "Oh, he's back." I know I am going to have a sexual sensation like others I have had before. I look forward to it. I know I am dreaming. I am lying on my back. Soon I feel the sensation of cunnilingus. I do not see my lover, but I sense his presence. I feel as if I'm waking up. I tell myself that I'm going to stay asleep dreaming this. Again I start to wake. I say no, I'm going to finish this dream. Then I dream to orgasm. When I awaken, the sensations are fresh in my mind and body.

FOR NEARLY TWENTY YEARS I HAVE BEEN LISTENING TO dreams like Felicia's above and calling it work! Women have told me about their sexual dreams most often in my office during individual or small group dream sessions. Students of the Delaney & Flowers Dream Center who have come from various states and countries to study with Dr. Flowers and me over the last decade have told us about their erotic dreams. Then there are those daring women who have described their sexual dreams to me in modest detail over the radio, in lecture halls, and on live television.

Because my entire practice is devoted to teaching people how

13

to understand their dreams and use them for practical problem solving, I have had the occasion to work with thousands of dreamers—some only one or two times, and others for periods of several months to several years. Felicia's openness in describing her sexual dreams is quite rare and utterly refreshing. In all the years and variety of my practice, again and again I have been struck by the embarrassment and hesitancy most dreamers, both men and women, feel when it comes to recounting an obviously sexual dream.

How many of your own sexual dreams have you allowed yourself to remember, or to write out, or to recount to a friend in vivid, graphic detail? How did you feel while doing it? I have enjoyed working with many people's sexual dreams, and I generally delight in my own. But at times, I, too, still feel shy when recording them or telling them to a friend. This pervasive social awkwardness and shyness about sexual matters inevitably affects the results of the few surveys that have been completed because the subjects who are willing to respond to interviews and have allowed themselves to recall erotic dreams still tend to withhold delicate material.

To illustrate, for years, one of the most generally accepted notions about the differences between the dreams of men and women is that men's dreams have more manifest (frank) sexual content or imagery than do women's dreams. This was one of many findings reported in a classic 1966 landmark study by Hall and Van de Castle, who analyzed the frequency of various dream images and actions in 1,000 dreams recorded at home by 200 college students.[1] In 1978 a University of Arizona study indicated that this finding might have been biased by the fact that both males and females in the study had given their dreams to a male class instructor or had been interviewed by males. When the Arizona team conducted a study on the dream content of thirty female and thirty male undergraduates, both males and females did the interviewing. These researchers found that same-sex student-interviewer pairing resulted in increased reports of sexual content, and: "Overall, the dreams reported by male and female subjects did not differ in either the intensity or degree of sexual content."[2] Another study, by Paul R. Robbins and his colleagues, analyzed the frequency of manifest sexual content in the dreams of 123 undergraduates at George Washington University. They, too, found no significant differences between the men's and women's dreams in this area even though the questionnaires were apparently collected by male instructors. [3]

The Benefits of Overcoming Shyness

Overcoming our reticence to explore sexual dreams can bring tremendous rewards. While dreaming, we blurt out the truth about how we really feel and think about the most important issues in our lives. In dreams' visual imagery, sometimes literal, sometimes metaphorical, we try to figure things out by looking at how our current experience relates to our entire history of life experience. Our dreams about sexual matters offer us the chance to understand the effects of early conditioning and current conflicts in our sexual lives. Erotic dreams can also show us what we really want, what we have been missing, and what we may already have without realizing it.

By refusing to be open about sexual matters, we forfeit many opportunities to shed encumbering fears and misconceptions and we cooperate in creating a social atmosphere of secrecy and shame that not only limits our enjoyment but actually encourages the development of destructive sexual behavior. The terrible secrets of incest and rape are hardest to reveal in a society that discourages open discussion of sexuality.

Coming to terms with our sexual realities is a more important task than it may at first appear. All the joking, prudery, and steamy media presentations of the subject often camouflage and oversimplify the harsher truths about sex. Most people still act as if only other people can be killed, or infected with chronic disease, or rendered forever contagious by sexual encounters. Sane people can act crazy when it comes to sex. Intelligent, assertive, and brave people act like timid wimps when it comes to talking about protecting themselves from disease or foolish emotional risks in sexual relationships. Honest people lie about their sexual health and behavior. Good people break hearts and break up marriages and families for dimly understood sexual discontents and attractions.

Working with your sexual dreams gives you direct access to the complex structure (the motherboard!) of past experience, beliefs, attitudes, and feelings that determine how you feel about yourself, your sexuality, and how you choose and relate to your sexual partners. The first step in tapping into this valuable resource is to increase your comfort in thinking and talking about sexual dreaming.

As you read the dreams of my clients and those collected in questionnaires completed by my lecture audiences,[4] you will probably be reminded of several of your own sexual dreams. If you jot down a few notes about them, you will have them at hand when you read chapters three and four, on surveying and interpreting your own sexual dreams.

FAVORITE SEXUAL DREAMS

As a student from the University of California at Santa Cruz wrote: "Sexual dreams are wonderful. They are free and easy and feel wonderful. No pregnancy can result, no guilt for cheating, no diseases can be transmitted, and they are somewhat satisfying." How's that for a look at the sunny side of erotic dreams?

Your pleasant sexual dreams can introduce you to new levels of sexual pleasure and help you liberate yourself from unnecessary inhibitions. They can remind you of a sexual vitality you may have let wither, and they can use the metaphor of a vibrant, unconflicted sexuality to trigger or announce new emotional or artistic growth. Welcome your delicious sexual dreams, record them, enjoy the pleasure they offer, and ask yourself if they signal new developments in your life.

Former Lovers

One of the favorite dreams enjoyed by women is that of a meeting with a former boyfriend, often the greatest love and/or lover of the dreamer's life:

After all these years, Leo is there, across the street. We are in Vienna in the fall. We meet, we kiss. We are in a beautiful hotel suite. Not a word is spoken. He caresses and kisses me everywhere. He enters me and I remember what it is to love and be loved passionately. Somewhere a Mozart horn concerto is playing.

Or,

I have a chance encounter with an old boyfriend, a great lover, that includes a romantic dinner, catching up with each other's lives, and my being swept up and carried off to bed.

Or,

I have a reunion with a former highly intelligent, very insightful, very virile lover. The scene is not heavily sexual, but we are profoundly connected and very turned on.

Or,

I had a week of spectacular sexual dreams that built in intensity. The coup de grace was one in which the focus was on an incredible feeling of very loving, very intense physical contact with my old boyfriend more than on the specifics of what we were actually doing with each other or where we were.

Romance

The emphasis on romance and emotional connection over explicit sexual acts in pleasurable sexual dreams is very common among women. Often women describe the sexual acts almost in passing as they move into a rich and enthusiastic description of a sweet intimacy or of a feeling of being deeply understood, accepted, or loved. Many women have told me of feeling loved in dreams in ways and to depths they have never known in waking life. Sometimes these dreams help their dreamers to recognize something they have been missing, something they have not known how to create in their lives, something they may not have felt capable of giving, or worthy of receiving, in their relationships. As you can see, even your sweetest dreams should not be written off as mere wish fulfillments. You can use these dreams as beacons that offer you some assistance, even inspiration, on your way to a fuller life.

Bill Domhoff, a professor of sociology at the University of California at Santa Cruz, has collected questionnaires on the sexual dreams of 273 students.[5] These undergraduates are twenty to thirty years younger than most of my clients and lecture attendees, nevertheless, their dreams seem to follow a number of similar patterns. For example, the next two dreams emphasize the beauty of the surroundings and of the feelings of tenderness and eroticism over the specific acts involved.

> My current lover and I were walking together in the woods and came to a beautiful lake. We swam together in an extremely erotic way. An old couple appeared on the shore and invited us to dinner. My mother was there and we ate until we were completely satisfied.

In responding to Domhoff's request to describe her most striking or memorable erotic dream, another student wrote:

> Before I actually became lovers with my now husband, I had [an erotic] dream about him. It was especially memorable because there was so much tenderness mixed in with the passion and erotic content.

Theresa, a fifty-year-old client of mine, dreamt,

> I was in bed with Jim. We were making love, and I felt the most exquisite openness within myself. I held back nothing, was willing to risk my entire emotional nakedness. I could be intimate for the first time in my life. Jim was

inside me and I felt the joy of surrender which had nothing to do with submission, rather with my radical willingness to let go of my self-protection, of my reservations, of my fear of loss of self. I felt entirely secure that I could lose myself and yet not threaten in any way the integrity of my being. This was the most erotic experience of my life.

Specific Acts

Specific acts are more commonly described in recountings of uncomfortable sexual dreams, although they do appear in some women's favorite ones:

> A young man with a huge hard penis is lying on a bed in a three-sided room. The fourth side is open to the world. We make love. I'm on top, and enjoy it greatly. We climax, and I relax on top of him. A moment later he says, "That's not enough for me." So we do it again, with even more pleasure.

Or,

> I am with a former lover, the best. He loves to love my body. He loves to have me love his. We are two extreme sensualists. I kiss and lick and suck his penis and suddenly his lips are everywhere, his hands are caressing me all over. I have several orgasms as he puts his fingers inside me, then his penis. We roll over and over and it goes on and on. I wake up feeling both incredibly satisfied and turned on.

A woman in the undergraduate survey dreamt:

> I was being kissed and sucked all over by a man I've lusted after for years. We made love for hours in all different kinds of positions I'd never tried before!

Sensitive, Tuned-in Lovers

The frequency with which women describe the deliciousness of being with a lover who takes great pleasure in pleasuring them is striking. When they talk about these dream lovers they contrast them to other lovers who engage in foreplay thinking it quite different from "the sex act" and who treat it more as fore-*work,* or forechores,[6] as the price of admission to the woman's vagina. Most women complain that it is not much of a turn-on to be fondled by a man who is just putting in his time to get her sufficiently aroused, or who is doing her a favor or meeting her demands, or who is really going at it in order to demonstrate what a skilled lover he is. Sometimes, a woman who has Mr. Try-ing-to-be-Patient, Mr. Dutiful, or Stud for a partner is able to tell him about a great lover dream and help him understand that if he could identify with her pleasure, they would both have a lot more fun.

Taking the Initiative

Dreams in which the woman is in control can be both satisfy-ing and confidence building. Many women would like to take a more active role in lovemaking but hesitate because they are shy or because they fear or know that their male partners would not welcome their direction. Dreams in which the woman takes the initiative can help her become more aware of her own sexual desire, and this can greatly enhance her sexuality. Sometimes these dreams serve as metaphors for the woman's desire to take more control of her life in general and of her relationships.

> My boyfriend and I were making love. It was very erotic and sensual. It was I who promoted the activity. I was very much involved and in control. I was confident of my sensu-ality and my lovemaking ability.

> There was this guy I was desperately in love with, and *very* sexually attracted to. I found him in a garage. I pulled down his pants slowly and brought him nearly to climax

with oral sex. Then we had wild intercourse on a desk in the garage till we were both ecstatic.

I went to a place with my mother and her best friend where we had intercourse with male prostitutes, one after the other. I was lost, and before my turn came I was in a corridor from which I could hear but not see. This was the most exciting part. I felt that my orgasms would be extremely intense since the men were "professionals," and since I was excited, and in a brothel with my mom.

Forceful Men

Dreams of being slightly coerced by one or several men are not unusual. Here are three:

A number of men from college or work forced all the women to undress except for our undies and stand in front of them. They rated us and I won. I was the epitome of erotic women. Now, believe it or not, every time I buy underwear, I make sure it is silky and sexy. Not that I ever would want the dream to happen, but just in case . . . I'm ready!

I was in a room with more than one man. All of them were sexually caressing my body. Although I felt a little uncomfortable with the situation, I was overcome by sexual pleasure.

In waking life, I was lying in my boyfriend's truck at about three-thirty in the morning because he needed to stop somewhere before we went to my house. I fell asleep in his truck for about twenty minutes and had this dream: Two of the guys who work with my boyfriend came over to the truck and performed what I call cunnilingus on me. I was in heaven. Naturally I can't truly imagine even wanting that to actually happen, but in dreams it is great and safe!

While some women dream of enjoying being made love to forcefully or of being originally somewhat coerced, dreams of being raped or violently coerced into sexual activities are more often considered nightmares.

This is one of the ways that sexual dreams differ from sexual fantasies. A woman can enjoy being utterly coerced to have sex with one or more unsavory men in fantasy. Such fantasies often serve to titillate the woman's sense of danger, and they can also serve to relieve her guilt about wanting sex, which can inhibit her sexual enjoyment. The dream experience of such a scene, however, is entirely different. The dreamer usually feels all the anxiety and terror that one might feel if caught in such a waking experience. This sort of dream functions to express great conflict and fear, and the dreamer is not turned on but terrified.

Plenty of Time

Time is another important, if subtle, element in many women's pleasant sexual dreams. Not surprisingly, I have rarely heard a woman tell me that she was having great sex in a rush. Except for the rarely reported erotic dream quickie, dreams of unrushed pleasures seem to liberate many women from waking pressures to hurry and "achieve" an orgasm in five to fifteen minutes—before her partner runs out of patience, loses his erection, or the children wake up. While these dreams sometimes highlight via contrast the shortcomings of a lover, or of a couple's sexual timing and styles, sometimes they help the dreamer see that she has to liberate herself from her self-imposed need to rush, to please, and learn how to take her own sweet time.

Kathleen dreamt an antidote to her orgasm-retardant anxiety one night after a miserable lovemaking session with her very sexy and sexually adept husband.

I was in a very pretty bedroom of white lace and flowers. Five handsome men who in the dream were clearly kind and with whom I was safe were explaining to me that they would make love to me as long as I wanted. I needn't rush anything. They would see to it that I had an orgasm if it took all night. In fact, they almost insisted that I let them do this in a rather coercive but friendly way. I was aroused and delighted at the prospect. I could have got out of it if I had made a big fuss, but I was glad to cooperate.

Upon awakening, sexually conservative Kathleen felt lusciously naughty and had created a fantasy she thereafter used to help her relax by pretending she had all the time in the world to reach orgasm.

Famous or Unknown Dream Lovers

Dreaming of kissing or of having sex with famous people can be a very satisfying way to spend an evening. Some women dream encounters with men such as Warren Beatty, Richard Gere, Nick Nolte, Robert Redford, Placido Domingo, Denzel Washington, or Tom Cruise. Others only very rarely dream of their favorite romantic male hero.

Dreams of having sex with unknown attractive men is high on some women's list of favorite sexual dreams. In fact, one respondent wrote: "Sometimes I make love with people I know. Then I feel guilty about it when I awake. But if I do it with people I don't know, that's just fine!" As you will see in chapter four, the interpretation of sexual dream encounters with famous or with entirely unknown men depends upon ascertaining what the dreamer thinks and feels about the dream lover. If the dreamer has learned to resist jumping to conclusions and first gives a good description of the famous or unknown dream lover, she often discovers his looks and demeanor, or his apparent personality style, remind her of someone or of some important issue in her life. At other times she discovers that the attractive famous dream lover acts as a nocturnal ego boost—the fulfillment of a wish to be found desirable by such a man.

Women with Women

Heterosexual women are often surprised to recall dreams of making love with other women. Here are a few from the Santa Cruz women:

> Although I consider myself an exclusively heterosexual woman, my last erotic dream was with another woman. She was older and proceeded to touch me throughout the dream. Although there was no sex, the eroticism was in her looks and caresses.

> I was on a bus and a woman I didn't know was coming on to me. It was strange because there were other people on the bus watching, and one of them was a guy I had a crush on at the time of the dream. Anyhow, the woman went down on me, and I felt really confused. After a while I got into it, but then realized I was imagining I was with the guy instead. I woke up suddenly and felt really strange. I guess it was my own homophobia which made me feel gross about the dream. But the more I thought about it, the more I thought that it wasn't that strange to have a lesbian dream even though I consider myself heterosexual.

> I dreamt about being on top of and kissing my good friend, Sylvia. It was strange because it did feel good, yet I'm not attracted to women.

> I had a sexual encounter with an older woman in a dream. I felt guilty and ashamed.

A student who considered herself predominantly heterosexual dreamt:

> I was dreaming about my first boyfriend and we were making mad, passionate love when suddenly he transformed into a lesbian friend who had been attracted to me at the time of the dream. It actually shocked me, but I was kind of intrigued and excited by the change.

Almost every heterosexual woman I have ever worked with has told me she has dreamt of enjoying making love with another woman. These dreams often trigger the dreamer's anxiety that perhaps she has unrecognized and unwelcome lesbian leanings. While the dream experience itself may have been extraordinarily pleasurable, its recall is often mixed with waking judgments, and the dreamer then thinks of it as an uncomfortable dream.

Similarly, my few lesbian clients usually have the same anxious response to pleasurable sexy dreams involving men. Such dreams can mean many different things. While this kind of dream can signal a repressed attraction, it can just as well be a metaphor for other areas of the dreamer's life. For example, a heterosexual woman's dream of having pleasurable sex with another woman could represent the dreamer's growing level of self-acceptance or her desire to become more like, or to be accepted by, the woman in her dream.

Wet Dreams

Having orgasms while dreaming is perfectly normal for both men and women. The Kinsey Institute estimates that 40 percent of all women have had at least one nocturnal orgasm, with women in their forties having the highest rate.[7] As women become more comfortable talking about sexual issues, we may find that a far greater percentage have this experience. In my practice, women in their fifties and sixties tell me that they are enjoying wet dreams for the first time in their lives. It is not yet clear what factors increase or decrease the incidence of these dreams. Some men and women report that an absence of waking sexual release increases the frequency of nocturnal orgasms, while others do not. If you decide to begin a dream journal that includes day and dream notes (as described in chapter three), you will be able to follow your own patterns and see what factors influence the frequency of your wet dreams.

> I was swimming with a dolphin in clear water. All I did was feel him rub along my belly and . . . Well, you get the picture.

I was on my childhood swing set teeter-totter. The experience became sexually arousing and ended with an outrageous nocturnal orgasm.

These dreams illustrate that orgasmic dreams can provide unexpected stimulation. Among my clients, who are mostly in their thirties and forties, wonderful dream lovers are commonly involved in bringing about nocturnal orgasms, which are sometimes experienced as multiple. Dr. Lonnie Barbach, a sex psychologist and author of several very good books on sexuality (listed in the Resource section), has told me that in her psychotherapy practice, which includes a great deal of sex therapy, she has seen a number of women who are unable to have orgasms in waking life but who are able to experience orgasm while sleeping.

My clients and our students at the Dream Center have often commented that a number of their orgasmic dreams are lucid ones. (A lucid dream is one in which you are aware of the fact that you are dreaming while you are asleep having the dream.) Felicia's dream, which opened this chapter, was of this type. Monique wrote me describing her experiences with orgasmic dreams:

> Briefly, all my sexual dreams that culminate in orgasm are lucid. The orgasms are quick, intense, full-body sensations and very pleasurable. The "Kundalini" [energy] begins to rise and I just go with the flow, sometimes with a partner whom I conjure up, sometimes with nobody. Sometimes I look around in the dream for some unsuspecting male whom I approach and seduce.

I have never heard a woman tell about an orgasmic dream that was not pleasurable, although I can imagine circumstances that might produce unpleasant ones.

WOMEN'S UNPLEASANT SEXUAL DREAMS

If women love dreaming about having sex in beautiful environments with men who know the difference between abduction and seduction, who take their time and are exquisitely tuned in to the woman on both emotional and physical levels, who enjoy all of lovemaking, and who find great sexual pleasure in pleasuring their partner, then you can probably predict what women don't like to dream about.

Violence and Threat

At the top of the list are dreams in which the dreamer feels forced, threatened, or obliged to have sex with someone. When that someone is a father, brother, or other family member the dreamer usually awakes very upset. These dreams can help the dreamer discover a variety of things—from feelings of being "screwed" by her senior partner at work to memories of actual sexual abuse in childhood. We shall explore the interpretation of these dreams in later chapters.

The respondents in the lecture audience survey described dreams of being chased or sexually cornered by big male spiders and by dangerous or crazy men, or vampires:

> There was a cold, terrible vampire in the room. He grabbed me and wanted to drink from the vein in my neck. It was erotic, but I was terrified. I was paralyzed with fear, but a part of me did not want to move. It was as if I were coming under his spell. I awoke cold and trembling.
>
> Thirsty Vampire

Sex with Undesirable Partners

Dreams of undesirable partners come in two main varieties: unpleasant dreams of having sex with a former husband or old boyfriend, and ones of having sex with a man or woman whom the dreamer does not find at all attractive.

I was having sexual intercourse with the singer Prince. It was disgusting. I don't like him at all.

And

My ex-husband and I were in bed. We were having sex and it was awful. All the old feelings of resentment and obligation were there again.

Embarrassment, Pain, and Repulsion

Some women dream of being embarrassed by their own body's odors or looks while having sex. A few women describe being coerced to engage in acts they found painful, unpleasant, or repulsive, such as anal intercourse or fellatio.

I was with my husband. He was putting his finger in my anus. It felt awful. He was intruding, intrusive. I got angry and told him to leave me alone. I was irritated at his doing that to me without asking me.

"My Husband's Intrusive Finger"

A commonly embarrassing and/or frustrating dream of which there are several variations is that of having a nice time in bed with a desirable partner, perhaps a spouse or stranger, when suddenly in walks Mother, or Father, or a friendly enough stranger! *Oniros interruptus.* In these dreams the intruder often represents attitudes that are actually deep in the heart of the dreamer and keep her from feeling adult or free with her lover. For example, Kim dreamt:

I am foreplaying with my boyfriend. We are about to intromiss and I feel very sexy. Then my mother walks into the room and says hi and as if this were the most normal situation in the world. I feel so self-conscious that I can't go on, and the dream ends. I feel very frustrated.

"Mom Interrupts Us"

The people who interrupt dream lovers typically are totally at ease and seemingly oblivious to the discomfort they cause the dreamer. The dreamer is the one who has to contend with the feelings of self-consciousness, which usually parallel similar ones in waking lovemaking.

Dreaming of being asked to have sex in an uncomfortably public place or of being unable to find a private spot also made our list of unpleasant dreams. Cindy dreamed:

> My ex-husband and I were in a college dormitory. There were many cots in the room, sort of like a fraternity house setup. My ex started kissing me and let me know he wanted to make love right there with other people sleeping in the room! I was not turned on. I felt pounced upon, and profoundly embarrassed at the public nature of the proposal. I was offended that he would suggest such a thing.
>
> *"Sex in a Dorm"*

While scenarios of having sex in public places, of being watched by others, are often highly pleasurable in sexual fantasies, in sexual dreams they are almost always described as painfully embarrassing.

WHAT WOMEN CAN LEARN FROM THEIR SEXUAL DREAMS

Highly pleasurable, erotic dreams may simply reflect and expand a woman's current luxurious sexual life or her wished-for sexual life. Dreams of former, but much better or more romantic, lovers can help the dreamer face the fact that she longs for something that is missing in her current relationship, and that continuing to deny her desires is costing her a piece of her life. Dreams of fantastic lovemaking could help the dreamer to let go of self-consciousness and unwanted inhibitions from childhood. Dreams of being greatly loved by an admired hero or current partner can help insecure women to believe that such feelings and such relationships are indeed possible for them.

Pleasant sexual dreams seem to be briefer and have much less of a plot than sexual dreams in which there is some awkwardness or conflict. There may be less pleasure in, but more to learn from, what may be the more common, conflicted erotic dream. Dreams of sexual conflict can diagnose both sexual and interpersonal problems and offer the dreamer who knows how to interpret her dreams invaluable insights. But even when the dreamer has few interpretive skills she can use her pleasant and unpleasant sexual dreams to increase her level of comfort in thinking about sexual issues and in talking about them with a close friend, therapist, or lover.

The sexual revolution is far from complete. We still have a long way to go in being comfortable with our sexuality and in discovering the joy of more mature, less inhibited, more creative sexual intimacy. Our highly charged, pleasantly sexy dreams can reanimate a relationship that has suffered from too much familiarity or too many daily distractions if the dreamer can take the inspiration from the dream and run with it.

Just as dreams can be reminders of passion, they can, if we let them, introduce us to new levels of sensuality that both extend pleasure and earthiness and add a new grace and elegance to lovemaking.

What Men Need to Know About Women's Sexual Dreams

The advantage to women of learning to understand their sexual dreams is obvious, but what can a man learn from them? He can learn a lot about satisfying a woman's sexual desires, about her inadequately expressed needs, anxieties, and wishes. We dream about the most intimate and important issues in our lives often before we can recognize and talk about them in the waking state. Thus, the sharing of even a simple dream in which the dreamer is being pleasured in a particularly satisfying way can smooth the path of sometimes awkward communication and provide practical information while reducing the dreamer's anxiety. A woman who is longing for more romance, a slower hand, or more surprise and excitement will dream either of her frustration or of scenes in which these longings are at least partially satisfied. By paying attention to such dreams, a smart lover can keep his job. In fact, just the simple act of attentively listening to a woman's dream will lead her to think that a man is interested in her inner life—in her feelings, perceptions, and concerns. A fellow who is uninterested in listening to a woman's dreams usually looses points.

Through these dreams, a man can often get a clearer picture of how his partner really experiences him in bed. When Rebecca dreamt that she was in bed with an angry, seething gorilla she admitted to herself and then to her husband for the first time that she was afraid of him, of his anger, which she spent much of her day trying to evade. In her dream she told the gorilla to get out of the bed and take his temper with him. Her husband saw the writing on his wife's dream wall and got himself into therapy just in time to save his marriage.

If a man knows how to listen to his lady's dreams with kindly openness and gentle acceptance, she will feel safe enough to include him as she explores any emotional and interpersonal conflicts that are getting in the way of good sex. After Julio heard Sarah's dream in which her mother had mercilessly criticized her for being too fat, he gained a new understanding of Sarah's exquisite sensitiveness to any criticism of her body. He made special efforts both to praise her body and to invite Sarah to consider how her mother's obsession with five pounds on her daughter's body was her mother's problem, not hers. Sarah was grateful to Julio for his understanding and concern, and she found herself much more comfortable and confident in bed with him.

In other words, a man who studies women's sexual dreams in general, and his partner's in particular, can become the kind of emotionally and physically tuned-in lover most women would kill for.

CHAPTER

2

Men's Sexual Dreams
and What Women
Need to Know About Them

MOST MEN WILL DESCRIBE THEIR FAVORITE SEXUAL dreams in terms of the unexpected, the daring, the highly genitally erotic. This is in striking contrast to most women's descriptions of their erotic dreams as romantic and timeless. Men tell of prized known and unknown dream lovers (sometimes movie stars, sometimes coworkers) who are willing and eager to do anything—who are extremely uninhibited.

The most vivid contrast I have noticed between the favorite sexual dreams of men and women is that while women relish dreaming about men who take their time, who are passionately pleasured in the act of giving the woman the kind of sexual attention she longs for, men revel in the delights of dreaming of being with women who are immediately accessible, easily turned on, and game to do anything. Men enjoy dreams not of the patient, sensitive, tender woman who knows how to provide pleasures so much as of the uninhibited woman who is ready and eager to participate in sexual activity. I've never heard a woman note how uninhibited a dream lover was, nor that he was immediately accessible. Such attributes are often present in the dream, but not commented on as part of the surprise and pleasure of the experience. Dreaming women seem to take these things for granted! Nor have I ever heard a man say how he enjoyed dreaming of being with a sensitive woman who knew how to take her time and be sure he was entirely turned on before intercourse. It is clear that in our favorite dreams we sometimes get what we wish we had in waking life.

Getting men to talk about the details of their sexual dreams is often like pulling teeth. To begin with, men are less likely to be interested enough in their dream life to recall many dreams. Then they are also less likely than women to take dreams seriously. Further, those I know are far more reticent to share such intimate experiences than are most women, despite all their good-humored comments such as "Sexual dreams? Boy, have I got some hot ones!"

In addition to the dreams of my clients, colleagues, and friends, we shall also consider in this chapter dreams collected by Professor Bill Domhoff in his survey of the sexual dreams of 273 University of California at Santa Cruz students. The 101 men who filled out the questionnaire in ten to fifteen minutes in class were mostly between the ages of nineteen and twenty-one—ten to twenty years younger than most of my clients and lecture audiences who responded to my questionnaires on sexual dreams. [1]

FAVORITE SEXUAL DREAMS

Eager, Available Women

Most men usually recall fewer and shorter dreams than do women, probably because as a group they tend to value dreaming less and therefore pay it less attention. Thus, it is not surprising that the men responding to the lecture audience questionnaire wrote much briefer accounts of their sexual dreams than did the women, such as: "Having great sex in the car"; "Entering a room with a large number of women, all of whom were willing to have sex with me"; "Making love to two extremely uninhibited women"; or "Being with a beautiful woman who is very sexually aggressive toward me." Two men were very brief. One wrote, "I have them. I love them. They're great." Another simply replied, "Yes Yes Yes."

A few fellows, however, went into more detail. Here are some representative examples:

> I was in an intellectual conversation with a female employee and friend. The next thing I knew I was embracing her and "totally" involved in massaging her buttocks. She was entirely into it. Then I woke up.

Or,

> I've never had the same sexual dream twice. My unconscious likes to play the field, I guess. My favorite kind of dream is when something startling happens such as a woman coming on to me unexpectedly in a public place.

Or,

> I meet an attractive lady and establish intimacy (not sex, just hugging and kissing) immediately without all the usual agenda of long-term commitment (no doubt this will remain just a dream given today's atmosphere).

One of Domhoff's university students dreamt:

> I was in an officelike room with a bunch of people who work with me at the bank. We were all waiting for someone to finish something so we could all masturbate together. Finally the time came and only two women were actually totally hot on the idea. One started to undress and touch herself. The other girl just talked about how this was going to be awesome. The other people just got up and went about their business. I couldn't decide whether or not I would masturbate because this other guy sitting beside me wasn't going to. But the girl totally did it and I was really turned on.

Another undergraduate took the willing, eager, uninhibited woman to an exotic level in this highly erotic dream:

I had sex with a demoness. Extremely wild. Fire. Sweat. I felt like life was being sucked from my body and being replaced by fire. *Ecstasy.*

Sex in Public

While dreaming of having sex in public is usually described by women as unpleasant and embarrassing (in contrast to their enjoyment of such scenes in waking fantasies), men often tell of enjoying the experience, as did this undergraduate:

I was at a gathering at my house with lots of friends from my hometown. There was a woman there whom I did not know. I was curious so I talked to her. Then she wanted to have sex, so we did, right there in front of everyone.

Romance

Men, too, will sometimes report that their favorite dream is one in which the emotions outshine the sexual specifics. Here are two examples:

I was with a well-built, sexy woman. There was a lot of erotic buildup. She wants to make love and I will respond. We aren't talking about it. Through caresses, the tension slowly builds. We make love. This won't be a long-term relationship, but we have lots of love and respect and attraction for one another. The woman brings me pleasure, she initiates the action. It is a very special, pleasurable, touching time. *The being wanted by her is the most pleasurable part.*

I meet a special woman. We are mutually attracted to each other. There is lots of kissing, cuddling, and sexual energy. Sometimes when I have this dream we have sex, sometimes we don't. But the special feeling is so warm, sweet, beautiful, and loving. It is almost spiritual.

Kisses

Kisses and romance may not be the very first things men rave about when telling their sexual dreams, but they could be the second or third. Kissing gets top billing in this fellow's dream:

> Perhaps the most interesting thing about the dream is that I'm in love in the dream—really powerfully in love, feeling all the same things that I normally would. It's erotic in a fairly limited way. I'm standing with the woman that I'm in love with on a street corner, kissing her with rain pouring down on us. The rain, the kiss—very erotic.

Notice how this dreamer went from characterizing his dream as "erotic in a fairly limited way" to "very erotic" after having described the scene and (presumably) after having relived some of the feelings in it. Was the respondent initially thinking that because the recalled dream did not include anything more graphic than kissing that it might not qualify as a very erotic dream? How many other respondents (both men and women) disqualified and decided not to report such dreams? As you can see, obtaining accurate, detailed reports on sexual/erotic dreams has its challenges.

Former Lovers, Famous and Unknown Lovers

Whereas women often recount sweet dreams of former lovers, of the men who responded to the lecture questionnaire, only one mentioned a positive dream of a former lover, in this case a former wife, dearly loved and deeply missed.

Just a few of Domhoff's respondents wrote of dreams of having sex with former lovers. Some wrote of dreams with unknown women and some with familiar women. Early research suggested that women dreamt more of familiar figures, men more frequently of strangers. In my experience, women dream more often of former lovers than do men, while both sexes often dream of unknown lovers.

Among the undergraduates, famous dream lovers included Mary Lou Retton, Kim Basinger, and Joan Collins. The older respondents wrote of dreams about Bernadette Peters, Jodie Foster, and Tina Turner in dreams that were short, the sex straightforward and satisfying. In my private practice, however, dreams of famous dream lovers tend to be more complex and often more conflicted than those described by respondents to our questionnaires. Men, like women, will usually tell of disconcerting interruptions and awkward circumstances in these dreams when they take the time to remember and tell all the details of the dream action.

Being Seduced by Older Women

Quite a few of the undergraduate men dreamt of gladly being seduced by older sexy women. In fact, the fellow who dreamt of the bank team also dreamt of being seduced to the point of orgasm by his French teacher. One fellow dreamt of "being the willing subject of fellatio to the point of orgasm by a suitably beautiful older woman . . ."

The older women in these men's dreams are not coercive, or even pushy. They are seductive, they may take the initiative, and they are skilled and very erotically motivated. While women often tell of dreaming of being gently and pleasurably coerced into sex by a forceful (not a violent) man, I have yet to hear a man tell of a dream of being coerced even gently into sex by a forceful woman. [2]

Erotic Sensuality

A few dreams in the Domhoff survey suggest that the new generation of young men may be more interested in foreplay and sensuality than their fathers:

> I was with my now ex-girlfriend, and we were involved with extensive foreplay—oral sex, sucking of breasts, etc.—I awoke when we initiated intercourse in the dream.

And,

> I had sex with a black girl I had seen in class. Her lips were very voluptuous and soft. She was so fleshy and tight, I thought she was beautiful. I remember her lips, her eyes, and the passion I felt.

And,

> I was making love with my girlfriend and we were *very* excited—all hot and sweaty. My penis was huge inside her. I could feel all of the inside of her vagina. As I glided in and out of her I found one area that she really liked. I caressed it softly with my penis for what seemed like hours. She was just going crazy. At one point she began squeezing her vaginal muscles and thighs. Things started getting very intense. . . .

Men with Men

Unlike heterosexual women, heterosexual men have never told me of pleasant erotic dream encounters with the same sex. In fact, I have heard very few accounts from these men of any homosexual encounters in dreams. This is very suspicious. Masters and Johnson have found that the sexual fantasies of heterosexual and homosexual men and women are remarkably similar. They report that homosexual encounters are the fourth most frequent sexual fantasies for heterosexual men. For heterosexual women, lesbian encounters are the fifth most frequent. For homosexual males and females, fantasized heterosexual encounters are the third most frequent.[3] It may be that most heterosexual men are too uncomfortable to report, and even to recall, such nocturnal dreams. If, on the other hand, heterosexual men, unlike heterosexual women, do not often have such dreams, what would explain this marked difference between men and women and between fantasy and dream content?

Wet Dreams

In the dreams discussed above, sometimes men awake frustrated just before they climax. But in wet dreams, the dreamer awakes as he is orgasming. Like the student who dreamt,

> I was surrounded by at least five women. They were all stroking and licking and sucking every part of me. I orgasmed.

Another student's orgasm was precipitated by a fairy-tale dream:

> The most beautiful woman, a princess, [is] lying on a huge bed in a castle. I see her naked body lying there and I climax just looking at her.

Many of the wet dreams I've heard from my private clients and from the students and professionals at the Dream Center include scenes of the man being pleasured by one or more enthusiastic females. It may be that wet dreams of men simply touching or looking at a woman are more common among younger dreamers. Men experience their peak of nocturnal orgasms in their twenties (women reach their peak in their forties). However, one of my clients, who is in his fifties, had the following wet dream right after having enjoyed making love to his wife:

> I was with a woman in a wet T-shirt. Her nipples were wonderful. Whoosh! I had an orgasm.

Although some people worry that there is something wrong with having wet dreams, they are normal, healthy, and usually very pleasurable. Psychiatrist and neuroscientist Allan Hobson suggests that REM sleep erections and wet dreams may be our nervous system's way of guaranteeing the readiness of the central circuitry underlying our sexual behavior. [4] Martin Cole, at the Institute for Sex Education and Research in Birmingham, England, reports that while higher rates of masturbation generally lead to lower rates of wet dreams, a group of men who were premature ejaculators had both a high frequency of wet dreams and a high rate of adult masturbation. Cole suggests: "This information would lend support to the view that it is the low sympathetic threshold in the premature ejaculators that is responsible for their high incidence of wet dreams and not their low masturbation rate."[5] Researchers estimate that 80 percent of men and 40 percent of women have had at least one nocturnal orgasm.[6] In a study of 625 male traumatic paraplegics and quadriplegics, 56 percent reported having sexual dreams. Of these, 20 percent had dreams of foreplay, intromission, ejaculation, and orgasm; 19 percent had dreams of ejaculation, but only 2 percent had dreams of ejaculation after which the ejaculate was noted.[7] Not all orgasmic dreams are wet. In fact, this same study found six patients who ejaculated without any kind of orgasm.

Erections and Engorgement During Dreams

Most of our dreams occur during periods of rapid eye movement (or REM) sleep. During a seven-to-eight-hour period, we pass through three to five cycles of various stages of sleep. Lasting about ninety minutes, each cycle is crowned with a period in which our eyes move rapidly under closed lids, our muscular activity is usually tremendously inhibited, and our brain waves show particular low-voltage frequencies with bursts of alpha and "sawtoothed" waves. These REM periods last from just a few minutes in the beginning of the night to a half hour or more in the seventh or eighth hour of sleep. While in REM sleep, our breathing and heart rate become irregular, and if awakened from this state, we will likely be able to report a dream.

Another interesting thing happens in REM periods: men have some degree of erection 90 percent of the time,[8] and women regularly experience some degree of vaginal vascular engorgement, clitoral swelling, and increased lubrication. Do these erections and engorgements cause, or are they caused by, our sexual dreams? Apparently not in most cases. In a huge study that examined 10,000 dream reports to see what normal people dream about and how often, Hall and Van de Castle found that only 12 percent of the dreams in their sample contained overt sexual interactions.[9]

MEN'S UNPLEASANT SEXUAL DREAMS

Whenever I have asked women about their least favorite sexual dreams they quickly respond with a list of two or more. Often when I ask men about their bad or uncomfortable sexual dreams they look at me, puzzled, and say, "What do you mean? A bad sexual dream? I didn't know there was such a thing! I mean, if there is sex in a dream it's got to be good." Only one woman respondent answered in a similar vein. What does this tell us? That men have more fun? That women are much more conflicted about sex and therefore use sexual dream imagery to express both sexual and other forms of conflict? That men don't remember such dreams readily, and if they do, are hesitant to report them?

According to Dr. Lonnie Barbach, a highly experienced sex psychologist and author of *For Yourself, For Each Other,* and *Erotic Interludes,* men just don't focus as much conflictual emotional baggage on sex as do women, so it would seem likely that men's sexual dreams would be generally less conflicted. My colleague at the Dream Center, Dr. Loma Flowers, who is a psychiatrist, adds that since men in waking life are less vulnerable to attack and coercion in heterosexual situations, heterosexual imagery would not likely serve to represent conflict in most men's dreams.

While they may have fewer of them, men still have plenty of unpleasant sexual dreams to tell. Here are a few "most uncomfortable sexual dreams" from the lecture audience survey:

My ex-wife is having sex with somebody.

I suddenly find myself naked in public.

I am naked, but the woman is clothed. I am ready, but she is very elusive and disappears.

I am having sex with a woman. We are getting along well. Then she changes before my eyes into a man [or animal].

As you would expect, some of the dreams emphasize the emotional content over the physical action:

Being abandoned or humiliated when I become sexually intimate with a woman.

And,

I often dream of being with a woman sexually but wanting to get out of the situation. The trouble is that I can't do it because I'm afraid of hurting my partner's feelings or of embarrassing myself.

And,

Finding that the woman I desire is always out of reach or unavailable in some way or the other.

Unappealing Partners, Interruptions, and Cheating

Like the women, the men in these surveys also told of having sex with unexpected partners, some of the dream lovers being ugly and unappealing. The men also told of frustrating dreams in which a potentially good sexual encounter was interrupted by a friend or by a mother's entrance on the scene. A few men in the surveys described dreams in which they were in compromising positions with a friend's girlfriend or wife. Some decided to stop, some did not. Three married or otherwise committed men wrote of being about to have sex with another woman and having to decide whether or not to cheat. As in the dreams of both men and women in my practice, the decisions went both ways.

Domination (But Not Violence)

In the surveys and in my practice I have come across no dreams in which a man was raped or otherwise coerced to have sex, a feature that is striking in its contrast to women's dreams. Such dreams may be kept secret or they may be found in different populations. I would imagine that men who have been sexually abused in childhood would constitute one group that would be likely to have such dreams.

In our surveys several men wrote of enjoying being sexually dominated. One dreamt of being dominated by Pippi Longstockings, and another of being "my ex-girlfriend's sex slave, giving her oral sex on demand." Since apparently neither our surveys nor the Dream Center have attracted people who are open about being active in S and M, we will have to wait for new research to see what their dreams are like. Studies by Beck, Ward, and Hurvich showed that men and women who suffer from masochistic character disorders and those who are depressed have more masochistic dreams than do other people. [10] However, I am unaware of any studies that have explored the incidence of sexual S and M in dreams of healthy normals.

No men have reported to me dreams in which they raped women or other men. Such dreams would be hard to discuss, and may have gone underground in a world that would be likely to censure them.

WHAT WOMEN CAN LEARN FROM MEN'S DREAMS

While men can use their dreams to identify and work out their sexual conflict as well as to explore new areas of potential pleasure, women can also benefit from them in a number of ways. Women generally are quite unaware how much their sexual inhibitions distress their male lovers. By reading about or by listening to their own lovers' delight in dreams of free, enthusiastic women, women can get new ideas and insight, and perhaps choose to ride the wave created by certain dream scenes. Some women experience a new level of permission and invitation-without-obligation upon listening to a partner's steamy dreams.

Listening to your lover's sexual dreams can help you not only to open your mind but to learn to listen more with curiosity than with judgment. Men can be shy about sexual matters, too. If you show your lover that you are interested in knowing and understanding how he feels and what he wants, and that you will not reject him when he reveals his inner life to you, you will gain a happier and most likely more intimate lover. You may well be the first person in your partner's life with whom he has shared such private dream memories and the thoughts and feelings they generate. Dreams can give you a glimpse into your partner's unspoken feelings and concerns regarding sexuality and intimacy. The openness that comes from sharing dreams with a lover can be very exciting if both are willing and if neither is intrusive or judgmental. However, I would suggest that you not attempt sharing dreams before reading part two of this book. The intimacy of dream sharing can expose some very tender spots and requires delicacy and tact, especially when you embark upon the enterprise of interpreting the meaning of sexual dreams.

As you will see in chapter four, your partner's dreams of having sex with another partner often do not mean he is having, or is even seriously desiring to have, an affair with another woman. However, if a man is having affairs with other people, he will probably dream about it in one form or another. He may dream of the other woman, of women like her, or of scenes portraying conflicts he may feel about his behavior. Only careful exploration of the dream with a fair amount of honesty on his part will reveal the meaning of such dreams. Remember that in a time of rampant sexually transmitted diseases, it is better to know everything you can about your partner's sexual activities. Dream talk can facilitate discussing such touchy subjects.

When you know how to draw your lover out without threatening him, you will find that his dreams will help him discover for himself and then communicate to you his sexual desires, anxieties, and conflicts. If you can then share your inner dream life with your partner, you will have a greatly enhanced chance at developing a vibrant sexual and emotional relationship.

3

How to Recall and Record Your Dreams

HOLDING ON TO YOUR DREAMS

When I ask people what they would like to know about sexual dreams, one of the most frequent answers is, "Tell me how to have more of them!" If you would like to study your sexual dreams, or if you just want to remember more of them, try keeping a dream journal. Writing down your dreams immediately upon awakening is the surest way to increase your recall of the four or five or more dreams you have every single night. Recording your dreams saves them from oblivion, where most dreams seem to go as soon as you step out of bed. Then, with your dreams preserved, you will be able to explore and enjoy them at your leisure.

The very act of placing a piece of paper beside your bed before you go to sleep with the intention of recording your dreams in the morning will increase your recall. If you actually write down the dreams you remember, you will boost it further. Try, when you first awake, to think backwards—"What was I just thinking of?"—rather than thinking forward to what you plan to do in the new day. Even if all you recall is just a meager fragment of a dream, don't disqualify it; write it down. This will help you form the recall habit and might sometimes result in your recalling the rest of the dream as you write.

You will achieve the best success if you add one very important step to the journal process. Take five minutes *before sleep* to record the highlights of what you did and felt during the day. This will improve your recall and you will later be able to use these "day notes" to establish the waking context that gave birth to the dreams. This will help tremendously in their interpretation. Keep your day notes brief, so that writing them never becomes a chore, and you will be more likely to write them and benefit from them.

Ross Campbell and Robert Hoffman at Carleton University in Ottawa recently conducted a telling study on this idea. In the study, there were three randomly formed groups of dreamers. Group 1 simply noted the occurrence of a dream in the morning. Group 2 did the same as group 1 and in addition wrote out as much of their dreams as they could recall in the morning. Group 3 did the same as group 2 and in addition kept an evening diary of daily events, which they recorded before going to sleep.

Campbell and Hoffman found that people who kept an evening diary of daily events in addition to noting the occurrence of dreaming and recording their dreams in the morning remembered more dreams than did those who simply noted the occurrence of a dream in the morning or those who both noted the occurrence and actually recorded their remembered dreams.[1]

Before being coached in dream recall, women are usually better at it then men. Raymond Martinetti studied ninety male and female undergraduates and found that the women recalled more dreams, had a greater degree of imaginal life, and had more positive attitudes regarding their imaginal lives. The men scored higher on the suppression scale. Martinetti joins many experienced dream recallers in thinking that a positive attitude toward imaginal processes and past introspective experiences increases one's likelihood of recalling dreams.[2] Another study found that recall was correlated with one's interest in dreams and that women speculated about their dreams and discussed them with others more frequently than men.[3] While men seem to have been socialized in ways that discourage recall, Loma and I find that our male students and clients rarely require more than a couple of weeks of journal keeping in order to recall more than enough dreams to work with every week. By the way, there is no need to remember a dream every day. It is interesting to do so, but not necessary. One dream a week, or even one a month, can offer so much information that incorporating into your life the insight from that one dream can keep most people very busy. The trick is to relax, enjoy recalling your dreams, and make good use of the dreams you choose to analyze.

Following these suggestions usually results in rich recall and can even result in your remembering more dreams than you want to spend the time to write out. Decide how many dreams you want to record each week and let the rest go. If you overload yourself with dream journal obligation, your dream recall may suddenly dry up, conveniently leaving you with no more journaling chores but also without your dreams.

I have been unable to locate any research exploring the question of how to increase the recall of sexual dreams. However, Rosalind Cartwright, one of our most creative dream researchers, and her colleague, Carl Browman, did serendipitously come upon one way to do it. They found that dreams with sexual content were precipitated following exercise taken before sleep.[4] So if you really want to stir up your dreaming, try taking a swim or jogging around the block before you go to bed.

As you might well imagine, a number of our dreamers have commented that exposure to sexy films and other stimulation just before sleep seems to increase the erotic imagery in that night's dreams.

OUR DREAM JOURNAL FORMAT

Here are the instructions for using the journal format we use at the Dream Center. Choose as your journal a bound blank book or loose-leaf lined paper and a long clipboard, and place it by your bed every night. If you travel frequently, you may like the ease of loose-leaf paper, which you can later place in a yearly three-ring binder. Night-light pens make early-morning recording less disruptive for a bed partner.

The organization of the journal aims at brevity, simplicity, clarity, and flexibility. When you review your dream journal, an important part of dream study, you will appreciate the quickly recognized date and other markings in the margin.

DATE

Day notes—Before sleep write three or four lines about what you did and felt during the day. For example: Arrived at work late today. I was irritable with my co-worker Jim over nothing. Got lots of work done, but was preoccupied thinking about this morning's fight with Tara, my wife.

TITLE OF DREAM

Record all the details you can remember about your dream, no matter how brief or insignificant they seem. Place a big # sign in the margin and leave space to write the title of the dream in big letters above your entry.

Commentary—Whenever you have time, write down any thoughts or feelings you have about the dream, and record any associations or interpretations you care to make. Place a zigzag in the margin to signal your commentary of the dream.

If you remember more than one dream, date another page and begin your next dream account across from another sign (#) in the margin. This will leave you plenty of room to add to the commentary of past dreams at a later time by adding pages to your loose-leaf notebook or by inserting extra pages into a bound book.

The key to rich recall is taking the time and effort to keep a journal faithfully. You don't have to write in your journal every day, but try to do it at least three times a week. Your dreams will be more vivid and stay with you longer the more you attend to them and the more you write in your journal. If you awake and force yourself to write down at least one line every morning you will overcome the common resistance to making the effort to put pen to paper. If you know that you will write one line about your mood upon awakening, even if you recall no dream, you may find that you recall more dreams since you aren't going to get out of writing by forgetting them!

And of course, remember to give yourself enough time to get all the sleep you need in order to awake refreshed in the morning. And leave yourself an extra ten minutes to record your harvest before rushing to the shower.

Explore Your Own Sexual Dreams, Then Join Our Study If You Like

Create a Sexual Dream Journal

In order to get the most out of your erotic dreaming, I suggest that you create a sexual dream journal, which could be combined with a general day or dream diary if you are already keeping one. By recording and reviewing your erotic dreams, you will likely discover revealing patterns and developments of themes that might otherwise go unnoticed. For example, how often do you have dreams that are entirely enjoyable? When you have frustrating or unpleasant sexual dreams, what causes the problem in the dream? Are there recurring themes such as coercion, interruption, lack of privacy? Are there particular people who keep showing up in your sexual dreams? Look for dreams that feel sexual but do not have any obviously sexual imagery in them. These dreams will offer you clues to how you use apparently nonsexual imagery to deal with sexual issues. What are the themes of your uncomfortable sexual dreams? Ask yourself if these themes are reflected in your romantic relationships. You will probably be surprised to see how many of your dreams contain obviously sexual imagery, and you will gain a better perspective on the ways in which you use erotic imagery to convey meaning to your waking mind.

You might want to record your sexual dreams and your thoughts about them in a separate notebook, or, if you already are keeping a dream journal, you might prefer to simply make a mark in the margin beside each sexual dream entry. Integrating your sexual dreams with your other dreams and with your notes on your daily activities will provide you with useful information about the interactional and emotional context of your life at the time of your dreams. Your sexual dream journal will serve you best if you include in it not only your erotic dreams but also your commentary on them and your thoughts about your sexuality and about your sexual experiences past and present. You might begin your journal by listing the themes of all the sexual dreams you can remember. If you want to take the time, describe in detail two or more of those dreams. Try to estimate approximately when you dreamed them and what was going on in your life at the time.

The sexual dreams questionnaire in the appendix will bring to your attention qualities and patterns in your sexual dreams that you may not have considered before. It will also help you to notice a broader spectrum of characteristics in your future sexual dreaming and thus form an important part of your journal. You may be surprised at some of your answers and at the feelings you experience in making them. Most of us know very little about the features of our sexual dream life and our reactions to it because we forget it so quickly and rarely notice its significant patterns of feelings and its relation to our waking life.

This questionnaire can serve a second purpose—that of breaking the relative silence in the reporting and study of sexual dreams. After responding to the survey, you could help us further research in the field of sexual dreams by sending us a copy of your answers.

CHAPTER

4

Is It Really About Sex? Interpreting Your Sexual Dreams

How can we tell when a dream is using nonsexual imagery as a metaphor for dealing with sexual issues, as in the case of the man who dreamt that he should play the piano more sensitively and realized he had used this scenario as a metaphor for improving his sexual style with his wife? How can we tell whether a penis is just a penis or a representation of power or creativity?

How can we understand common sexual dreams, including uncomfortable ones such as dreams of being naked, or having sex in public, or having sex with unexpected, unfriendly, or inappropriate partners or with partners of surprising sexual preferences? I believe that the answer in each case is: Ask the dreamer—or yourself, if you are working on your own dream— to describe each of the dream images and the feelings associated with them, then you and the dreamer will know. Your most embarrassing dreams often are not about what you fear. I receive so many letters from people who suffer terribly from guilt upon awakening from a dream that shocks them with scenes of their having pleasurable sex with a parent or a sister or brother. Yet often the images in such dreams are really just metaphors for issues that would not at all fill you with either guilt or shame.

You may be so troubled by your sexual dreams that you don't want to interpret them. I would like to relieve you of the embarrassment and guilt you may suffer upon recalling such dreams and help you discover that they can open new doors of insight and maturity. Many people are comforted simply by learning that we all have shocking sexual dreams. If you think your sexual dreams are more embarrassing than anyone else's, read on. If you are ready to find out what your dreams mean, roll up your sleeves; you have come to the right chapter.

Suppose that you dream of having sex in an airplane. And let's also imagine that three other people reading this book have also dreamt of having sex in a plane. Let's say that you love to fly, that dreamer number two is terrified of flying, that dreamer number three is an air force pilot, and that dreamer number four is a businesswoman who was caught having sex with someone in an Al Italia airline bathroom somewhere over the Mediterranean Sea. Can you imagine that having sex in a plane could possibly have the same meaning for each of these dreamers? So much for those dreadful dream dictionaries! Before interpreting these dreams we would have to find out what each person feels and thinks about airplanes and about having sex in the air. For example, do airplanes represent the excitement of travel to exotic places, the drudgery and fatigue of business travel, or the anxiety of doing something that strikes terror in your heart? Dreamer number two, who is afraid of flying in planes, might use the image of having sex in a plane to express an analogous fear of sex or to portray her perhaps unrecognized fear that she feels very unsafe in her current love relationship. Dreamer number four might dream of being caught having sex in such a public setting at a time in her life when she is feeling that her adventurous sexual life is becoming or might become too widely noticed. But then again, she might be using such images to portray her own conflict about her sexual rebellion, using the thrill of sex in the air as an image of her newfound interest in sexuality in the context of breaking the rules of propriety and thumbing her nose at them. So, is such a dream about excitement, work, anxiety, embarrassment, or rebellion?

We would also need to know what the dreamer thinks and feels about his or her specific dream partner, and how the lovemaking is going. A dream in which the sex is going deliciously would mean something quite different from one of being forced at a hijacker's gunpoint to have sex with a seatmate.

Clearly, if we are to find out what a specific dream means to a given person we had better find out the following things:

- What does the dreamer think and feel about the dream setting (the airplane over the Mediterranean), the characters (the dream lover), the objects (the gun), and the action (having sex in this situation)? What memories, thoughts, and feelings make up her experience of the different elements in the dream?
- How does each setting, feeling, character, object, and action fit into the particular dramatic thrust of the dream?
- How do the images and feelings in the dream relate to the current life concerns of the dreamer? What insight does the dream offer the dreamer?

DREAM INTERVIEWING

Who better to ask in order to discover this often idiosyncratic web of personal experience and feeling than the dreamer? However, if we ask the dreamer, "What does this dream image mean to you?" we usually don't get very far. If the dreamer knew that, she wouldn't be asking for help with her dream. I have developed a set of questions and a method for asking them that is very effective in eliciting from dreamers their own most relevant associations and in helping them to see how they fit together and make sense in the dramatic context of the dream and in relation to the dreamer's waking life.

We ask our students at the Dream Center who want to learn how to interpret their own and other people's dreams to give up the role of interpreter in favor of adopting that of an interviewer. The dreamer can play both roles, interviewer and dreamer, or she can assign the role of interviewer to a friend or therapist. While it is easier, especially in the beginning, to ask someone to be your dream study partner so that you can alternate roles of dreamer and interviewer, you may feel reticent at first to share your sexual dreams with another person. You can be your own interviewer by asking yourself the questions suggested in this chapter. You may find that jotting down your answers will help you to discover what the dream means.

When you play the role of the interviewer for yourself or for another dreamer, remember that the worst thing you can do is impose an arbitrary, prefabricated, or half-baked interpretation. Remember above all else to explore the specifics of the dream and of the feelings and associations it evokes before you try to make any conclusions as to its meaning. To help you in resisting the terrible temptation to project your theoretical or premature prejudices onto the dream's imagery, pretend that you are an interviewer who comes from another planet and has little information and few preconceptions about life on earth. Ask yourself or your dreamer to define and describe all the major images in the dream as if she were describing them to someone who has never heard of them before. This is the most important step in the dream interview process.

For example, if a person dreams of Brigitte Bardot, ask, "Who is she, and what do you think she is like?" What the dreamer says and the exact words she uses to describe Bardot will be the precious keys to discovering what Bardot means to the dreamer. Will the dreamer say she is a French national sex symbol? If so, you would need to ask how the dreamer feels about her. Does she like, disdain, or envy her? What is Brigitte up to in the dream? Is she playing the part of a heroine or a villain? Say you dream of and describe Bardot as a likable sex goddess who has been locked in a closet, neglected and starved. Your dream may make you think about the sexy part of yourself that you have been neglecting. Or suppose you describe Bardot as one of Europe's most effective advocates of animal rights and say you admire her for having overcome a very painful childhood. And let's say that in your dream she is at long last being applauded for her good works. Then you would ask yourself if there is anyone in your life or any part of yourself that is like that description of Bardot, and if it is time to give yourself more credit. The meaning of Bardot will emerge as you discover how the dreamer sees her. Once the dreamer's description of Bardot is made, the dreamer can decide for herself if Bardot reminds her of a part of her own personality or potential, a characterization of someone in the dreamer's personal life, or a force or attitude with which the dreamer has been trying to grapple. Since the interviewer comes from another planet, she also refrains from pretending to know how one should feel and experience life on earth and is keenly interested in knowing what reality is like *according to the dreamer.* It is by eliciting information from a naive position that the interviewer is most likely to:

- Recognize how little she can take for granted about the nature of the dreamer's experience, history, and feelings.
- Draw forth from the dreamer highly personalized, straightforward, and relatively nondefensive descriptive associations and feelings.
- Avoid making premature interpretations based on inadequate or prejudicial information.
- Arrive at interpretations in collaboration with the dreamer that make sense to the dreamer and are useful in the context of his or her life.

The above is just as true when you play the role of your own interviewer. By asking yourself these questions you will find surprising thoughts, words, and opinions you hardly knew you held, which will make spotting the metaphoric meaning of your dreams much easier and more accurate.

Let's take a simple example of a short dream. Trish, a successful actress, was surprised to awake one morning with the following scene.

I was on a cruise with Bill Moyers. We were having dinner in bed together in our wood-paneled cabin. Actually we were having a break in our sex fest. He was a great lover, warm, fervent, extraordinarily sensual. I was as happy as a clam. Bill was wonderful.

"Cruising with Bill Moyers"

I asked Trish to pretend that I was from another planet and had never heard of Bill Moyers. Our interview proceeded along these lines:

INTERVIEWER: Who is Bill Moyers and what is he like?
TRISH: He is a very good television journalist who specializes in intelligent and meaningful documentaries. He works from his heart and does wonderful things. He helps us see ourselves as Americans better than anyone else has done. He seems kind, bright, and creative. And practical. He gets what he wants done, and is a tremendous success.
I: So he is a bright, kind, creative TV journalist who is tremendously successful. Anything else?
T: Well, I used to think he was sort of clumsy verbally, and shy. Either he has matured or I have come to see his better qualities.
I: Is there any situation in your life which reminds you of cruising with Bill, this bright, kind, successful, formerly clumsy journalist who helps us see ourselves?
T: You know, he is not like any actual man in my life, but he sounds like a model of what I would like for myself in my career as an actress. I want to keep doing the type of more meaningful roles I've just begun to get. In fact, the role I've just accepted does reflect an important part of American women's experience, and is more like a documentary in that respect. And I used to see myself as verbally clumsy.
I: How does it feel to be with Bill in the dream?
T: Fantastic. Stupendous. I have arrived in the Big League with the admiration and involvement of Bill Moyers, who is an honest and wonderfully creative man who does good in the world. This dream clarifies my goals. I'm not there yet, but I'm on my way.

Pleasant dreams of famous lovers usually involve very intense feelings of loving and of being loved by someone you admire. The key to understanding these dreams is to describe your famous dream lover as if you were describing him to someone who has never heard of him before. Listen to your own description and see if it reminds you of someone in your current or not-so-current life. Frequently famous dream lovers remind the dreamer of special positive qualities of a current partner, of special feelings she once had toward him that she had begun to lose sight of. Sometimes a dream lover represents the dreamer's desire to be loved and accepted by someone very special, or a desire to live a more lively, romantic, artistic, or accomplished life.

Trish's dream incorporated her desire to be accepted and to be successful while it clarified for her a certain Bill Moyers–like quality of achievement, which she sees as a good model for herself. When she heard herself describing Bill as verbally clumsy she realized that she had been dreaming of someone with whom she could identify since she had seen herself the same way. As she described Bill she recognized parts of herself and of her hoped-for future self in her description. Dream images often highlight or characterize an aspect of our own personality to help us get a better look at it and to show us how that part of ourself is working for or against our best interests.

A dream lover, famous or not, can represent an aspect of yourself, a role model, an experience of being accepted or loved—or all three, as in Trish's dream. A dream lover can also represent an aspect of your current or past lovers, as when you find yourself describing your dream partner in words and with feelings that perfectly describe someone surprisingly familiar. For example, John dreamt of a very steamy sexual scene with Sharon Stone. When he described her as an actress who was alluring, sassy, strong, intriguing, but deep-down crazy with a hatred of men, he recognized that he had just described his new very sexy girlfriend who, while not murderous, was deep-down angry with men. As he thought about it, not only had his dream helped him open his eyes to his current girlfriend's hostility, but he began to see that he had chosen many similar girlfriends in the past. By taking the time to give a description of this dream image, John alerted himself to a troublesome pattern of attraction to dishonest, destructive women.

When your description of a dream lover reminds you of a family member, don't panic. As you will see in chapter eight, such dreams can suggest sexual or emotional abuse, but often they do not. The context of the dream is, of course, important. If you are being coerced into sexual or violent acts by someone who looks like or reminds you of a parent or sibling, ask yourself if you have felt or have actually been abused emotionally, sexually, or physically by that person. If the answer is yes, it would be good to see a therapist to explore the matter further. If the sex in the dream is pleasurable or only a little awkward, look for a metaphoric meaning, again by describing the dream lover and the dream action. What does it remind you of? Angie dreamt of finding herself in bed between her mother and her father. She felt awkward and knew she should not be there. When she awoke, she saw the dream as a metaphoric expression of her recent competition with her mother for her father's attention. The dream made her admit that she had gone too far and that she needed to find her own man. She did not see the dream as a cloaked expression of a desire to actually have sex with her father but as a commentary on her inappropriate alliance with her father, which tended to crowd out her mom.

If you dream of having sex with a person at work you could indeed be expressing an unrealized desire. But far more likely, your description of the office lover will turn up unexpected meanings. You may find that you describe the coworker in terms that remind you of your husband or wife. Sally dreamt that her coworker, Will, had seduced her in an empty boardroom. Because of her dalliance, she was late to a very important meeting. Sally woke up furious at herself for having let herself be distracted. When she described Will to herself as a fun-loving, zany guy who was always behind schedule, but smiling, she realized that she had just described an important aspect of her husband. Sally further realized that, just as in the dream, she had lately been letting herself be seduced into too much playfulness with her husband to the point that she was falling way behind on her work.

The interpretation of this most common of sexual dreams, that of having a sexual encounter with an unexpected partner, depends entirely upon your descriptions of the dream lover and the events of the dream. Sometimes you may use the image of a dream lover to represent someone you have not yet realized you are attracted to. For example, you might dream of a warm, appealing pilot who, upon closer inspection, reminds you of your therapist. Of course you might dream directly of your therapist as himself or herself. Your attraction to your therapist might include romantic feelings that, while a normal response, should be made conscious so that you can talk about your feelings and not act them out in any actual sexual behavior with your therapist. *Discussing* with your therapist your sexual and romantic feelings for him or her can lead to important and useful insights. *Acting* on these feelings leads to the destruction of the therapeutic alliance and to emotional damage for you, the client.

The Five Major Elements of a Dream

When you first try to interpret a dream, the task can seem daunting. While we sleep we make up picture stories that often seem incomprehensible to our word-oriented waking minds. Relating the visual metaphors or parables of dreams to our waking lives requires that we look carefully into our thoughts and feelings about a visual image *before* we attempt to relate it to something in our waking concerns. Where should you begin? First, identify the major elements of the dream. Then you can begin your interview by asking exploratory questions tailored to each type of element.

Most dream imagery can be categorized as follows:

1. Settings: Where do the various dream scenes take place? The locale of a dream could be an automobile, a schoolroom, your childhood home, Texas, or the French Alps.
2. People and animals: What characters appear in the dream? Dream figures could include an unknown prowler, a horse, your ex, a brother, Madonna, a coworker, Suzi from the fourth grade, or that gorgeous Dane you met in Istanbul.
3. Objects: What are the major objects in the dream? Dream objects such as a gun, an airplane, a red dress, a piano, a seesaw, a key, or a golden coin can convey unexpected meanings.
4. Feelings: What did the dreamer feel at various points in the dream? Identify the feelings by putting words to

them such as *curious, frightened, anxious, sad, happy, relieved,* and so on.

5. Action: Who was doing what at any given moment, and what is the overall plot of the dream? Was the plane taking off or crashing? Was the dog chasing you or was she licking your hand? Did the sexual encounter go well or were there problems and interruptions?

DREAM DIAGRAMING

When you are just beginning to use this method, you will find it much easier if you have a copy of the dream in front of you and mark out or diagram these elements. Here is how we do it at the Delaney & Flowers Dream Center:

1. Settings: Draw a rectangle around the words indicating the setting of any particular scene.
2. People and animals: Circle the main characters throughout the dream.
3. Objects: Underline the major objects mentioned in the dream account.
4. Feelings: Draw a wavy line under or circle around any words that describe or suggest feelings. If none or very few appear, be sure to inquire and jot them down as you go through the interview.
5. Action: Underline with an arrow the major actions in the dream.

Let's look at how we diagramed the dream of Alexandra, a lively schoolteacher who was a member of a weekly study group:

Lynn and I have been whoring. We have been making tons of dates. My husband saw me writing down something. I felt naughty. I had all the appointments written on the underside of a box. I noticed that I had scheduled several extra dates for the same day. My husband saw me looking at the box so I put it back on the shelf. He did not catch on.

Lynn and I <u>didn't know how we were going to ditch our husbands</u>, who were walking down the street with us. As we were slowly ambling down the street, we just took off running into the shopping center. We left our husbands behind.

As we are running, I say to Lynn, "<u>Did you bring rubbers?</u>" She said, "No." I said, "<u>If we are going to be doing this, we've got to get our act together.</u>" . . .

"Whoring"

This brief highlighting of the major elements of the dream will provide you with a preliminary map of action for conducting your interview. We have identified the major elements of the dream for which we are going to obtain good descriptions from the dreamer. (Diagraming is especially useful to help organize your interview when you play the role of your own interviewer.) It usually works best to inquire about each element in order of appearance.

Of course, getting a good description of the dream images is only part of the process. To help the dreamer recognize an image as a metaphor for something in her life, the interviewer should *recapitulate* or mirror the description to the dreamer in the dreamer's own words. Then the interviewer will ask the dreamer if she can *bridge* from the dream experience to waking life by asking the dreamer if a given description reminds her of anyone, anything, or any part of herself. These three steps of *description, recapitulation, and bridge* are central to the Dream Interview method. This systematic questioning helps the dreamer explore both the dreaming and waking sides of the metaphor, minimizing time lost chasing after excessively tangential associations and prefabricated or arbitrary interpretations. Asking for descriptions from the point of view of someone from another planet, we can rather quickly find out what the dreamer (or we ourselves) think and feel about the images that make up the dream.

In most interviews, the dreamer and the interviewer will have to make choices regarding how thorough to be. Time will not always allow the full exploration of every image. With experience, you will learn to recognize which images are most essential to the structure and feelings of the dream and be able to focus on them more efficiently. You will also gain confidence as you discover that if you have omitted an important part of the interview, the dream will not make much sense, and you will know to go back and investigate some of the elements you omitted earlier. While usually there are a few obviously predominant dream images in a dream, marked by the clarity of their recalled vividness and by the intensity of the feelings associated with them, *all* the images in a dream are relevant and offer clues to its meaning. Sometimes you will be surprised to discover that apparently secondary details (such as the color of the car you were driving, or the style of clothing your dream antagonist wore) will remind you of a very specific attitude or person and thus point to the bridge and the meaning of the image. When a small detail is recalled with particular clarity take a little extra time to get a good description of it. You will usually be well rewarded.

To give you a feeling for how an interview unfolds before getting too specific about the other steps involved, let's look at part of Alexandra's work with her dream.

INTERVIEWER: Well, Alexandra, that is quite a dream! The first element you mention is the person, Lynn. Could you tell me who Lynn is and what she is like? *(Eliciting a description of a person.)*

ALEXANDRA: She's my best friend, a fellow teacher. She was really into sex when she was younger. She's very creative and like me she's on a diet.

I: So, she's your best friend, a fellow teacher who was really into sex when she was younger, and she's creative and on a diet. *(Recapitulation of the dreamer's description.)* Does she remind you of anyone or anything in your life? *(Asking the dreamer to bridge from the dream image to something in waking life.)*

A: No. Well, of me a little. (We can't be sure yet whether Lynn is herself in the dream or if she represents an aspect of Alexandra's or someone else's personality.)

I: Okay. Tell me about whoring. What on earth is it? *(Eliciting a description of an action.)*

A: It's having sex with miscellaneous men. When I was younger, I always thought it would be exciting and fun. It could offer lots of independence and money. But nowadays it would be crazy because of AIDS, and then there is the physical danger. But in the dream it seemed fun and exciting.

I: Is there anywhere in your life where you feel as if you've been out doing something like whoring? Like having sex with miscellaneous men for fun and excitement, even though it's crazy, and where you've overbooked yourself? *(Bridge question.)*

A: No, not yet. (Both the dreamer and interviewer know that there are many clues yet to be explored and that it often is difficult to bridge early in the dream.)

I: What was the box like?

A: It was the sort that holds a necklace. It was a discarded gift box with a floral design.

I: So you are keeping your appointments on the underside of a discarded gift box out of your husband's easy sight? *(Recapitulation.)*

A: Yes.

I: How did you think your husband would feel if he found out what you were up to? And did you care? *(Eliciting description of dreamer's expectation and motivation/feeling in the dream.)*

A: He'd be furious, jealous. Of course I cared, I don't want to lose him. I love him.

I: What is a shopping center? *(Eliciting a description of a setting.)*

A: A grouping of a wide variety of stores where you can buy lots of different things.

I: So is there anything going on in your life that is like going off with Lynn to have tons of dates with miscellaneous men? Where you are overbooked, wonder how you are going to ditch your husbands, and take off in a shopping center where one can buy a lot of different things? *(Recapitulation and bridge question.)*

A: Well, both Lynn and I are on sabbatical this year and we're both playing very hard, though not sexually. We are taking all sorts of classes and doing fun, exciting things. Actually, my husband is sort of irritated and angry. Both husbands are jealous that we play, they work. That's a funny metaphor. (*A strong bridge.*)

I: It is. Next, you ask Lynn about the rubbers. Remember, I come from another planet, what is a rubber? (*Eliciting a description of an object.*)

A: A condom, a device which makes sex safer, it protects you from the negative consequences of sex, such as pregnancy and disease.

I: How do you feel about Lynn's not having brought the rubbers? (*Eliciting a description of a feeling.*)

A: Well, I am upset. We could get into lots of trouble by not taking precautions and getting our act together.

I: I see. Is there any way that you and Lynn, while seeking fun and excitement on your sabbaticals, have overbooked yourselves and failed to take the necessary precautions? (*Bridge question.*)

A: Yes. At the beginning of our sabbaticals, when I had this dream, Lynn and I took too many courses, all sorts [like the miscellaneous men], and we got overloaded, and our husbands got bent out of shape. We decided to cut back and be more careful of our own energies and of our relationships.

As you can see, the interviewer does not have to supply the dreamer with interpretations, but has only to help the dreamer discover how much she really knows about the images in her dream and about how they shed light on analogous waking situations. As the dreamer discovers the metaphoric bridge from each image to waking life, the various images and the dramatic structure of the dream fall into place as a sort of parable of a current or earlier life situation.

If a dream depicts childhood feelings and situations, it is because they have been triggered or are currently influencing the dreamer's present life. It is typical of dreams to pinpoint a problem well before we consciously recognize it. Had Alexandra seen the metaphors in her dream when she first had it, things might have gone more smoothly. It might be tempting to suggest that Alexandra should have taken her sabbatical freedom and run with it without regard for her husband's jealousy and anger, but that would be imposing upon Alexandra's dream. In her dream, and in waking life, Alexandra felt that she was too overbooked and unprotected for her own good. She felt she and Lynn had to get their act together if they were to continue this sort of fun. In fact, she did not cease her fun-seeking behavior, she merely modified it to better suit her personal and interpersonal needs.

OVERVIEW OF THE DREAM INTERVIEW METHOD

Working with your dreams is a fascinating endeavor, but it can be a frustrating one without guidelines. If you supplement your solo dream study with an hour or so a week with a friend or dream specialist you will likely find that you learn faster and have a lot of fun. In case you, like most of us, feel shy about sharing your sexual dreams, remember that you can practice with your dream partner by working on any of your other dreams. Whether you work on your dreams alone or with a partner you will have more success if you organize your interview. Following the six basic interview steps in a flexible but thorough way will help you explore the dream effectively with a minimum of distortion from extraneous or misleading projections and premature formulations.

1. *Get a rich description* of all the major dream elements. Ask the dreamer to describe—and in the case of objects, define—the major elements of the dream as if he were describing them to someone from another planet who depends on him to learn about life on earth. Ask the dreamer for a definition/description that includes his feelings or judgments of each element (for example, ask "What is whoring?").

2. *Recapitulate* each description using the dreamer's words and tone. Do not add your own words or associations. The words the dreamer chooses will usually be the most potent associative triggers. Edit and synthesize slightly if necessary to make the descriptions terse. Do not interpret, just mirror the dreamer's descriptions.

3. *Bridge* from the dream images to specific situations in

the dreamer's life. Ask "Does [recapitulate the description] remind you of anything or anyone in your life?" or "Does it remind you of any part of yourself?"

4. *Test* the strength of the bridge. Verify and clarify. A dreamer will sometimes make a bridge not because there is a good fit but in an effort to please the interviewer. Have the dreamer tell you specifically *how* the dream element relates to the dreamer's waking life. Say something like, "You say this dream image [or action or feeling] reminds you of X. How so?" Dreamers will also sometimes bridge from only a small part of a description, ignoring the many other aspects of the dream image that don't seem to fit the bridged-to waking situation very well at all. Upon testing such a bridge, the dreamer can usually see that the dream image really doesn't correspond very well to the identified waking situation. When this occurs, simply return to the definition and ask for the dreamer to give it to you once again and to elaborate if appropriate. Then, armed with more information, recapitulate and bridge again.

5. *Summarize* descriptions and bridges as you go along, especially at the end of each scene and at the end of the interview. Ask the dreamer to correct you if you misstate or give an inappropriate emphasis to any part of the summary. And be sure to invite him to add any thoughts that occur to him as you are making your summary, for these are often very helpful and integrative in nature. As the dreamer listens to a summary or conducts one for himself, the pieces of the dream continue to fall into place and the overall thrust of the dream usually becomes clearer.

6. *Reflect.* Invite the dreamer to consider what, if any, actions or attitudinal shifts might be appropriate in light of the insights gained from the dream interview. Ask the dreamer to reread the dream two or three times over the next week and deliberately keep in mind the major dream images and insights for the entire week. Writing a one-page summary of the dream interview is extraor-

dinarily useful for most dreamers. By putting in writing your thoughts and insights generated by the dream work, you are more likely to remember them, understand them better, and make use of them.

How will you know when you have accurately interpreted your dream? The best guideline is this: when the dream makes sense to you and when you have gained one or more insights that lead you to say "Of course, why didn't I see that before?" Dreams offer you good common sense about your life. A good interpretation should open your eyes to something that, once seen, makes perfect sense in the context of your daily life.

You may and probably will make some farfetched interpretations in the beginning of your dream study. Check your interpretations to see if all of the major elements of the dream fall into place and are concordant with your hypothesis. If a predominant feeling or action just doesn't fit into your interpretation, start over again to see if you took a wrong turn or if you have simply failed to get a good description and bridge of the part that seems not to fit. Also, be wary of interpretations that seem too pat, that relate your dream to psychological or mythological jargon rather than directly to your life situation. It is easy to interpret the two pears on the windowsill as your mother's breasts, the conductor's baton as your penis, and a cave as your mother's womb. But what good will that do you? Describe each of the images first, forgetting about superstitious or traditional meanings, and find out what your images mean *for you*! A correct interpretation will not necessarily be a complete one at first. It often takes days or weeks to appreciate the full impact of a dream and its relevance to various aspects of your life.

Let's look at two short dreams that required only brief interviews. Bert, a twenty-five-year-old man, dreamt:

> I saw my wife and my father in bed having sex. When they were finished, my father left the room. My wife said, "Can't you be better than your father?"
>
> *"My Wife and Dad"*

INTERVIEWER: What is your wife like?

BERT: She's fun, sexy, kind. I love her a lot. We get along well.

I: What is your dad like?

B: He's a really good guy. Very successful in every way except monetarily. He's loving, honest, dependable, fun. He's really great.

I: So he's very successful except monetarily, loving, honest, fun, a really good guy. Does he remind you of any part of yourself or of any situation in your life?

B: Well, you know, he's really great, but I feel he has missed so many opportunities in life. It's almost impossible not to make it monetarily if you just stay alert. Yet I find myself in the same situation. I'm a good guy who just can't seem to make it monetarily.

I: So you have that in common with your dad to your surprise?

B: Right.

I: How do you feel watching your wife and your dad in bed?

B: Sort of numb. A little jealous.

I: What is your wife up to by asking you "Can't you be better than your dad?" What does she mean? (Here I, the interviewer, am asking for a fuller description of the wife's action, that is, her motivation for posing this question.)

B: I'm not sure, but I think she is daring me, and I don't know how to respond I am so surprised by the scene.

I: Is there any way in your life that your wife has been daring or challenging you to be better than your dad?

B: Not that I remember. Wait a minute. In the dream she's assuming I've got a problem with trying to do better than my dad sexually. That means doing better economically, as a potent, powerful man. I'm sure of it.

I: In your waking life have you, in fact, had trouble being willing, let alone being able, to outdo your dad?

B: Boy! That may be the big invisible barrier that's been in my way. How stupid! I guess that a part of me has been unwilling to outdo the dad I admire so much. He would be fine with it. I'm the one with the hang-up. I wonder if my wife has seen this problem all along?

Bert used manifestly sexual imagery to express concerns and dynamics of interpersonal and intrapersonal issues. But this was not evident before the dreamer gave his descriptions of the dream elements. Here is Renata's dream, which went from apparently nonsexual imagery to a sexual issue:

> I removed the red nail polish from my toes and finger-nails and redid them with a pearly white polish. I smilingly showed my fingers and toes to my husband, hoping for approval and appreciation.
>
> *"White Toe Polish"*

At the time of this dream Renata and her husband had just started living together again after having been separated for two years. After only two interview questions, she understood her dream.

INTERVIEWER: I come from another planet. Why do human females wear toe and nail polish?
RENATA: To look sexy and attract the opposite sex.
I: What is the difference between wearing red and pearly white polish?
R: Oh! Red is the very sexiest color, and white is not at all sexy. White is the color of purity; red, the color of passion. I remember a poem, "Oh the red rose breathes of passion, the white rose of love . . ." meaning purity. The dream shows me forfeiting my passion in order to win the approval and love of my husband. I've given up my newfound interest in sexuality which precipitated our separation. My husband and I just have no really sexy energy between us. Now I am wearing that ghastly white that would go best with an old-fashioned nurse's uniform. I really have wiped out my sexual passion and am trying to be good and sweet. I think I've overdone it.

Renata's dream helped her see how her efforts to be a good little wife felt like they would lead her to a pretty, but bland, life. Her need for approval from her husband (who disdained red nail polish) now looked like a liability to her. She eventually divorced and later married a man for whom she wore very red polish.

As you can see, you need not interview yourself or your dreamer about every single image in the dream before the meaning emerges. Although every image constitutes a clue to the dream's interpretation, sometimes getting a good description of one or two of the major images will do the trick and the significance of the other images will become suddenly clear. If you have a dream of having a sexual encounter with an unexpected partner, you may get to the significance of the dream by giving a rich description of that partner. Winston, a heterosexual man, had the following dream:

> I was at the office one morning when a coworker, Paul, gave me a big wet kiss on the lips. I found this objectionable and I just wanted to get the hell out of the office. Actually, I wanted to tell him, "I'm just not your sort of guy."
> *"Wet Kiss"*

INTERVIEWER: What is Paul like?
WINSTON: He's a very gung-ho corporation man. He's straight. He's really into the program at the company where I work. I would hate to be like him—a conformist follower.
I: Is there any way you feel like someone or something that is gung-ho corporate and conformist is coming on to you?
W: Yes. I've been thinking that I should take a full-time job at work where I've been a part-time consultant. But I am very uncomfortable that I might turn into a dull, conformist corporate man. I'm not that sort of guy! I like my freedom, and I detest conformity. Full-time feels like a wet kiss. But the security and increased income of a full-time job looks important now that my daughter is going to be off to college soon.

Winston's dream was underlining his distaste of conformity and his strong feelings of not wanting to become a company man at a time when he was trying to convince himself to take a full-time job in order to help his daughter out with her education expenses. Winston's dream led him to ask how he could work full-time and not turn into a corporation man.

Pleasant steamy dreams of coworkers often leave us feeling uncomfortable and puzzled. If you have such a dream, relax. They are very common. Describe the coworker's personality. She may well remind you of someone with whom you are or have been romantically involved. But you might find that the woman in your dream reminds you most vividly of the woman in your dream! Perhaps you are more attracted to her than you had realized; perhaps you were with her at a meeting the night before and used the dream to blow off steam in a safe, uncomplicated fashion. Sometimes an erotic dream is little more than a nocturnal sexual fantasy. There is no harm in enjoying these dreams and waking with a smile on your face.

Dreams of unknown lovers can be dealt with in the same way. Diana dreamt:

> I am walking down a wooded path with a handsome, fascinating man. He is very interested in me. I can hardly believe it. We kiss and make love by the river. It is wonderful.
> *"Who Me?"*

INTERVIEWER: The setting is a wooded path by a river? What was it like?
DIANA: Beautiful. Very romantic.
I: Can you tell me more about this man's personality?
D: He was handsome, kind, competent. A real catch.
I: How did you feel about his interest in you?
D: I could hardly believe that such a neat guy would fall for me.
I: Is he sincere?
D: Without question.
I: Does this handsome, kind, competent, fascinating man remind you of anyone in your life, or of any wished-for someone?
D: Actually, a man, Matt, whom I've dated a few times seems a lot like him. But I've been very suspicious of his sincerity. Gorgeous men like him have never been attracted to me before. I hadn't seen the parallel before between the man in the dream

and this guy. Maybe I'm telling myself Matt is sincere after all. We'll see.

Diana did not interpret her dream to be a kind of psychic omen that Matt was indeed sincere. But the very experience in the dream of having felt that such a man could be attracted to her made her a bit less defensive around Matt. She became more willing to give him the benefit of the doubt while nevertheless continuing to check him out over time.

Jason dreamt of having great sex with Margaret Thatcher, even though, in the dream, he knew he didn't like her very much.

INTERVIEWER: Who is Margaret Thatcher?
JASON: She used to be the prime minister of Great Britain. She is smart, tough, powerful, but too hard and rigid for my political tastes. Sexually, she doesn't interest me at all.
I: Why not?
J: I can't imagine her being tender or playful. She takes herself too seriously. At least that's the image I get from the press.
I: Does Margaret Thatcher remind you of anyone in your life who is smart, tough, powerful, but too hard and rigid for your tastes? Who takes herself too seriously and doesn't seem to be tender or playful?
J: Now that you put it that way, yes! The woman I've been seeing for the last few months is a successful partner in a big law firm and she is just like that! Smart and powerful and I love having sex with her. She excels at that, too. But if I were really honest with myself, I would have to admit that I don't like her all that much. And, no, she's not very tender or playful. I'm not proud of the fact that in my dream, as in my waking life, I'm having sex with women I don't like very well at all.

Jason's dream held up a mirror for him. He did not like the reflection of his behavior that he saw there.

How could we leave this section without discussing that ever-so-popular and ever-so-embarrassing dream of being naked in public? It may well be that everyone who lives in a culture that significantly clothes the body has had this dream. Certainly everyone I have ever worked with has. Common dreams like flying, falling, being chased, and finding oneself naked in public often elicit similar emotions in people. But why a particular individual would have this dream on a given night becomes clear only when the details of the dream are explored and when the dreamer places it in the context of his waking life.

If you can recall one of your dreams of being naked in public, ask yourself:

- What was the setting of my nakedness like?
- How did I feel being naked? (I'll pretend you have said you felt embarrassed and overexposed, but use your own adjectives if they are different.)
- Do the setting and the thoughts and feelings associated with it remind me of any situation in my life at the time in which I felt the same quality of embarrassment or uncomfortable exposure?

If you are able to remember the emotional atmosphere in your life the day preceding the dream, or if you can use the day notes in your journal to recapture it, this mini-interview may solve the riddle. If you have not been able to put your finger on the meaning of your dream, keep your journal and next time you have the dream, work on it while it and the ambience and the facts surrounding it are still fresh in your mind. As you have already guessed, people usually have these dreams following days in which they have felt uncomfortably exposed or vulnerable. Sometimes these dreams come in anticipation of a situation (public speaking, meeting prospective in-laws) in which the dreamer fears being criticized. Whether or not the dreamer's actual exposure was excessive, or whether he only feared being criticized, will be reflected by the reaction of the public in the dream. Usually the public is entirely unperturbed by the dreamer's nakedness, and rarely does the dream seem to have to do with specifically sexual concerns. The bigger issue is most often the dreamer's anxiety and fear of revealing his inner feelings and rendering himself more vulnerable to judgment and criticism.

Asking Effective Questions

As you may have noticed, dream interviewer questions appear rather casual in structure and conversational in tone. This is no accident. These questions have been refined over two decades to elicit the most relevant and concise information from the dreamer while minimizing the dreamer's discomfort and the interviewer's intrusion. Below is a list of basic questions tailored for exploring each element of a dream and for executing the basic steps of description, recapitulation, bridging, and testing, as well as summarizing.

Notice the exact wording of the questions. One word can make a huge difference in the response elicited. For example, the word *like* is extraordinarily effective. If you ask a dreamer or yourself, "What does high school mean to you?" you will usually get a dull, rambling response. But if you ask, "What is high school *like*?" most dreamers will respond to the alien interviewer with a more focused and emotion-laden description. You may have to remind yourself and your dreamer that you come from another planet when you ask questions such as "Who is Robert Redford, and what is he like?" Don't accept "You know who he is!" for an answer or you will never really find out how the dreamer sees him. When you are interviewing yourself, it is just as important to ask and answer these questions in full. You will be surprised at the words you come up with to describe your dream images. And it is these words that will trigger your recognition of the metaphorical nature of your dream pictures.

Here is a streamlined version of the most often used interview questions.[1] You can use this cue card when you work on your own or a friend's dream. You can also ask a friend to use the questions to interview you.

DREAM INTERVIEWER'S CUE CARD

Settings: Descriptions and Bridges

1. Describe the opening (or next) setting of the dream.
2. What is this place like in waking life?
3. What is this place like in your dream?
4. How does it feel to be in this setting?
5. Does this (recapitulate the description) remind you of anything in your waking life?

People and Animals: Descriptions and Bridges

6. Who is X?
7. What is X like in waking life?
8. What is X like in your dream?
9. Does X, whom you describe as (recapitulate the description), remind you of anything, anyone, in your life?
10. Does X remind you of any part of yourself?
11. How so? (Test the strength of the bridge by asking the dreamer to elaborate on how the dream image fits the waking one. See if this is a good metaphorical match.)

Objects: Descriptions and Bridges

12. What is a Y?
13. What is the Y in your dream like?
14. How do you feel about the Y? Do you like or dislike it and why?
15. Does the Y in your dream which you describe as (recapitulate the description) remind you of anything in your waking life?
16. How so?

Feelings: Descriptions and Bridges

17. How do you feel at this moment in the dream?
18. Tell me more about this feeling.

19. Tell me about a time (or the last time) you felt this way.
20. Does this feeling of (recapitulate the description) remind you of anything in your current life?
21. How so?

Action: Descriptions and Bridges

22. Describe the major action or event in this scene.
23. Does this action (recapitulate the description) remind you of any situation in your life?
24. How so?
25. How would you describe the central plot of this dream?
26. Does this plot (recapitulate the description) remind you of any situation in your life?

Summary

27. Shall I summarize the descriptions and bridges made so far, or would you like to do it?
28. So in this part of the dream (this happened), which you described as (recapitulate), which reminded you of (bridge). Then (this happened). Does all this remind you of anything else?
29. Now, how do you understand your dream? Tell me the whole dream, adding the bridges and commenting on what you understand and what remains unclear.

Mastering the art of interpreting your dreams will take practice, but if you describe just one image at a time, and recapitulate and bridge when you can, you will learn how to do it. All the analyzed dreams in this book have been interpreted using the Dream Interview method. I shall frequently present dream interview dialogues so that you will become more familiar with the method as you read about the various ways in which dreams deal with sexual issues. If you would like to learn more about dream interviewing, my book *Breakthrough Dreaming: How to Tap the Power of Your 24-Hour Mind* teaches the method in detail.

5

Perfecting Your Sexual Style and Technique and Targeting Your Dreams to Free You from Old Inhibitions

DREAM-TAUGHT TECHNIQUES

Believe it or not, a number of my clients have actually dreamt of doing very specific things with their partners that they had not previously tried or had tried without enthusiasm. When these dreamers experimented with the dream techniques in waking life, their partners were delighted. Men have dreamt of new ways to pleasure their partner's breasts and labiae, for example, and women have reported dreaming better ways to stimulate their partner's penis, buttocks, and other erotic areas. The most valuable aspect of such dreams is not that the techniques practiced in the dreams are completely new to the dreamer. The value of these technique dreams is in the fact that they provide the dreamer with a firsthand experience of enjoying doing something different that is pleasurable to his or her partner. It may be in a dream that, for the first time, the dreamer discovers that a particular behavior he has avoided can be pleasurable. In dreams we can try out activities that in waking may be offensively colored with old inhibitions or premature judgments.

Sometimes we will resist giving our partner a particular sexual pleasure, not because we are inhibited but because we are locked in a power struggle with him. We may feel that giving him what he asks for is giving in to him in a more general way.

We may be responding to unresolved childhood conflicts and/or expressing sexually a feeling that a partner demands too much of us in general. As we shall see in chapter six, your dreams are quick to pick up relationship issues that impact your sexual relationship. However, if the interpersonal seas are calm, partners may have dreams that focus primarily on issues of sexual style and technique. These dreams seem to be rare, but when they are recalled, they can inspire one to set new goals and to work to overcome the conflicts that obstruct their attainment.

SEXUAL STYLE

I'm with a tall, sexy, lively woman. A friend. She is in a pretty, loose-fitting dress with nothing on underneath. I'm attracted to her, but she's complaining about Southern boys who just stand you up and pull down their pants and put their penises in. She says that doesn't satisfy her very much. She turns to me with a sexy smile and says, "And what could you do, Big Boy?" I respond, "I can sure do better than that." I think I'll have a good time having sex with her and demonstrating that I am better than the Southern boys.

"Southern Boys"

Stan had been married to his wife for nine years when he had this dream. He complained that his wife wasn't allowing herself to be open enough to sexuality. He blamed her conservative up-bringing and tried to be patient. She, on the other hand, complained that her husband's lack of interest in foreplay made of sex a quick and relatively uninspiring affair. Knowing this, we can guess what the dream was about, but we can't be sure. Furthermore, until Stan figures out the problem for himself, he probably will not respond to other people's requests or advice. I, as interviewer, asked Stan:

INTERVIEWER: What are Southern boys like?

STAN: They are rural, impulsive, friendly, uncultivated, ambitious. Regarding sex, they won't compromise what they want in order to please the female.

I: How do you feel when you say, "I can do better than that"?

S: I realize that to get up her skirt I'll have to do better than the Southern boys. But awake, I note that I am not entirely happy with her demands. I'd like her to just get to it and come quickly.

It wasn't hard for Stan to make the bridge from the Southern boys to himself. His Southern-boy style, as Stan described it, was evident in the description, his feelings upon waking, and in much of the descriptive tone of the dream. The fact that his motivation to please the lady was strongly colored by his goal to gain entrance to her and by his competitiveness with the Southern boys did not promise any quick resolution to his impasse with his wife. His attraction was stimulated by the apparent easy access to the woman without the undies, not by her interest in a more sensual encounter. For her part, his wife acted more seductive than she felt inside, and these misleading signals complicated matters still further.

I have many more examples of women's dreams than I do of men's because more women study their dreams. Dreams like Stan's, in which the male dreamer considers his unsuccessful sexual style, may be very common, but I have heard only a few in my practice. Again and again women tell their close friends and therapists that they wish their lovers or husbands were more attentive, more interested in sensual, mutually giving sexual encounters. They say that their requests for these have proved to be out of their lovers' or husbands' audible range of sound. A woman's desire for a sexually sophisticated and sensually luxuriant lover who can identify with her pleasure while enjoying his own motivates many an affair.

Although I have never heard a woman tell me of a dream of wanting her man to hurry up and get to the orgasm, I did once hear a dream that indicated that the man wanted more foreplay. Ellie dreams of her new boyfriend:

We're on my bed planning on making love. John tells me that there are potato chips in the bed. I brush them aside into a pile on the floor.

"Chips in Bed"

Coming from another planet, I of course asked Ellie what potato chips are like. She said that they are junk food you eat in a rush. She immediately bridged the image to the way she has been treating sex. She's been having sex on the run, and it hasn't been very good. Her boyfriend had begun to protest. . . .

INHIBITING SELF-IMAGES

Dreams often reveal how we see our bodies and our images as sexual beings. We also get new perspectives on how others see and react to us. Coping with aging is not easy. One woman dreamt:

I looked in the mirror and saw that something about my hair showed that I had cancer and eventually would die from it. Although I knew I could handle this information, I worried in the dream about telling my husband. I felt the news would be too much for him to handle and decided not to tell him.

"Hair Cancer"

When she asked herself what would be like a cancer of the hair she thought of her newly noticeable white hair and of her decision to dye it. What surprised her was that a part of her took the matter seriously enough to dream of it as a cancer and that she wanted to hide it from her husband. She realized that she had underestimated her worry that her husband might not be able to take it if she looked gray and older.

Somewhere in their thirties some women start dreaming of having sex with younger men. Sometimes things go very well in the dream. Sometimes women become aware for the first time that they are being seen as older women, and they feel less attractive and insecure. These dreams can help a woman to begin facing the fact of aging. They can also be indicators that there is a crisis of self-confidence on the horizon.

Recently divorced women will sometimes dream of the handsome and interested younger lover, or of contemporary or even older attractive men who surprise them with their interest. If the dreamer cannot bridge these dream lovers to any one in her waking life, the dreams often put the dreamer in touch with a part of herself that feels attractive or that is seen by the world as attractive. These dreams can be powerful mood lifters and confidence builders. While we could call them wish-fulfillment dreams, I think that would short-circuit some of the more beneficial aspects of such dreams, which usually come when we are grappling with issues of self-esteem. A woman who feels sexy and attractive is more likely to appear so to the outside world. Dreams can remind you what it feels like to feel great, and then it's up to you to take the ball and run with it. In other words, after the dream, it's your turn to do whatever it takes to nurture positive feelings about yourself.

Sometimes the dream imagery that seems to be pointing to body image issues turns out, upon closer inspection, to be dealing metaphorically with self-confidence and sometimes interpersonal issues as well. Here is a middle-aged woman's body image dream with an unusual ending:

> My husband, Pierre, says I'm fat. I say, "Well, let's see." I show him and we examine together different parts of my body. I say things like, "Is this part fat? Would you call my arms or my chest or my hips fat? Now look at my legs. Would you call this fat? I wouldn't. I wouldn't call this a fat leg. You usually say you like shapely legs. I *could* make it thinner, but one could hardly call it fat!"
>
> *"Pierre Says I'm Fat"*

The evening before this dream, Julie had had a fight with her husband about what she saw as his excessive drinking. Pierre had been suffering a hangover from the night before. He had denied that he had a problem and said that his wife was hyper-critical and overreacting to having grown up with alcoholic parents. Julie had decided to incubate a dream by writing in her journal just before sleep: "Is this terrible fight due to my stuff [emotional baggage], as Pierre suggests?" Julie understood the dream to mean that she was okay in this matter, that she was the one who was unjustly criticized, and that it was time for her to stick to her guns.

Obviously, it is hard to have an exuberant sexual life if you have an extremely bad self-image. A very negative self-image can lead to poor partner choices and unsatisfying or even unpleasant sexual experiences.

USING YOUR DREAMS TO EXPLORE YOUR SEXUAL SELF-IMAGE

How do you see yourself as a sexual being? What is the image you project to the world and what is the one you privately hold? Are they the same? Are you a stud, a nerd, a lamb in wolf's clothing, an artist, a Southern boy, or a femme fatale, a Ms. Prim, a Ms. Cosmopolitan, a tigress, a lamb in tiger skins? In your dreams you picture yourself in ways that may sometimes surprise you. Your dreams can show you how you feel underneath your facade, how you have expressed yourself sexually, and how you might yet express yourself if given the right conditions. How we behave sexually is not always how we *feel* sexually. Men have long been pressured to exaggerate their sexual drive and women to downplay theirs in order to win approval. Some women who play the insatiable tigress are really not as interested in sex as they are in winning love and attention. One relatively easy way to gain a better understanding of your sexual self-image is to ask for a dream that will give you a reading on the matter. You will find instructions on how to do this later in this chapter.

Sharing Dreams

Simply telling your pleasurable erotic dreams to your partner can help you to communicate your sexual wishes. And letting your partner know what you want sexually is as much a part of sexual style as is learning what he or she wants and how best to provide it. In the context of sexual therapy, Dr. Alexander Leavy and Dr. Joseph Weissberg have noted: "Frankly sexual dreams frequently provide clues to preferred methods of arousal as well as to areas of inhibition."[1] Sharing your dreams can make it easier to let your partner know what sort of touching and atmosphere or settings might appeal to you. In addition to helping you express wishes or desires you find difficult to verbalize, sharing dreams can lead to a discovery and sharing of insights that help you see beneath the surface of sexual and relational problems.

Of course, there is some risk in telling your partner about your erotic dreams and the insights that flow from them. Take a moment to consider the impact such revelations might have on your partner and on your relationship. If your partner is unfamiliar with the various ways in which dreams work (mixing literal and metaphorical imagery, and so forth), he or she might feel needlessly threatened, criticized, or outdone. If your partner tries to interpret your dreams without first eliciting your descriptions and bridges, *you* may feel run over, inappropriately analyzed, and put down. So proceed with caution.

For example, it can be difficult to share a wonderfully erotic dream in which you reunite with an old flame. Just as in sharing sexual fantasies, you must carefully gauge the effect of telling such dreams. It is not uncommon for a partner to become very hurt and angry upon hearing that his or her lover spent the night in dreamland with another lover, especially a former lover. One way to deal with this problem is to tell the dream but leave the lover unidentified, but this may still trigger difficulties. It is a good idea to interview yourself about the dream first. After your interview, you may be in a better position to decide what to share and how to share the meanings you see in the dream. Not infrequently, when you describe the characteristics of the dream lover, you may be surprised to discover that you are describing none other than your waking lover.

For example, Kiri dreamt:

> I am in bed with Joe, my best lover. He is attentive, and when I give him a luscious, deep kiss, he feels so loved that he just opens his heart and becomes incredibly sensual and sexual. I awoke very turned on.
>
> *"Joe Again"*

Kiri lay in bed and interviewed herself before opening her eyes.

INTERVIEWER: What is Joe like in waking life?
KIRI: I haven't seen him for years since I've been married, but he was a very creative lover. He was warm, giving, and funny. That reminds me of Nate, my husband.
I: What was Joe like in the dream?
K: Wonderful, except he seemed as if he couldn't be there with me one hundred percent. He was a little stiff. But then when I kissed him, he really opened up. It seemed that he needed that expression of passion and eagerness from me.
I: So Joe reminds you of your husband. And Joe is a little stiff.
K: So is Nate! I've thought that he's a little stiff and not flowing lately. And maybe what he needs is a sign from me to reanimate him. I have been pretty passive lately.

Kiri savored and enjoyed the dream for itself. Then she interviewed herself, and from that decided not to tell her husband the dream and bring up her old boyfriend, but to act on her insight. After her interview, Kiri opened her eyes and gave her husband a special kiss. . . .

If a dream of a past lover reminds you of important deficiencies in your current relationship, it may be time to discuss the issues raised by your experience of the dream rather than the dream itself. Or you may decide to tell the dream to open a discussion of delicate issues dealt with in the dream action. One of the most valuable aspects of most dreams is that they can vividly express a complaint or dissatisfaction without finger pointing or blame. In a dream you can speak eloquently of your hopes, disappointments, and needs without blaming and offending your partner who later hears the dream.

Susanna had been more frequently avoiding rather than seeking sex with her boyfriend for almost a year. She seemed to have lost interest in sex and did not know why. One night she incubated the question and had the following vivid dream:

> My boyfriend and I are standing along the Seine in Paris. It is night. We notice a couple a short distance away. They are so in love. We watch them kiss. They are passionate, alive. At first I cry because I realize we don't have that anymore. Then I feel determined and say to myself, I *will* have that passion in my life again.
>
> *"Passionate Parisians"*

I have heard several versions of this dream of seeing others enjoy love and passion that seems lost to the dreamer. Usually the dreamer resolves to find it again. But upon waking, the inertia of the ongoing relationship often acts to vitiate the dreamer's courage and determination such that he or she fails to act. A dream can show you what you need to recognize, but it can't do the work of changing your relationships for you. Sharing your dream as a means of communicating something you want your partner to hear can get the ball rolling. Susanna did share her dream with her boyfriend. Both of them understood that it was time to look at a number of problems they had been sweeping under the rug before it was too late.

INTERVIEWING EACH OTHER

Going from simply sharing dreams and your insights from them to actually exploring them together and interviewing each other is a giant leap—a leap fraught with danger, but one that has the potential of spectacularly heightening the intimacy and trust you share with your partner.

Keep in mind that in sharing dreams with lovers, or even with friends, you are dealing with exquisitely intimate and often very tender feelings. Dreamers are almost always more vulnerable than they seem. They easily feel judged and criticized when no such thing was intended. Add to this the fact that a listening lover may feel threatened by the dream action and you have a potentially explosive situation. In addition to using your good sense in deciding whether or not to share a particular dream with a partner, remind each other that the one who plays the role of the interviewer must listen to the dream without interruption and proceed with the interview questions as if he or she came from another planet.

All interpretations or bridges should come from the dreamer, no matter how tempting it may be for the interviewer/lover to suggest them. Just as when adults work with children's dreams, a lover who suggests a possible interpretation is very likely to be perceived as pushy, controlling, scolding, self-serving, or intrusive. The minute the dreamer's feelings take a turn in this direction, he or she will become defensive and resentful. Good dream work will cease. To the degree that the dreamer feels listened to, accepted, and assisted in discovering his or her own meanings, dream sharing will enrich the relationship by reducing defensiveness, and promoting curiosity and openness.

Working with Dreams by Montague Ullman and Nan Zimmerman, *Romantic Dreams* by Patricia Maybruck, and my book *Breakthrough Dreaming* will give you detailed suggestions on how to avoid the pitfalls and take advantage of the opportunities inherent in sharing dreams.

HOW TO INCUBATE A DREAM

Have you ever gone to sleep with a problem on your mind and awakened the next morning with a dream on the topic or with the actual solution clearly in mind? Most people have had this experience at least once or twice. If you are willing to spend five or ten minutes with your journal just before sleep, you can turn this rare assist from the night into a dependable skill of having helpful dreams on the topic of your choice on the very nights you ask for them. This is called incubating a dream and generally works the first time you try it if you follow these instructions which are taken from my book, *Living Your Dreams*. [2] You can incubate dreams on any question in your life, from how to improve your ice skating or tennis game, to solving a math problem, to how to better understand why you can't get through to your child. Regarding sexual issues, you can ask for dream responses to questions such as "What is my main sexual hang-up?" "What is my greatest sexual gift?" "Why do I feel smothered, frightened, bored, when I make love with my partner?" or "What do I need to understand in order to improve my sexual relationship?" and so on. Here are the instructions for incubating whatever issue is important to you.

The Five Steps of Dream Incubation

1. Choose a night when you are not too tired.
2. After your day notes, write a few lines on what you would like your dreams to deal with. Churn up your feelings. List the different aspects of your problem or issue. Clarify your question and make it as specific as you like. This is called your incubation discussion, and you might want to write "ID" in the margin beside it in your journal.
3. Next, write out in big letters a one-line question or request such as "How do I really feel about myself as a sexual partner?" or "I'd like a dream that will inspire me to improve my sexual self-image." This is called your incubation phrase.
4. Turn out the light and repeat your incubation phrase to yourself over and over as you fall asleep. Feel the desire to learn something new, perhaps surprising or threatening, but helpful. Each time your mind wanders, repeat the phrase again until you fall asleep.
5. When you awake, in the middle of the night or in the morning, write down whatever is on your mind. You may recall a full dream, a little piece of a dream, a title of a song, or the direct answer to your question. If you first

awake in the middle of the night without any response in mind, as you fall asleep again reincubate your question by repeating your phrase over and over again. This will greatly increase your chances of success in the morning.

As you record whatever is in your mind when you awake, be careful to make no judgments at all as to its relevance to your incubated question. Often it is impossible to know what a dream is about until you have explored its images and metaphors that may at first seem to have nothing to do with your request. When you have time to interview yourself or ask a friend to interview you, I would suggest that you not assume that your incubation worked. First find out what the dream is about, then ask yourself if it sheds any light on your question.

When I work with my clients I usually prefer that they not tell me what the incubation question was until we have concluded the interview. This reduces the temptation to force-fit a perfectly good dream into an answer to a question to which it may not pertain. Almost any dream will deal with issues of import to the dreamer, and if an incubation did not work, there usually is a reason. Sometimes, a dreamer will incubate a dream on a relatively low-level concern, such as improving his golf swing or a skating move, on the very night that he has a painful fight with his wife. At such times, the more immediate and important problem will take precedence in the dream work of the night, thus aborting the incubation effort.

Now let's take a look at a young man's first effort to incubate a dream. Oscar, an attractive, single, real estate broker, complained that he kept finding himself in relationships with women who saw him more as a father figure and a protector. His girlfriends felt safe with him, but they didn't seem to have very strong sexual desires for him. One night he incubated a dream on the question "What's wrong with the sexual image I project?" He dreamt:

I was at a lively singles party. There were some gorgeous women there I wanted to meet. But as I approached one, another guy would cut me off and introduce himself. He was a psychiatrist, and the women liked him because he knew how to listen to them and put them at ease. I was amazed because he seemed sort of, well, not very sharp or energetic.

"A Psychiatrist Beats Me Out"

Oscar described psychiatrists as gentle, understanding, but not very dynamic people. Listening to the recapitulation, he suddenly said, "That is how women describe me when they leave me!" Oscar had not previously realized how much he came across as a psychiatrist, and decided to look for other ways to present himself in hopes of attracting a different kind of relationship.

Whether you incubate your dreams or take them as they come, they are a rich resource for understanding and developing your sense of yourself in the sexual arena. Ginger, a mother and housewife who had been married for a decade, dreamt:

> Two women enter a restaurant by the sea. One is wearing a bathing suit and the other a business suit. The maître d' shows them to a dreadful table in the dark bar with no view of the ocean. The lady in the bathing suit is willing to accept the table, but the lady in the business suit refuses it. She pays the maître d' five dollars for a wonderful table in the bright room with a good view. The two ladies sit down and get to know each other.

"Two Suits"

Ginger had no idea what the dream was about until she took the time to describe the two women.

INTERVIEWER: What is the lady in the bathing suit like?
GINGER: She is in a very sexy outfit. She is a sexual partner, mother, and housewife. She reminds me of my role as a woman since my marriage.
I: What is the lady in the business suit like?
G: She's superaggressive, independent, self-confident, and has lots of status and power. I could use some of that but don't have much.

I: Okay. The business-suited woman refuses to take the bad table and buys her way to a better one.

G: Yes. That's how men do it. She's smart, and not intimidated as the sexy one is. The maître d' reminds me of my husband now. He runs the show, but can be persuaded . . .

I: Do these two women remind you of anything?

G: Yes, of course, of the two extreme pictures I have of the choices of female style.

I: What do you think about that the two women are getting to know each other?

G: That's just what needs to happen. I need to get to know more about the parts of myself that are like these women, and I need to blend them a little. My images are too extreme, I avoid exercising power for fear of being perceived as a tough, overly aggressive woman. But I definitely want more status and power; I don't want to sit in the dark, I want a good position with a view.

Ginger's dream offered her insights that would significantly alter and expand her sense of herself in and out of bed. Sandra was also working on her self-confidence in life and in bed when she dreamt:

> My husband and I were in a bedroom. I noticed that he had his own black shiny phone by his side of the bed. And I didn't have one. Then, somehow, I found a black shiny phone of my own. I plugged it in next to my side of the bed. I had a great feeling of satisfaction that I now had a shiny black phone and Mike, too, was very happy that I had found one.
>
> *"My Own Phone"*

Sandra bridged the phone by saying that her husband, Phil, had long been a good communicator, especially with people in his business, and that his great rapport was like the envied, shiny phone. She wrote in the interview that "his own self-security and knowledge of this successful rapport have long been known to him, as has his comfort with his inner self. *My* phone was found later, just as in waking life I've only recently reconnected with my self-confidence. My communications with people are greatly increasing, as is my ability to communicate with my husband. I still have a lot of work to do, but at least now when he makes the first move to communicate, I can respond more fully and openly. And yes, this has its effects on our life in the bedroom as well."

Katherine was confused by her live-in boyfriend's on-and-off-again sexual interest in her. She began to feel more and more insecure, but couldn't get him to admit to any problem. She incubated a dream, asking, "What's going on under the surface in our sexual life?" She dreamt:

> By telephone, I'm invited to have sex with four guys I know. I accept, and we have fun, nice sex. Then the guy who invited me criticizes me for being loose sexually. He says that he had not intended any such thing as my having sex with four men. I am angry and call him on it. I say, "Did you not telephone me and invite me over to have sex with the four of you?" He hesitated and finally had to admit that he had.
>
> *"Sex with Four Men"*

Upon awakening, Katherine saw in the dream something she had failed to notice in her relationship. Her boyfriend suffered from a strong, if hidden, double standard. He regularly encouraged her to be sexually abandoned, but often after a good sex session he would withdraw for a few days. He, himself, was probably unaware to what extent his early religious training about sex still led him to invite and then criticize Katherine's sexual interest. By the way, people often dream of sexual activities that, while pleasurable in a dream, would be out of the question in waking life. Katherine used the image of sex with four men not to reflect past behavior or to inspire her to new feats, but (according to her description) to express a very open, very daring, and eager sexuality.

Now and then we have the good fortune to recall a dream that provides us with strikingly vivid and appealing images that make the work of self-discovery fun. Sandra, who needed help in appreciating and integrating two images of herself, reported such a dream:

> I was Doris Day—the blond, freckled girl next door. I was wearing a white old-fashioned swimsuit, the type with the bust that pushes you up. It was tight in the crotch and I had a sexy short skirt flowing over it. I remember being confused, wondering how could I be Doris Day while having a body like Marilyn Monroe. At first I was really self-conscious. Then I started to really feel my breasts in the tight suit and feel how sexy I really was . . .
>
> *"Doris Day/Marilyn Monroe"*

Our interview followed these lines:

INTERVIEWER: Pretend I come from another planet. Who is Doris Day, and what is she like?

SANDRA: She is a famous actress who always played the tomboy, flat-chested, friendly girl next door.

I: Does Doris, who is a friendly, flat-chested, tomboy girl next door, remind you of anyone?

S: That really is my image. I'm not flat-chested, but that is how I tend to come across.

I: Then can you describe Marilyn Monroe to me? What is she like?

S: Well, she was just incredibly sexy. In the dream there was no sense of her unhappiness, just of her/my voluptuousness. And yes, I suppose I am also sexy like her, but I have downplayed that in favor of my Doris Day persona. In fact, in the dream I originally discounted the Marilyn Monroe image by saying it was Doris Day when she was *fat*! I often tell myself that I'm fat, but I'm not really. In the dream, I felt sexy but also very vulnerable. Yet over all, it felt great to become aware of how sexy I was. I like the idea that I am or could potentially become both the friendly girl next door and the sexy Marilyn.

I: It might be worthwhile looking into your feelings of vulnerability when you feel sexy to see if they have been blocking your appreciation of your Monroe qualities.

Inhibitions

Do you have any sexual inhibitions from which you would like to liberate yourself? While sometimes inhibitions have deep roots in a painful childhood and require long self-study and often psychotherapy to safely root out, others are not so complicated. If you have inhibitions that seem to stem from a sense of prudish modesty or from early training regarding sex that you no longer respect, then you might want to set to work on them by using your dreams.

Like Ilena, who asked for a dream to help her past her resistance to licking a penis and had a dream of enjoying a penis as if it were a lollipop, you can certainly incubate dreams to look into whatever specific inhibitions are most bothersome to you. There are, however, a number of common dreams that are usually about sexual inhibitions, and knowing about them may alert you to them when they come your way spontaneously.

Dreaming of starting to have sex with an agreeable partner when suddenly in walks your father or mother or a friend is a classic. In most cases, the interrupter is quite at ease, not at all bothered or particularly interested in what you are up to. However, you, the dreamer, are completely nonplussed and unable to carry on. Sometimes you decide to go off in search of another private room, but most often the dream stops, leaving you rather frustrated. If you describe the personality of and sexual attitudes you learned from the interrupter, you will probably notice that there is a part of you that is haunted by those attitudes, which cause you some sexual discomfort. Ask yourself how you might be letting your parental images into the bedroom with you in such a way that you feel embarrassed about your sexuality.

If it is a friend who interrupts you, describe his or her personality and see if there is not a similar part of you or of your partner that disrupts your sexual flow. For example, if you describe an interrupting friend as a chatterbox, ask yourself if you or your partner break the magic of a sexual encounter with anxious chatter.

Many people dream of being interrupted while having sex by

a mother or father who enters the room and who acts as if nothing unusual is going on. Usually the dreamer becomes so self-conscious that he or she terminates the sexual encounter. Most dreamers understand these dreams to be portraying their own sexual inhibition in the presence of an internalized parent who haunts them into adulthood. Sometimes you will discover that the interrupter is not so much a metaphor for a part of yourself as an image that allows you to work out feelings related to the actual person visualized. Jeana had just moved into a new house-sharing situation and dreamt an interesting version of the interruption scenario.

> My new housemate, Kim, and I are in separate rooms. I'm watching TV and I'm masturbating by moving back and forth on the bed and letting my clit rub against the sheets. It's a new way for me and very stimulating and fun. I keep stopping, though. I am afraid Kim will come in as it's almost time to get up. I am watching a sexy scene on the TV which excites me. But I keep on stopping for fear of being walked in on. Then I finally realize that Kim would knock before coming in. I feel relieved.
>
> *"Masturbation"*

Jeana's feelings of discovering a new way to pleasure herself, of being more open and risk-taking, in the dream reminded her of parallel feelings in her waking life. She had just come out of a sad end to a romance and had moved, and was looking forward to new adventures in life. Our interview continued:

INTERVIEWER: You say you felt that Kim might walk in and that you felt at risk of being embarrassed?
JEANA: That's easy to bridge. I worry daily about disturbing someone in my new housing situation. I worry about being embarrassed, caught. I've not shared my personal habits with anyone for a long time.
I: What is masturbation?
J: It's a private, personal thing I do for myself to make me feel good. I like it whether or not I'm in a relationship. When I mas-

turbate I don't have to share my thoughts or reactions, and most importantly, I can take my own time. It's fun. I have total freedom and don't have to be answerable to anyone else.

I: So you are enjoying a new form of masturbatory pleasure where you are not answerable to anyone, can take your own time, and have total freedom. But you worry you will be intruded upon, embarrassed, caught. Do these feelings remind you of any situation in your life?

J: Of my new relationships with people like Kim and Joe, our other roommate. I'm opening up more emotionally, letting people in, but I'm still worried about my boundaries. The fact that I realize that Kim would knock makes me think that I am trusting more that I won't be transgressed upon. That I'm not really that vulnerable. And I think that in my relationships now I am better able to say yes *or* no.

Here Jeana dreamed up a dream that used her shyness and fear of being embarrassed while masturbating to highlight her concerns regarding privacy versus sharing issues. While dealing metaphorically about boundary anxieties, she also got a chance to look at how her fear of being caught and embarrassed interfered with private pleasures of masturbation.

Looking in vain for a private place to have sex is also a common dream. Ask yourself from whom do you want to hide your sexuality, and is your concern necessary in the context of the dream. Lina dreamt of being with her husband of fifteen years:

> Paolo and I are with a nice small group of friends. I am unobtrusively seated under the table between Paolo's legs and playing with his penis. I am getting turned on. I say, "Oh it's so big and thick. Oh boy!" Oops! Everyone heard me! Oh dear. Paolo, being very nice and pleased, suggests that the group continue its discussion while he and I go off and have sex. I am horribly embarrassed that he said that to them and am completely turned off.
>
> *"Did I Say That?"*

Often these dreams lead dreamers to see that the very fact that they enjoy sex is something they find embarrassing to admit. As they work at becoming more comfortable about their adult sexuality, people seem to have fewer of these dreams.

If you find yourself in dreams in which other people are pointing their fingers at you and criticizing you for kissing or bathing in the nude or some other harmless activity, ask yourself to describe the attitudes and motivations of the criticizers. Then look carefully to see if your descriptions portray an aspect of your own attitudes that may be left over from a time when you accepted other people's beliefs and pronouncements on a child's faith in adults. Look at Julius's dream:

> My wife and I are at the Pike Street market in Seattle. We see another couple embrace. We look away. We look back and now they are sunbathing in the nude. Other people start pointing their fingers, saying how disgusting it all is. People try to hurt them. It's not fair, they aren't hurting anyone.
>
> *"Embarrassing, Embattled Lovers"*

Julius's ambivalence toward the couple's open sexuality is clear in his first looking away, and according to his response to my questions, in the anonymous crowd's angry response. Julius and his wife were in a period of growth and opening up in their sexual relationship, and this dream illustrated some of the still strong negative attitudes yet to be understood and overcome.

These broad outlines are meant only as suggestions for a line of self-inquiry that my experience leads me to think will likely be relevant and useful for many of these types of dreams. But common dreams can, at times, have uncommon meanings. You, or the dreamer you are interviewing, may use one of these scenarios in an entirely idiosyncratic manner. Until you explore the personal associations to a dream, you cannot be sure what meaning the images carry for the particular dreamer. So please use these comments as pointers, not as fixed interpretations.

Before leaving our discussion of dreams that help to reduce our inhibitions and improve our technique, I'd like to draw your attention to a type of dream that strikes me as a special gift and that may be akin to instinctual programming and sexual development. As we saw in chapter two, young men regularly tell of delicious dreams in which an older, experienced woman seduces them. Where these dreams are without conflict, interviews have not revealed a repressed wish to have sex with Mother, and I do not think it appropriate to insinuate such a wish via an interpretation on my part. Rather, these dreams seem both to provide the dreamer with a sexual outlet in the form of wet dreams and to increase the dreamer's self-confidence and sexual pleasure. The emphasis is on the woman's greater sexual knowledge and confidence, which helps to bring the young dreamer along.

Whether or not young heterosexual women have such dreams, I cannot say. Certainly they dream of the eager, capable lover, but he is often a past lover or a romantic famous figure. The emphasis is not, in my experience, upon the fact that he is older and more experienced than the dreamer, although he may well be both. My impression is that when an explicitly older man is sexually involved with a woman in her dream, the feeling tone in the dream is one of fear or disgust. In the interview, we discover that these dreams often have to do with the dreamer's concerns relating to childhood molestation. Perhaps in the future someone will explore this question, and I will be able to report to you the results of his or her study.

PART TWO

INTIMATE PASSIONS

6

How What Goes On in Bed Reflects the Essential Dynamics of Your Relationship

DYNAMICS SEEN WHILE LOOKING THROUGH THE KEYHOLE

It is not true for everyone, but for most modern couples what goes on in bed usually reflects the essential dynamics of the entire relationship. Lovers who are generous, exuberant, and creative in bed will likely have very different relationships than do lovers who are selfish, passive, or critical.

EXERCISE **6-1**

**Compare Your Sexual with
Your Emotional Relationships**

Look back on your major sexual relationships. Did the qualities of your sexual relationship mirror those of your emotional relationship? Sometimes these parallels are easier to see and to admit when you have the benefit of hindsight and are no longer so threatened by seeing possibly uncomfortable truths.

EXERCISE 6-2

Early Warning Signs of Trouble

Pick any major past relationship that went sour. Think about how and why it ended. Now, go back to the first week or month of that relationship and try to recall what signs your lover gave you early on that foreshadowed the major problems in your relationship, signs that at the time you chose to disregard as unimportant because you preferred to focus on the good and exciting things between you.

If you are like many of the people I know, most of the dragons in your ill-fated affair were visible early on to anyone who cared to look. Workaholics would have shown you that they were obsessed by their jobs, alcoholics would have drunk too much, chatterboxes would have bent your ear, know-it-alls would have held forth, wimps would have wimped out in some way, complainers would have complained, and selfish lovers would have made love as if you weren't there or had no needs. Conflicts of style and goals were probably evident as well. He loved living in the city; she, in the country. He wanted children; she didn't. He loved to hunt and ride horses in Montana; she went to tropical islands or exotic cities whenever she could. He was a jock; she, a smoker. While you were awake you might have been wearing blinders in hopes that you had found or could sculpt Mr. or Ms. Right. But I would be willing to wager that in those first nights you took off your blinders more than a few times while you dreamt about your new romance.

My clients and students who keep dream journals have often looked back at the dreaming they did at the beginning of a new relationship and found information they wish they had understood and known how to use at the time. These dreams quickly pointed out the pros and cons of the romances, as well as their similarities to past relationships. However, since most of us miss the early warning signs and refuse to listen to our friends' advice or our dreams' insight, we often find ourselves in difficult relationships and can't quite make out what underlies the dissatisfaction or pain. At this point, we can get valuable insights about what is really going on by taking a close look at the qualities of our sexual encounters. In order to be able to reap from our sexual dreams the subtlety and depth of understanding they offer, we would do well to become more aware of and able to discuss (at least with ourselves) the nature of our waking sexual experiences.

Personality Traits Expressed in Sexual Interactions

Men who complain that their partners were tight and inhibited in bed after more than a month or so in the relationship often say that one of the major reasons they ended the relationship was because they found the women to be that way in most parts of their life and in their interactions. Greg had such a complaint, and his wife's timidity and unwillingness to try new foods and new activities in daily living were clearly reflected in her unwillingness to try oral sex or to have sex outside of the bedroom. Both in and out of bed, Greg interpreted his wife's timidity as a stubborn rigidity that denied him and her many new and pleasurable experiences. And I have never heard a woman complain that her husband is lethargic and dull in bed and then describe him as an exciting, scintillating person outside of it.

People who are extremely passive and dependent, or aggressive and controlling, usually show it in bed. Excessively dependent people often are far more interested in being hugged and cuddled—almost cradled in your arms—than in being erotically engaged in bed. Excessively controlling people can be very active lovers who have trouble being sexually receptive to your initiatives, and may be uncomfortable even in letting the other be on top. Sometimes highly controlling individuals seek out lovers who will dominate them in bed and relieve them of the leadership role. But often such a submissive lover is really the one in control. He or she may insist on always directing the style and timing of the other's dominance. All this is a question of degree. When a lover seems to be inflexible in his or her style, and when you find that style problematic, you have a good indication of possible troubles of a similar nature in your relationship.

People who are irresponsible and/or insincere may give you hints of these traits. What do they tell you about their sexual histories; how do they say it? Or do they avoid the issue until you bring it up? Are there inconsistencies or big gaps in the history? How convinced are you that you are hearing the whole truth? If you were scoring your lover on integrity and responsibility, how would you rate his or her answers regarding contraception and the prevention of spreading diseases? Is making sex safer left to you? Does your lover seem to support your efforts to deal with the issue, or does he or she imply that you are unkind to doubt or silly to worry? As difficult as it is to talk of disease and dying from sex, and as awkward as it is to take effective precautions, such discussions and actions do tell you a good deal about your partner. A lover who is interested in your health and shows it by showing you his HIV test results, by a willingness to use condoms, by following safer sex practices, and so on, will show you traits of caring that you are likely to see in other parts of your relationship, too. (If you would like to refresh your memory about how to make sex safer, see the information in the resources section at the end of this book.)

Interpersonal Dynamics

If you and your partner get into power struggles in bed, you probably suffer them in restaurants, on the dance floor, at home, everywhere. If your partner has to control the action in bed, and if you feel obliged to allow it, do you also abdicate your power of making decisions to him or her out of bed? If your lover doesn't ask how best to please you in bed, or listen to your suggestions, is he or she equally closed, defensive, or uninterested in your needs and preferences outside of the bedroom? Are you unable or unwilling to make your preferences known both in and out of bed? What price do you pay for this reticence? You may repetitively choose dominant, controlling partners who, while they may seriously constrict your personal growth and maturation, nevertheless relieve you of the task of learning what you want and of learning how to take the responsibility of getting it. If a woman tells you she can only make love in the dark, beware that you have met a woman whose timidity may be paralyzing to your relationship. If a man tells you what kinds of orgasms you should have, watch out! Besides being dreadfully misinformed, he may well have an oppressive need to instruct and correct you while avoiding dealing with his own problems.

The selfish, lazy, or inhibited lover is probably a selfish, lazy, or inhibited spouse or partner. The sexual doormat is probably always the doormat in the context of the relationship, even though he or she may be a real tiger at work. And if you are a partner to one of these types, what does that say about your need to play the supporting role a given personality type requires? What are you getting out of it? Or what are you getting out of, or hiding from, by continuing such a relationship?

Merging or Meeting in Bed

On more subtle levels, some people complain that what their partner wants sexually seems to be a kind of parental nurturing (soothing, reassurance, and acceptance) to the exclusion of excitement, drama, giving, or an electric meeting of an I with a Thou. Often lovers, especially younger lovers, like to think of the lover as a part of themselves and aim at merging into one. But if the other person, the Thou, is not granted and appreciated for his or her differentness and separateness, the erotic component of the relationship will tend to atrophy. The nurturing aspect of lovemaking is essential to most everyone, but when it is overdone, the resulting child/parent dynamic smothers the potential for a more adult, I/Thou encounter. The I/Thou relationship requires a greater sense of otherness and equality between the partners than is possible in the parent/child mode. And it requires more appreciation of the other's power of choice, initiative, and decision than is likely when a couple relates in parent/child patterns.

Domination/Submission

Carried out too regularly or too far, dominant-submissive relationships threaten the viability of the I/Thou quality of a relationship. By dominant-submissive, I refer to relationships that manifest a marked degree of this dynamic, which is found to a limited degree in most relationships. I am not referring to extreme versions that include sadism and masochism as a sexual fetish. Often couples who play dominant/submissive roles sexually do not carry out the same roles in the rest of their relationship. Rather, they treat their sexual role-playing as a mutually desired game that heightens the erotic quality of their partnership. This erotic encounter is often easier to find in the early stages of a relationship, when the (often illusory) sense of equality between lovers has not yet been shattered by the brandishing of status, financial power, and social or marital roles. Thus, a powerful man who falls in love with a woman of more modest status (boss/secretary, politician/volunteer) will sometimes while in the heat of infatuation see her as different, and perhaps as having power over him. In time, their shared beliefs about one or the other's superior status in the relationship produces a nonvoluntary dominant/submissive dynamic that can begin to eat away at the electric quality of their I/Thou connection. (If the couple is turned on by dominance games, the roles have more of a voluntary, gamelike character.)

Often one partner eventually claims a higher status in the relationship, as in the case of the corporate executive whose lover is her former household handyman. When mundane chores of living are relegated to the lower-status partner, resentments build up, every one of which silently, sometimes secretively, creeps into bed with the lovers. When one partner has come to feel he or she has been relegated the drudge work, both partners begin to move from attraction and interest in the other to feelings of dominance, control, submission, resentment, and sometimes, revenge.

In her book *The Bonds of Love,* Jessica Benjamin explores the interpersonal and social forces that limit men's and women's erotic potential. She points to the forces that discourage the woman's sense of her own drives and desires, "her subjectivity," and to those that discourage the man from recognizing the woman's subjectivity while rendering him fearful of losing himself in intimate emotional encounters. These forces, by-products of the current split of human faculties according to rigid gender rules and models of the active independent father and the engulfing, dependent mother, encourage the stereotypical power games between male-female couples. Benjamin writes:

> If I completely control the other, then the other ceases to exist, and if the other completely controls me, then I cease to exist. A condition of our own independent existence is recognizing the other. True independence means sustaining the essential tension of these contradictory impulses; that is, both asserting the self and recognizing the other. Domination is the consequence of refusing this condition.
>
> In mutual recognition the subject accepts the premise that others are separate but nonetheless share like feelings and intentions. The subject is compensated for his loss of sovereignty by the pleasure of sharing, the communion with another subject.[1]

The ability to recognize the individuality or subjectivity of both the self and the other, to be aware of the differences, makes it possible not to fear the loss of self and to enjoy the momentary merging with another in the peak experience of erotic ecstasy. As Benjamin puts it:

> In recognition (of another's subjectivity), someone who is different and outside shares a similar feeling; different minds and bodies attune. In erotic union this attunement can be so intense that self and other feel as if momentarily "inside" each other, as part of a whole. Receptivity and self-expression, the sense of losing the self in the other and the sense of being truly known for oneself all coalesce. In my view, the simultaneous desire for loss of self and for wholeness (or oneness) with the other, often described as the ultimate point of erotic union, is really a form of the desire for recognition. In getting pleasure *with* the other and taking pleasure *in* the other, we engage in mutual recognition.[2]

The capacity to enter into states in which distinctness and union are reconciled underlies the most intense expe-

rience of adult erotic life. In erotic union we can experience that form of mutual recognition in which both partners lose themselves in each other without loss of self; they
lose self-consciousness without loss of awareness. [3]

The qualities and forces of dominance and submission are
often swept under the rug in many relationships and their influence on the erotic life of the couple is thereby vastly underestimated. However, with a little reflection, it is usually not difficult
to identify your own participation in this dynamic. If you then
explore the degree to which you and your partner recognize
each other's subjectivity, you will probably discover a few answers to some of your questions about the intensity of your
erotic connection.

EXERCISE 6-3
How About You?

Having considered just a few of the many dynamics that can
shape a couple's interaction in bed, perhaps you will find a fresh
perspective on your own sexual relationships. If you write out
your responses to the following questions in your sexual dream
journal, you might be surprised to see how much more you will
discover about your own sexual relationship patterns.

When you are having sex with your partner is he or she warm
and generous or reluctant and passive? Is your partner demand-
ing or threatening? How about you? Are you exuberant, creative, generous, open, distant, resentful, or frightened? Take a
moment to describe in your day or dream journal the quality of
what generally goes on or went on in bed between you and your
current or most recent lover. Describe very briefly what your
partner is or was like in bed, how you are or were, and how it felt
or feels to have sex together. If you don't have a journal, jot
down a few lines right here:

_____

_____

_____

What adjectives did you use? Have you just described the quality of your entire relationship with your partner? If your first answer is no, take another moment and ask yourself again. If you still see no parallel between your relationship in bed and the overall relationship, write a few lines describing how the two relationships are different. Then look for aspects of your current relationship that, in spite of the differences, do match your descriptive adjectives. In doing so, you may be surprised to find parallels you had not noticed before.

How did you feel in bed with your most recent major lover? Did you feel wanted sexually, loved, celebrated, serviced, tolerated, resented? Write down in the space below just how you felt.

Does this description remind you of how you felt in any other relationships? Most people find that the core emotional feelings that surrounded their last major sexual relationship were not only the same in and out of bed, but were present in most of their past relationships and are often present in their current one. This usually comes as a bit of a shock. Yet once you begin to recognize your relational patterns, you wonder how you could have failed to notice them for so long.

GOING ONE STEP FURTHER:
LONG-TERM PATTERNS

EXERCISE 6-4
When Did You First Feel This Way?

Now, if you are game, review your descriptions and ask yourself when was the first time you felt this way in relationship to anyone in your life? If you find yourself saying that you felt similarly loved, ignored, used, and so forth by your mother, father, grandparent, brother, or sister, don't be alarmed. You are not alone.

There is nothing more common than to choose major emotional entanglements with people whose emotional style resembles that of someone from whom you first learned to relate, even in nonsexual ways. The bad news is that it is very difficult to change these patterns, and if your pattern leads to repeated unhappy relationships, you have your work cut out for you. The good news is that self-study (including reading John Bradshaw's *The Family* and *Homecoming*), serious dream work, and, where indicated, therapy can help you change the pattern and make better choices.

Anna kept finding herself playing the role of the placator in romantic relationships with men who had tempers. For example, in order to head off angry and irritable outbursts of her current lover, Ian, she was ever ready to placate him by changing her behavior and apologizing if she had made any ill-received demand—and, of course, by being willing to make love whether she felt like it or not. It had been the same for her with Sam and Richard and B.J. After reflection, Anna saw that she had played the same role with her easily angered father. In fact, she saw that her major boyfriends were all rather depressed workaholics who expected the women around them to richly compensate them for the fact that they worked so long and hard for the family. They were all perfectionistic, overtired, overwrought, with complete denial about their underlying depressive character style. Underneath superficial differences, they were all like Anna's father. And now she could see it in the way she felt with them in intimate encounters in or out of the bedroom. Once she recognized her pattern in choosing men, Anna could embark on the arduous task of changing that pattern and looking for men with whom she could have relationships that would be more rewarding to her. In order to do this, she would need to resist powerful urges to repeat her pattern by falling for the usual type of guy, then she would have to develop an emotional taste and a sexual attraction for the sort of man who could be a more satisfying partner for her.

The Blood-from-a-Stone Syndrome

Anna's case is not one of frustrated sexual desire for her father. She was compelled to re-create this type of relationship because she was unaware of the ubiquitous and stubborn human tendency to try to find the love and approval we either received or missed from an early caregiver in the person of someone else who shares the same traits. It is as if, growing up wanting blood from a stone, we get the idea that it is a stone we want. But this time we hope to find one that can give blood. It takes a long time for most of us to realize that stones, by their very nature, do not, cannot, give blood. Anna had to learn that depressive, volatile workaholics like her father could never give her the love and approval she longed for any more than she could get blood from a stone.

By the time he finished medical school Watson had decided that he wanted a modern wife who would be professionally ambitious and interesting. He married Francine, who was the opposite of his sweet but dull and very dependent mother. Unaware that he was overreacting in an effort to avoid re-creating the dynamic between his parents, Watson ended up with an ambitious lawyer who had little free time to spend with him and who challenged him whenever he assumed that he, as the man of the house, had the last word on a decision. While Watson admired his wife's accomplishments and found her an interesting and enjoyable companion, he felt threatened by her economic, intellectual, and emotional independence. He worried that she didn't need him enough in the ways he had grown up believing a wife depended on a husband, and he worried that his wife didn't really love him since she so often struggled with him and since she was so often too busy with her work to attend to him.

After about fifteen years, things became unbearable for Watson. He often felt unsupported by a wife who led a busy life, much of which did not include him. He found that he longed for a woman who would be much more available to him, who was much more supportive of his endeavors, and who looked up to him more. In short, he wanted a woman who treated him more like his mom had treated his dad. He divorced his wife and remarried a sweet nurse who respected his higher status as a surgeon and as a husband. She quit work so she could be free when Watson was, and she nurtured him well. They made a much happier couple. Watson no longer asked for excitement from a wife; he had discovered that a more traditionally nurturing woman like his mother fit him better. For Watson, women who were not as nurturing as his mom seemed unloving. He finally recognized that what he really wanted was a more supportive, less challenging partner, and he went out and found one. After a short time their sexual relationship waned, but Watson was willing to trade erotic intensity for domestic comfort and tranquillity.

Choosing partners who are like your mom or dad works well if those parental relationships were good ones. If they were troubled, you may have similar troubles in your romances. Choosing the polar opposite of one of your parents is no solution. In fact, it usually leads to worse troubles. At least when you pick similar relationship patterns you know your role and how to cope. When you pick an opposite type, after a while of enjoying the refreshing change, you begin to lament the fact that your partner can't give you the good things you got from your parent. And you usually pick an extreme opposite who brings with him or her all the problems of extreme characters. What is needed is a choice based on greater self-knowledge, a better grasp of the forces that shaped your needs and attraction for a partner, and the courage to know when it is time to end a bad relationship and to do it.

Your dreams can help you to engage in this undertaking with an uncommon degree of insight. In fact, your dreams follow you through the entire relational process, commenting as you go from early formative relationships, to choosing a partner, through the establishment of your major dynamics, and to the creation, experience, and, perhaps, resolution of conflict. Even when you use sexual dreams to express primarily sexual concerns, they also deal with broader issues. Because most of your sexual concerns are inherently also relational concerns, you use sexual metaphors to explore your relationships as well. Now let's look at what your sexual dreams may be saying about your relationships.

7

What Your Dreams Can Tell You About Your Sexual Relationships

Y OU MAY WELL DREAM ABOUT THE QUALITY OF YOUR SEX-
ual relationships several times a week. When these relationships
are causing you particular distress, you may dream several
dreams about them every single night. It appears that our
dreaming brain responds as quickly to relationship distress as a
fire department does to a fire. In both cases, the sooner one
deals with the problem, the less likely things are to get out of
hand.

One of the reasons I have chosen to devote my professional
life to studying dreams and to teaching people how to make
good use of them is that I have been so vividly impressed by the
incisive clarity and the maturity with which we are able to comment on our relationships while dreaming. And we seem to be
able to do this weeks, months, years, even decades before we
consciously come to the same insights if we ignore our dreams. I
certainly do not mean to suggest that dreams are panaceas to our
problems in our sexual relationships. While now and then certain dreams can buoy us up or work transformational magic,
most of our dreams throw us the ball and leave it to us to catch it
and run with it. Top-quality insights are plentiful in good dream
work. But they need to be actualized in waking life to be of
much use. And this is not always easy to do.

You may or may not use sexual imagery when you dream

about your sexual relationships. Your dreams about your sexual relationships may focus on your physically sexual activities, or they may deal with the emotional, interpersonal, or intrapersonal aspects of those relationships. In chapter one we looked at dreams with and without sexual imagery that highlight the mostly physical side of sexual relationships. Now we turn to the kind of dream that identifies and analyzes the emotional undercurrents that sooner rather than later determine whether a sexual relationship will thrive, stagnate, or explode.

The complicated dynamics that drive most relationships, that forge them and make them work or fall apart, reveal their structures readily to your X-ray dream vision. With your night vision you see important but unappreciated traits in yourself and your lover. You also see, if you know how to read metaphor, how the dynamics we spoke of in the last chapter may be affecting your romance. As you will discover, when you examine the qualities of your sexual relationships, sometimes you dream in sexual imagery, sometimes you don't.

EARLY WARNING SIGNALS

If you were to dream that your new lover was smothering you to death with a plastic bag the first night after you made love, you might wonder if you had missed something important about him or her and about your means of choosing a partner. You might begin to worry that the protestations of love at first sight might really mean dependency at first sight. Then you might start to remember significant things your lover said just a few nights before that should have tipped you off to the fact that this person was looking for a security blanket, not a lover. The dream might remind you that you find this sort of relationship suffocating rather than cozy and warm.

A woman who told me her dream on television said that she canceled her wedding because of it, even though the invitations had already been sent out. She dreamt that she was at the church altar in front of all the guests and noticed that everyone seemed to be following with their eyes something moving about on the floor. Finally she looked and saw her groom's head on the writhing body of a snake. She understood the dream not as an expression of her fear of a penis (as some dogmatic Freudians might) but as a rude awakening to her that she was about to marry a snake-in-the-grass. She later discovered things about her almost-husband that would have torpedoed the marriage. She was delighted that the dream had made her look at some very painful facts. Some dreams are nearly transparent and easy to understand if the dreamer is open to new insights. Most demand more investigation.

Collette, who had just resumed a relationship with a fellow she had dated two years previously, wondered why she was not having any dreams about him. She had broken up with Emile because he was not interested in forming a monogamous relationship. She told us that this time she was not going to get deeply involved because she knew he would not be good for her. She was just having fun, light times with him until she met a more appropriate guy. Then she told us this dream:

I'm in my room looking out the window into the hills, saying, "I love my room." A girl says, "Look!" I look and see a man using a slender tree trunk trying to get a bear out of a tree. He is tormenting the innocent bear that is just existing in his natural environment.

Somehow, I offer my room as an escape route to the bear, so he can get away from his tormentor . . . I am scared, but I go out anyway to look for the bear. I get close to him and let him smell my hand. He starts biting my gloved hand and I begin to realize that I could be in danger. The bear goes away, but I think he's bonded with me, and I think he will come looking for me again.

Next, I hear the bear following me. Frightened, I enter a building and run up many stairs. I enter an open door. An Asian midget who doesn't speak or understand English points a gun at me. I try to communicate by my expression the danger I'm in and he finally relents and puts the gun down.

"The Bear"

Collette's dream was quite complex. Three other members of our study group and I interviewed Collette for half an hour before the pieces began to come together. Here are the key points of our interview:

INTERVIEWER: What is the girl like who draws your attention to the bear?

COLLETTE: She is actually my sister, whom I hardly ever see because she is married to an alcoholic and is a classic co-dependent. She's in complete denial and is very dependent upon him.

I: What are bears like?

C: Well, I have an unrealistic view, but I think of them as cuddly, like pets, but I know that they can be very dangerous.

I: What was the bear feeling and doing in the dream?

C: He was innocently doing his own thing in the tree and being harshly treated by this man who was cruel.

I: Why do you offer your room to the bear?

C: I feel sorry for him. He could escape in one and out the other of my corner windows.

I: Is there anything or anyone, or any part of yourself, that you see as cuddly, that you feel sorry for and want to help escape torment, but could be dangerous?

C: No.

I: You see the bear as a victim, a cuddly being you feel sorry for. Remind you of anyone?

C: Emile is a victim of an awful childhood of incest and a dominating father. And yes, he is cuddly, and could be dangerous if I let him in too close.

I: Is there any connection between your sister's showing you the bear and her co-dependency? Does Emile drink too much?

C: Perhaps. I wouldn't call him alcoholic. He drinks maybe four or five beers a day.

I: As a physician, do you have a working definition of alcoholism?

C: Yes. I guess he does have a problem, but it doesn't affect us much, since I only see him once or twice a week.

I: So you protect yourself, as in the dream you wear a glove on the hand the bear bites. . . . Has Emile hurt you?

C: Oh yes. In the past. But now I'm not going to get too involved with him again.

I: In the dream, you think the bear has bonded and will look for you again. Sure enough, you try to escape him for fear that he will hurt you and you run into the Asian midget. What is he like?

C: Well, Asians like those I've met in Taiwan are just so different from me. We can't communicate at all. Our languages have nothing in common. And midgets are people who suffer the prejudice of normal people and so have more obstacles to overcome in life. This one has a mustache and is scared and angry that I barged in. He didn't understand at first that I was frightened and meant no harm. He felt threatened.

I: You say he had a mustache and felt threatened by your entering his space. Remind you of anyone?

C: Emile feels threatened if I get too close, and yes, he has a mustache. I guess the bear is back again, and I'm not safe with either the bear or the more civilized, but frightened and noncommunicative parts of him. I used to be in love with Emile. I guess I'd better look at what I've got myself into.

After her interviewers had asked Collette to describe the major elements of her dream and then to see if they reminded her of particular people and situations in her life, she was able to interpret the metaphors with which the dream told its story. She understood the bear to represent the apparently safe but in fact highly dangerous aspects of her boyfriend, Emile. Her fantasy about the cuddliness of bears paralleled her equally unrealistic denial of her history of being repeatedly hurt by Emile. She felt sorry for the bear in much the same way she felt sorry for Emile. Collette's co-dependent sister, who in waking life has shown Collette the pain of living with an alcoholic husband, drew her attention to the bear in the dream. The parallel helped Collette to admit that she, too, had been trying to deny the alcoholism of the man she loves. Collette's effort this time around to get help in escaping the dangerous bearlike part of Emile by communicating with him fails in waking as it does in the dream.

Emile is radically different from Collette, and he feels terribly threatened by her needs for intimacy and by her pleas for emotional support, much as happens in the dream with the Asian midget. It remains to be seen whether or not Collette will be able to act on her dream insights into her co-dependent relationship to her returned lover. Will she be able to focus on her needs for a healthier relationship with a man who can support and communicate with her? Will she be able to overcome her needs to rescue someone for whom she feels sorry, who reinforces the idea that she can't do better, doesn't deserve better?

Mitzi, on the other hand, was able to act immediately on a dream she had just as she was divorcing her husband and after only two dates with Kurt, who had already fallen madly in love with her.

> A slightly overweight woman who is nearing the end of her prison term announces that she is remarried, this time for life. In a parental mode, I say to her, "What? You remarried while still in prison?" I was distressed for her. She was just about to get free, and she marries! How sad. How stupid.
>
> *"Almost Got Free"*

Mitzi saw immediately that she was already too involved with a man who would be even more dependent than her husband had been and that no matter what, now was no time to get serious about anybody. She wanted to savor her freedom, and decided not to continue her relationship with her new boyfriend.

Zelda had a dream about a vampire that didn't pull any punches:

> I am being seduced by a vampire. I know what I'm getting into. I see his fangs in the mirror—he shows them to me! I have two daughters, young adults, and I want them to protect themselves. I'm screaming, "No! No!" and I can't scream loud enough to be heard. I am horrified at myself for letting him sink his fangs into me.
>
> *"Vampire"*

Zelda described a vampire as a deceitful monster who is evil behind a handsome exterior. She said that in the dream she felt excited, titillated by the seduction. She wanted to lose control, and at the same time was afraid to lose control to such a monster. Zelda had been suffering from a romance drought and was just getting together with a man she knew didn't love her. But since she didn't love him either, she thought she could handle a casual relationship. As it turned out, she ignored the dream and failed to protect the young, more vulnerable part of herself (the young girls), and was very hurt in the relationship since she soon cared much more for her lover than he did for her. In hindsight, Zelda realized that she had indeed known what she was getting into and should have listened to her dream warning.

Women who dream of having sex with a man and in the dream worry that they have not used a condom as protection from pregnancy or disease find these dreams very upsetting. Marabelle had a long dream about an old boyfriend that included such a scene. In earlier dream work she had already bridged her old boyfriend's characteristics of being exotic, fascinating, and much more interested in his humanitarian work than in personal relationships to her current heartthrob, Carlo. She didn't like to admit it, but Carlo, like her old boyfriend, just didn't have enough time for her or for their relationship. Both were incredibly warm at the beginning, but became cold and distant as soon as work took them to other countries. Physical distance brought emotional distance. In the dream, Marabelle was making passionate love to her old boyfriend and enjoying it, but she was not sure that they had used any form of contraception to avoid pregnancy. This led to a great deal of anxiety in the dream. I asked her:

INTERVIEWER: Why would an earthling want to have protection from pregnancy?
MARABELLE: If I had an unplanned pregnancy, I would have to deal with the abortion issue, or have the baby, and that would screw up my life.
I: Is there any way that in your relationship with your old boy-

friend and with Carlo that you have not taken precautions to protect yourself and have risked screwing up your life?

M: Oh yes. I didn't adequately protect my feelings. I rushed into both relationships and I was hurt by both of them.

Dreams of having unsafe sex often work out to mean that the dreamers have failed to adequately protect themselves from emotional harm, that they have failed to take the necessary precaution of getting to know their partners before leaping into relationships with them. Other common images of rushing too fast into a relationship might include scenes of buying a new car or a new house, or taking a new job, or accepting a hitchhiking ride without first checking out the situation to be sure it is right or safe for you.

Emerging Problems

Our first realization that a new problem has arisen in a relationship is frequently made in a dream. Jessica, who had been married for six years to a kindly, mild-mannered man, had often encouraged him to be more assertive and forthcoming in social situations. As you will see, her dream, which pictured her husband's assertiveness as a lion, suggested that he might take her advice *too* much to heart.

> I had encouraged a trainer at a zoo to let a lion out. But it was out without a leash. Only then did I realize that it was very dangerous as it roved around us. The male owner/ trainer was not in control. I thought the lion could bite me. Maim me. Eat my feet, my elbow (as I slept, I was aware that my elbow was exposed near my husband). I was extremely frightened and called to the owner to control the lion! I wanted it out, not loose. I liked the lion and wanted it to have some freedom, but this was too much! I knew that the lion was a wild animal and that it was crazy not to have it on a leash.
>
> *"Lion is Loose"*

Before the dream, Jessica had been aware that she had felt angered by what she saw as the excesses of her husband's new-found assertiveness. He had begun to actually bully her with outbursts of anger and with subtle threats of an outburst if she did not meet his demands. However, Jessica had been entirely unaware that she was actually and seriously frightened by these tantrums and intimidated by her husband's threats and roaring anger. This fear itself, and the resentments born of such fear, have undone more than a few sexual relationships. Thanks to her dream work Jessica was jolted into a realization of how much her fear of her husband had affected her sexual interest in him. She could feel little desire to get into bed with a man who bullied her and who might explode with anger toward her at any moment.

RED FLAGS AT EVERY STAGE OF A RELATIONSHIP

Boredom and Loss of Sexual Interest

When a relationship becomes dull, when the sexual encounters lose not only their zest but most of their pleasure as well, couples often just accept it as a natural consequence of familiarity in an ongoing relationship. They may ask themselves, "Whatever happened to the excitement, the specialness of our romance, and of our sexual sharing?" Sometimes the causes of such dullness are difficult to identify. But while dreaming, the unsuspected, or at least unrecognized, causes of their boredom and lack of interest are often crystal clear.

When the boredom is due in part to her own laziness and lack of creativity, a lover will sometimes dream of being in bed wearing very unappealing clothing, serving unimaginative food to a dream partner, or of engaging in foreplay in a boring, mechanical manner. If the lack of creativity is experienced as a characteristic of the lover's partner, she may dream of being in bed with a nerd, a klutz, or another type of guy that highlights her lover's less than exuberant sexual behavior. Commonly, men who find their sexual relationships with very inhibited women stalling will dream of being in bed with unexciting nuns, schoolmarms, or with acquaintances from their past who evoke similar feelings.

EXERCISE 7-1
Spotting Unappealing Dream Lovers

Look through your dream journal if you are keeping one, or search your memory if you are not, and see if you find dream images of boring or dull, or just plain unappealing, people in what might otherwise be a romantic or sexual situation. Interview yourself about these figures and see if they fit you and/or your lover. Ask yourself if there is anything you would like to do to enliven your style. Perhaps you will think of an alternate figure you would prefer to see in your dreams. If you come up with one—say, Tom Cruise or Madame Bovary—imagine how you might move in that direction in both your fantasy (for practice) and then, bit by bit, in your waking sexuality.

EXERCISE 7-2
Understanding Your Sexual Boredom

The problem of boredom often has more complex causes, which include fear, anger, and resentment in one or both partners, that can block sexual delight. One of the quickest ways to put your finger on the major source of the problem is to incubate a dream by asking something like "Why am I so bored in this relationship?" Then be ready for some surprises or for some uncomfortable reminders of feelings or attitudes you may have suspected were at work but have managed to sweep under the rug.

Jonathan incubated a dream by asking, "Why have I suddenly lost my interest in my wife?" He dreamt:

I am with a sweet little girl who won't let go of me. She is whining and complaining that the girls at school won't play with her. She wants me to play with her all the time. I just want to get away.

"Girl Play"

As soon as Jonathan described the little girl as sweet, but dependent on him for all her social needs, he realized that he was describing his wife. In the last year, they had moved from California to Louisiana. Jonathan's wife found herself transplanted into a conservative social world with which she felt out of step and in which she felt unwelcome. She had become increasingly dependent on Jonathan for just about all of her social needs. He in turn began to see her as a clinging child who did not turn him on. After working with this dream, Jonathan was more sensitive to his wife's predicament, and both of them were more motivated to find ways to remedy it. Their sex life began to revive soon thereafter.

Matt and Gemina could not understand why Matt was having trouble maintaining an erection. They had enjoyed a robust sexual life for six months. But about a month after they began living together the difficulties surfaced. One night Matt dreamt:

> I was playing ball with my big sister, Cindy. We were about five and eight years old. Everything was going fine until she decided to show me who had the power, and ran away with my ball. I was furious, but felt helpless to chase her. I said to myself, I'll never play ball with her again.
>
> *"She Took My Ball"*

Matt bridged the dream feelings of anger and helplessness to those he often experienced in the face of his sister's competitiveness. Then he bridged to Gemina's power play that led to their moving in together before Matt was quite ready. Gemina had presented Matt with an ultimatum: either we live together or we end our relationship. Matt was resentful and furious at Gemina for having extracted his commitment via her threat, but he felt powerless to resist. His feelings of powerlessness came from his feeling blackmailed by Gemina. He didn't want to lose her, and in order to stay in a relationship with her, he felt he had to agree to her demands. His older sister had taken unfair advantage of his relative weakness just as he now felt Gemina was doing. As he thought about the dream and his decision not to play ball with Cindy again, he saw that he had found an effective, if painful, way to retaliate. Matt's dream led him to see that his current temptation to retaliate against Gemina by leaving her would be a childish response. What he decided to confront directly this time was the power play itself. He needed to let Gemina know that emotional blackmail was hurting both of them.

Addiction to Substances

Frequently clients tell me that a dream has pierced through their denial of the severity of an addiction problem of their own or of a lover or partner. Dreams of this nature may present scenes in which the lovers find an addict lying between them in bed—an addict who is clearly not at all interested in reforming. Or a dream may depict the addicted lover as committing suicide or choosing to live in squalid circumstances. The meaning of such dreams is easy to recognize and should be taken seriously. Consider, for example, the dream of a young physician named Charles:

> Willi Hanmil, an old fraternity brother, becomes my psychiatric patient. He is on major tranquilizers. I don't like that prescription and try to get him off them. But he gets very angry (he's dependent on them) and he shows me a scene from his past in which there is much fighting with his parents, especially with his mother. I agree (sort of) to prescribe for a while, but secretly I plan to get him off the tranqs and make him face the feelings he is trying to run away from.
>
> *"Hooked on Tranqs"*

Charles quickly saw that the introverted Willi, who was hooked on tranqs, was none other than himself, who used alcohol to escape his anxiety. Charles, like Willi in the dream, had suffered greatly from the constant strife between his parents and especially between himself and his mom. Like Willi, he was unwilling to believe that he had a serious problem. He typically responded with strong anger when his wife would ask him to cut down on his drinking. Unfortunately he was not ready to accept this insight. He decided to ignore his dream.

Addiction to Emotional States and Behaviors

Slightly more subtle than, but perhaps almost as common as, dreams of physical addictions are dreams pointing out addictions to certain emotional states and behaviors. Some people use habitual reactions of tearfulness or moodiness or anger to manipulate others and to avoid feeling other more painful feelings underneath. These feelings are often rage, sadness, grief, fear of abandonment, or, in the case of the determinedly independent and self-sufficient, feelings of dependency. Now and then, these dreams conclude with their own prognosis.

Lila was like a co-alcoholic (a co-dependent) in the ways she enabled and reinforced her boyfriend's temper tantrums. When he was in a rage, she would try everything to mollify him, even when that meant giving in and apologizing for a fight he had initiated. She had long ago lost her interest in sex with her boyfriend, and had often thought of leaving him, but couldn't. She had many dreams of being threatened by unpredictable snakes and by aggressive, vicious animals. But this dream was the one she could not ignore. It came the morning after she had incubated a dream by asking, "Why don't I have any sexual interest in my boyfriend?"

> As if watching a nature show documentary, I hear the deep voice of a narrator who says, "Some people try to save, to cure, their rabid dogs. But this is an organic brain syndrome." Then I see illustrations of skulls of dead rabid dogs. The brains had been eaten away by the disease.
>
> The narrator continues: "But, in fact, the only thing to be done is to hold their heads, comfort them, then put them out of their misery and remove the threat they pose to society."

Then I see body parts of humans who had been attacked by rabid dogs. Arms and legs bitten, shredded. Very horrible. I understand that "rabid" here refers to a temper disorder—anger and rage—not to a rabies poison that is transmitted by saliva. The lesson of the scene is that one mustn't take half measures. This disorder is too dangerous, and there is no cure.

"Rabid Dogs"

Lila was crying when she awoke. As she worked with the dream she began to see that her boyfriend's difficulty in handling his anger, his "temper disorder," was indeed more severe and more threatening to her than she had previously admitted to herself. If things were really this bad, no wonder she didn't want to have sex with him. For years Lila had clung fast to the role of placator of the irritable beast and she had taken some pride in her skill at improving his moods and averting explosions. To an unhealthy extent, her life had centered around the care and management of her boyfriend and she had lost sight of her own needs. She took the first steps toward taking definitive action to protect herself by learning to communicate to her boyfriend that she would no longer tolerate his temper tantrums. This was not easy for her because she was good at soothing bad tempers, not at asserting herself in the face of them.

Rescuing or Parenting Your Partner

Co-dependent relationships in which couples are dependent upon each other to an unhealthy extent come in endless varieties, and have been described in many ways, most notably by Melody Beattie[1] in her book, *Codependent No More*. For the moment let's consider co-dependent relationships that consist of an emotionally or substance-dependent partner and another partner who is the caretaker or rescuer. Both partners are dependent, each needing the other to play out his or her role. One is dependent on a drug or on the financially or emotionally supportive partner, while the rescuer is dependent on the partner in trouble in order to play out his or her role of long-suffering rescuer. Rescuers may derive a sense of purpose or an enhanced sense of self-esteem by sticking with dependent partners, or they may find that the rescue effort allows them to avoid facing their own painful feelings of loneliness or depression. If you have a pattern of choosing partners who need rescuing, or if you choose partners you hope will save you from loneliness, sadness, insecurity, and so forth, you know firsthand about the pain of co-dependency.

Olivia, who, like so many other women, saw herself as the one who should rescue her alcoholic husband from his unhappy feelings, was shocked when she awoke with this dream:

> A public bathroom with a line of people waiting to get in. My husband, Ken, and I are inside and at his request we have uncomfortable sex standing up. We exit, and I smile to the crowd and say, "It's your turn." Ken still has an erection and wants me again. I am embarrassed—we are outside in public now. But I say okay in spite of my reluctance because I want to please and satisfy him.
>
> I thought Ken would be able just to slip in under my skirt, but we have trouble getting the right angle and have to turn this way and that, right there in public! I become just too uncomfortable in this public scene and pull away from him and say loudly, "Enough!" Then I see him left there with his erection in front of everyone. He was embarrassed at the situation, at the public rejection and at standing there with his penis in the air. For an instant I feel guilty and want to go save him somehow. But then I say to myself, "No. His demands are just too much. He went too far, and the consequences are what they are."
>
> *"Public Bathroom Sex"*

After many years of placating her husband, Olivia was beginning to stand up for herself. But at this point she had a long way to go. Since we tend to be well ahead of ourselves in dreaming insights, the fact that Olivia still felt guilty at saying no to her dream husband's extreme demands suggests that it will be a while before she can get even as far as she does in the dream in learning to say no and in learning that her need to take care of her husband's feelings is exaggerated to an unhealthy degree. While dreaming, Olivia could see the outrageousness of her husband's demands, but she would have to continually remind herself of this insight while waking in order for it to sink in and result in new behaviors on her part.

Ramsey, who had been married to May, a domineering wife, for over thirty years, had just begun working on giving his wife a better, clearer idea of his boundaries and wishes when one night she pulled one of her old tricks: listening in on his telephone calls. Although he was furious, he said nothing about it. That night he dreamt:

> Our boss had done something awful. I want to confront him but my coworkers from my last job (where I had kowtowed to a volatile boss) told me not to say anything. That if I did, I'd be fired. But this time I had had it. I told him off and felt greatly relieved.
>
> *"Coward No More"*

Ramsey was learning to risk expressing himself to his volatile wife he felt was his boss. But he was making a start at asserting himself and he felt good about it. He knew that he just had to risk being fired (divorced) by his wife if he was ever to have a decent relationship with her.

Competition for Control

Of the myriad dynamics that drive relationships, everyone, at some point in life, has been in a struggle for control with a lover. The struggle may be covert or out in the open: in the bedroom, in the kitchen, or anywhere one wants to control the acts and sometimes the thoughts of the other. When the need to control the other gets out of hand, it becomes another form of co-dependency that poisons the love in the relationship. When one partner focuses a lot of energy on controlling the other, the other becomes the partner's life project or obsession. The partner neglects taking care of his or her own business and generally makes life a torment for the other. If you pay attention to your dreams you will find pointers to the problem as well as descriptions of its origins.

Francisco and his wife, Carmen, were in couples therapy when Francisco had the following dream:

> After attending a lecture to which I had driven in a Jaguar I realize that someone else will be doing the driving on the way back. I am uncomfortable not being the one in control and try to figure out how I can get back into the driver's seat.
>
> *"How to Get Back in the Driver's Seat"*

Francisco had seen his wife as a control freak and himself as an easygoing sort of fellow. But as he was learning in therapy, his own needs to control his wife, while less obvious, were quite strong. When he described the Jaguar as racy, agile, sleek, and sexy, Francisco saw right away the parallel to his wife, whose movements he had often described as jaguarlike. He recognized that while therapy was helping his wife to take better control of her own life rather than his, he was nevertheless uncomfortable about his loss of control over her. As long as his wife had been focused on what he did or did not do, he had great control. Now she was moving her focus away from him, tending to her business rather than his.

Another couple dreamt about their control problem on the same night. Floria dreamed:

> My husband, Luccio, and I were in a dreadfully strict private school for girls. We decided to escape the stern headmistress by making a run for it to the bathrooms and out the window. As we momentarily rested, hiding in the stalls, the headmistress came running in out of breath. She asked, "Please let me escape with you. I hate the oppression here!" Surprised, we responded, "You can come with us, but you must swear to stop telling us what to do!"
>
> *"Escaping the Headmistress"*

Floria had no trouble seeing the headmistress as herself. Neither did her husband, Luccio, who had often complained about the controlling ways of his wife, who drove him crazy with her rules and regulations. That very night Luccio dreamt that he was trying to escape from a hoard of hostile Amazon women who were out to capture and imprison him or worse. . . . As soon as he described Amazon women as women who had total control over their men and who showed no mercy, he knew he was looking at only a slightly exaggerated picture of his situation with his wife.

The Incest Taboo

People who have never experienced incest sometimes report dreams of having sex with family members. Unlike the dreams of incest survivors, which we shall discuss in the next chapter, the actual sex in these dreams is often pleasurable and not traumatic, although it may be awkward. Upon waking, some dreamers feel guilty for having dreamt such things. A college student in Domhoff's survey wrote:

> The only dream I can remember at this time is one of getting together with my brother, although I don't know if we had sex. I woke up feeling ashamed and confused. I suppose I still do. I think his fiancée walked in on us during the dream, but we didn't care. It was passionate, and the feeling was mutual.
>
> *"With My Brother"*

The shame the dreamer felt upon awakening at the thought of having dreamt of having sex with her brother may have blinded her to the dream's probable focus on her difficulty accepting that the fiancée was threatening to intrude on her special relationship with her brother. Had this relationship actually been physically incestual, I think the sex in the dream would have been very conflicted. Instead the dreamer described her dream feelings as passionate and mutual, and wrote that she and her brother did not care that the fiancée saw them. The lack of

shame, conflict, or coercion within the dream leads me to suspect that this sister and brother were overinvolved with each
other on an emotional, not a physical, level. It is likely that the
sexual imagery served as a metaphor for excessive emotional intimacy.

Another undergraduate dreamt:

> I was with my boyfriend somewhere and somehow my
> brother was in the dream. He and my brother kept chang-
> ing roles. I'd be kissing my boyfriend and he'd turn into my
> brother so I'd stop.
>
> *"Boyfriend/Brother"*

She wrote, "Can this possibly mean that I somehow associate
personality traits in my boyfriend with traits in my brother?" This
is indeed the most likely answer to the riddle of her dream. The
fact that she stops kissing when she sees her brother suggests that
the incest taboo is invoked by her awareness of these similarities
and has already affected her sexual relations with her boyfriend.

It is a common phenomenon that when a couple has become
very familiar with each other, they can fall into seeing each other
as "family." Sometimes they may accidently call each other
Mom or Dad, or by a sibling's name. In these periods, the couple sometimes notices a reticence in their sex life that is often
due to a surfacing of the incest taboo and is often reflected in
sexual dreams involving family members.

When the brother/sister dynamic becomes a prominent or a
dominant one in a relationship, it usually means trouble unless
both partners had siblings they found sexy and with whom they
never transgressed the taboo boundary and so have no guilt. But
generally when a spouse comes to feel more like a sibling, sex
dies for one or both partners, one or both may have affairs, and
so on. Janette dreamed:

> A sister and brother team like Donny and Marie Os-
> mond decided to marry. They have sex with each other.
> This seemed fine and natural.
>
> *"Donny and Marie Marry"*

From that morning on, Janette understood that she and her husband had fallen into the trap of treating each other as sister and brother. She concluded that her dream feeling that this was fine was absurd because she did not find Donny and Marie sexy, nor was she finding her beloved husband sexy. Yet she did enjoy the wholesome, nonthreatening, low-risk, Donny-and-Marie emotional environment she had created with him. She was reluctant to disturb it by trying to re-create a less merged, more I/Thou, adult/adult relationship.

When you dream of having sex with your mom or dad, or with a sister or brother, ask yourself to describe your dream partner's personality. Is your dream lover a family member who is gentle, kind, and creative, or critical and selfish or smothering? Does your description remind you of some aspect of your partner or of anyone else? How does the sex go in the dream? If there are problems do they reflect problems you are having in a current relationship? Do the feelings evoked (happiness, sadness, resentment, shame, possessiveness, and so on) remind you of feelings you have with your waking partner? If they do, and that is a problem, it would probably be worth your time to talk about the matter with your partner. If the problem seems particularly awkward or painful, if the dream feelings include shame and coercion, there *may* be deeper roots to the feelings, which could suggest earlier sexual abuse. In this case, consulting an experienced therapist is a very good idea.

Sometimes dreams of sexual activity with family members are gateways to disturbing but important memories. Alexander Leavy and Joseph Weissberg[2] have described their use of dreams in sex therapy, saying that dream work speeds the therapeutic process by furnishing an understanding of unconscious factors that cause and perpetuate sexual dysfunction. One of their clients was an anorgasmic wife who was averse to touching her husband's genitalia. After completing an assigned therapeutic exercise that included mutual genital stimulation, she had two dreams.

Dream 1: She was playing with her father's penis and he had an erection. She was aroused, fascinated, and curious, not at all frightened.

Dream 2: She and her brother were playing with each other sexually. Their mother came in and was furious.

Leavy and Weissberg comment:

> Here the [therapeutic] exercise stimulated dreams of incestuous activity in the patient's childhood, indicating positive unconscious sexual desires for the penis (albeit the father's), combined with maternal disapproval and threatened retaliation. Clarifying the fact that her husband's penis, in contrast to her father's, was in reality hers to enjoy produced a dramatic break in her resistance to this phase of treatment. [3]

Her work with these dreams helped this dreamer identify a probable cause for her problem, and her therapist was able to help her begin to separate her guilt in touching her brother and father from her relationship to her husband. In the next chapter we shall look more deeply into dreams that help dreamers recognize and cope with sexual abuse.

Trust, Insecurity, and Sexual Satisfaction: Infidelity Dreams

Dreams in which your partner is unfaithful, or is thinking about being unfaithful, can be worrisome. Such dreams usually evoke doubt and jealousy that may or may not be discussed between the couple. Infidelity dreams are often metaphoric expressions about infidelity that is not literal, but of an emotional nature. Wendy, who had been living with her boyfriend, Carl, for five years, dreamt:

> In bed one night with Carl, I realize that he has been having an affair for the entire time of our relationship. Every day he has seen this mousy woman who is very dependent and needy in a girllike fashion. I am furious. Now I understand why he has so little energy to romance me, to

court me. I tell Carl I want this to stop. He says the other woman needs him so badly that he just can't deny her.

"Carl's Mousy Affair"

The key questions from our interview:

INTERVIEWER: Can you describe this mousy woman at all?
WENDY: From what I could tell, she was immature, needed lots of support and nurturance. She wasn't into sex as much as cuddling. She made intense demands which someone like Carl would have a hard time saying no to because he's a rescuer. That makes him feel strong and worthwhile.
I: (I recapitulated her words, then asked) Does this description remind you of anyone?
W: I hate to admit it, but that fits me, or more precisely a part of me. I'm sure that Carl is not having an affair with someone else. But the more adult, sexually oriented part of myself with which I identify in the dream is feeling betrayed because I have trained Carl to pay so much attention to the little girl in me who needs so badly to be cuddled. Why couldn't I see that before? It is so obvious now.

Another common version of an infidelity dream in which the other man or other woman represents an aspect of the dreamer is the one in which a nonblonde dreams of her man having an affair with a sexy blonde. While this dream sometimes turns out to be a reflection of her man's actual interest in a sexual encounter outside of the relationship, frequently it expresses something closer to home. My clients have noted that such dreams often come the night after they have had unsatisfactory, usually rushed, sex together. After describing a blonde to an imaginary alien interviewer, they see into the dream. What follows is a typical, extremely stereotypical response to the question:

INTERVIEWER: Pretend I come from another planet. What are blondes like?
NON-BLOND DREAMER: I know it's not fair to generalize this way, but I think of blondes as women who give men easy sex,

who are always available, and never need much persuading to have sex. I think they are cheap, and they threaten me. Men do prefer blondes for sex.

This response, once recapitulated, often bridges to the dreamer herself, who sees herself as a cheap blonde whenever she "services" her partner's sexual needs at times when she doesn't really want to have sex, either because she's not in the mood or because she does not find sex with her partner to be very fulfilling. The dreamer then finds herself in the position of being envious of herself and threatened by her own role-playing. She sees that she feels betrayed by her man, who falls for and spends time with the sexy blonde she plays for him and who ends up usurping her position. Liz had a vivid dream of this nature:

> I am in bed delightfully anticipating the arrival of my husband. He had promised to bring my favorite dessert, something with chocolate sauce on top. He's late. Then he sticks his head in the door to say that he won't come to bed for a while. He is going to have sex with a blonde. I am disappointed. And there will be no chocolate sauce. I think, "Another broken promise."
>
> Then there is a scene in which I am lying on top of my husband in bed. I am digging my nails into the back of his neck. I want him to know how much he has hurt me. I want him to feel some of the pain.
>
> *"Broken Promises"*

Liz told the members in her dream group that the blonde fit her stereotype of a purveyor of easy sex. She added that although she had been encouraging her husband to read about sex and join her in more interesting, longer-lasting encounters, she had been giving him the quick meat-and-potatoes sex he preferred. She described chocolate sauce to us as "a delicious, special treat" that she craved: "Chocolate is sexy, sensual. Chocolate sauce is not essential to life, but it is one of life's greatest pleasures. Chocolate sauce is what my husband has promised me sexually and has not given me."

Liz was now seeing that she had to give up her blonde act, not have sex when and in ways that did not interest her, and let her husband know that she really, really wanted that chocolate sauce. Up until then, he had believed that Liz had been relatively happy with their sex life. These scenarios, both the waking and dreaming ones, seem to be common ones among the women I work with. So if your partner seems to be having an affair with someone else in a dream, look before you shoot.

The other lover can also represent nonsexual relationships that you feel threaten your relationship. Colleen, who had been married for twenty-four years, was very upset by this dream:

> I discover that my husband is having an affair with Skip.
> I am jealous, and hugely angry.
>
> *"My Husband Is Gay"*

INTERVIEWER: Who is Skip? And what is he like?
COLLEEN: Skip is a part of a homosexual couple with whom my husband and I are very close. He is so easy to get along with, and I can talk to him about anything.
I: Does Skip remind you of anyone else in your life?
C: Well, my husband is very easy to get on with, but I am sure he is not gay and that he has not had an affair with Skip. Why would I dream such a thing?
I: Tell me more about Skip and your relationship with him.
C: Skip and his friend invited us to live with them while we build our house and we are thinking about it.
I: How did you feel at the end of the dream?
C: I felt jealous, angry, and left out.
I: Do you ever feel that way about your husband's relationship with Skip in waking life?
C: Oh! Well, yes, I do. In fact, they do spend a lot of time together. And I guess if we lived together that could get worse and become a big problem for me.

Once Colleen could recognize the feelings of being left out, of being jealous of Skip's close relationship with her husband, she was in a better position to decide if and under what conditions she could comfortably take Skip and his friend up on their offer. She could also now talk to her husband about her feelings, which, once out in the open, were not so hard to deal with.

Sometimes, painful dreams of learning that your partner is having an affair with another lover are expressions of your insecurity and jealousy. By interviewing yourself, you will probably be able to recognize these dreams without too much difficulty because the lovers and the dream feelings will keep reminding you of your waking insecurities. If you have these dreams regularly, look for scenes that suggest that you have work to do on your self-esteem, and consider consulting a psychologist to help you accomplish it.

Sometimes people first admit to themselves in a dream that their partner is actually having a secret affair. In such cases, the affair's telltale signs are somehow missed or ignored until the dreaming individual creates an undeniable eye-opener. For a couple of years, Beverly had this recurring dream:

> I am at one of my husband's and my frequent dinner parties, but I seem mostly to be an observer. I notice that although everyone looks normal, I know that they are all in costume. I awake crying terribly, without knowing why.
>
> *"Costume Dinner"*

Finally one night she dreamt:

> My husband and I are at another one of our dinner parties. The bread basket is passed around to the women only. When it gets to me, I see not bread inside it but my husband's penis.
>
> *"Penis in the Bread Basket"*

Beverly awoke shocked. She summoned up her courage and asked her husband if he was having an affair. He said he couldn't imagine why she would have such a silly dream. But this time

Beverly was so disturbed by the dream that she did some investigating and discovered that her husband had indeed had sex with most of the women who regularly had attended their dinner parties. Beverly cancelled her next dinner party and divorced her husband.

Now and then a person who is attracted to someone with whom he feels it would be immoral or unwise to have sex will have a dream that reinforces his flagging determination. Pascal, who was in love with a married woman, dreamt:

> I'm in bed with Marcia, whom I love deeply (as I do in waking life, where I have decided not to have sexual relations with her because she is married to a good, faithful husband). We lie in bed and become aware of our nakedness, of our bodies against one another, and of a beautiful deep harmony between our souls. Suddenly, I saw her husband's face behind her body, calmly looking back at me. I knew it was not right to be where I was.
>
> *"Her Husband's Face"*

I have heard a few dreams from people who were currently having extramarital affairs. One man told me of dreaming of trying to keep a wild animal in the bedroom closet so his wife wouldn't be hurt by it. Another dreamt of having a snake under his and his wife's bed. He had to protect his wife from the snake. Only he knew it was there. Both dreamers bridged the dream animals and the feelings of wanting to protect their wives from them to their affairs.

Betty, a wife who had just initiated her first affair, dreamt:

> I had walked out of a dark, cold medieval chamber into a sunlit meadow where I met a kind, smiling cowboy in a pickup truck waiting for me. I was a little anxious, but decided to hop in the truck and have an adventure.
>
> *"The Cowboy"*

Betty quickly bridged the dark medieval chamber to her role of wife to a formal, traditional, cold executive. The cowboy reminded her of her new, nontraditional, and younger boyfriend. In her dream she was happy with her choice. In waking, she was not willing to take the risk of actually leaving her husband, but the affair felt sunny and liberating. The dream sharpened her recognition that her life in the chamber was worse than she had been willing to admit to herself, and it gave her a glimpse of choosing the sunlight in spite of her anxiety.

Men's and women's most frequent sexual fantasy is that of having a sexual encounter with a different partner.[4] Sexual dreams also often present us with a new or unexpected partner, although generally with a broader spectrum of effects. Whereas in fantasies we almost always use the images of new partners to heighten our sexual excitement, in dreams new partners can do that and more. They can build our self-confidence; they can embarrass us, frighten us, or disgust us. New partners can also drive us wild with jealousy and insecurity when we learn that they regularly appear in our spouse's or lover's dreams.

You may dream of having sex with someone other than your partner without being aware of any concerns (in the dream) about being unfaithful. But in other dreams you will find yourself thinking about or deciding to have an affair or a fling and being unfaithful to your waking lover. A common dream line in such situations is "I'd love to, but I'm married" or "What if my lover found out?" Often the dreamer turns down the sexual opportunity. In these cases, besides obtaining a good description and bridge to the dream lover, you need to assess how you felt about declining the sexual invitation. If you awaken relieved to have escaped the encounter, then you are likely warning yourself in the dream to resist either a concrete sexual attraction or to resist whatever relationship, activity, or attitude you bridged the dream lover to. If you awaken saddened to have missed a sweet opportunity, describe and then bridge that feeling to some situation, sexual or nonsexual, in your waking life.

If you dream of deciding to go ahead with your infidelity in the dream, pay close attention to how you feel doing so and how the dream drama develops—was the sex satisfying, were there interruptions or painful consequences? Then ask yourself how you felt upon awakening. If things go badly, or if you awaken frightened of having made a terrible mistake, ask yourself if you are on the verge of threatening your primary relationship by getting overly involved with another person or another competing interest, or even with another aspect of your partner, if you find that your dream lover represents one side of your waking partner. A dream of your threatening your primary relationship is not necessarily undesirable if you happen to be in an unhealthy dependent entanglement.

If things go well or even much better after you have accepted an amorous invitation, ask yourself if moving closer to the person or attitude or aspect of yourself or your partner to which you have bridged the dream lover would be a good and enriching thing to do in waking life.

Fusion Relationships

When a couple is extremely dependent on each other; when they cannot bear to do things apart and are excessively possessive and jealous of each other; when they constantly complain, endlessly bicker, and fail to resolve their conflicts, their identities are usually merged in unhealthy ways. For some reason such couples are so enmeshed that they live life bound together in a sort of three-legged race. Martin Blinder, in his book *Choosing Lovers*,[5] describes such pairings as fusion relationships. After the first hot month or so of a new romance, these behaviors should be taken as warnings that one or both partners are trying to meet unfulfilled needs for succor and identity that are left over from childhood. The erotic life of such couples is often unsatisfactory to one or both partners because they are so merged that the exciting meeting of the "other" becomes almost impossible.

In dreams or waking, a merged partner may use sex as a way to feel nurtured or as an antianxiety agent (others may use drugs and alcohol). If while making love to your partner, or while dreaming of doing so, you feel too often that you are like a little girl or boy, and/or that you are like the mother or father giving nurturance, you may have a problem. Dreams of having sex with a friendly sibling or with an especially immature and needy friend could suggest that you and your lover are merged. This merged feeling forms some part of most relationships, and can feel either wonderfully secure or imprisoning; but when exaggerated it almost always mitigates against adult I/Thou eroticism. A strong relationship requires some bonding of a friendly, familylike nature. It is only when one or both individuals merge or fuse, losing a clear sense of their individuality, that big problems arise. When two individuals meet and abandon their separateness in a brief, magical merging, ecstasy can be the result. But when two are merged to begin with, and are seeking through the other to become whole, whence can come the magic of two whole individuals meeting each other?

Domination/Submission

Dreams of submitting to sex in exchange for love or protection usually point to the dynamics behind the dreamer's waking sexual and/or social conflicts. Some of us grew up thinking we had to earn or buy love from others, and this can result in an adult's submitting to sex and to a variety of inappropriate demands from partners and even friends in order to win love and affection. When one submits in a dream to sex in an effort to escape bodily harm or death, the dreamer's waking conflicts are likely to be experienced as dramatically more threatening. These dreams should alert us to the possibility that the dreamer learned early in life that if he or she did not meet the demands of others terrible punishment or abuse would result. If someone associates threats of violence to sexual activity in a dream it is a good idea to find out why. Dr. Bernard Beitman, a psychiatrist at a midwestern university sent me the following dream of a twenty-one-year-old woman who was a senior in college.

> I am handicapped and can't get around on my own. I move myself around on a flat platform on small wheels. I don't have a wheelchair. I am trying to keep up with a man, I can't. We are going through a bad part of town. I am attacked by a gang of men. The only way I can save myself is

to offer to give a blow job. I escape with cum all over my body.

"Handicapped"

The dreamer's interpretation: "I feel handicapped and that I can't do as well as men. The only way I can get along is by serving them sexually. I realize that some of the handicap is my own and self-induced." Dr. Beitman commented: "I found this an archetypal statement of women's position in the world." Not being at liberty to go further into the personal life of the dreamer, let me simply underscore that social issues find their way into many dreams in the personal context of a given dreamer's life.

Sometimes, as above, these dreams reflect feelings of domination and submission at a social level that affect the dreamer's sexual, interpersonal, and professional life. Sometimes, as we shall see in the next chapter, these dreams reflect painful, life-shaping, early sexual abuse.

Relationships between human beings are rarely free of shades of dominance and submission. But when this dynamic is too one-sided it inhibits the development of a supportive relationship in which each partner feels free to assert his or her own needs and to respond to the needs of the other.

Identifying Long-Term Patterns in Your Relationships

It comes as a great shock to most of us to discover that in our choice of partners we tend to re-create the dynamics of past relationships. In our major romances we usually unconsciously pick partners to whom we relate in much the same way we related to our mother or father—or in some cases to a sibling. If you had a distant, critical father, chances are your major boyfriends were also distant and critical. Or you might have the habit of picking men who are like your mom or your older brother. We seem inexorably driven to re-create familiar feelings in our intimate relationships, even if those feelings are very painful. We can more easily see this drive to re-create the familiar patterns when we watch our friends choose yet another lover who is the same type as the last ones who didn't work out. Eventually, many of us can recognize our repetitive patterns of falling for lovers who are much like a parent or sibling, as well as the popular variation on this theme: falling for lovers who are the extreme opposite of a parent or sibling. However, relatively few people ever come to a clear understanding of how many of our romantic choices are determined by patterns that go all the way back to our relationships with our parents and siblings, and we are thus likely never to break out of those patterns. For people who had satisfying early relationships this may be a blessing. For those who grew up in unhappy homes, it is a curse.

Our dreams regularly compare our current relationships to our earliest ones and offer us the chance to identify recurring patterns and motivations that influence our lives. By recognizing and dealing with limiting or destructive patterns, we can learn to act with greater freedom of conscious choice. We gain the ability to act from our own assessments of our needs and preferences, rather than from old habitual reactions patterned on childhood relationships.

If you find you have dreams of your mother and father or of one of your siblings, interview yourself about the person in the dream and see if you discover formerly unrecognized similarities to current lovers. A former lover who appears in your dream may well serve the same function: in describing the former lover you may find that he or she reminds you not only of a string of former lovers but of one of your parents or siblings as well. If so, you have an opportunity to examine your tendency to choose this sort of partner and to consider making changes if you so desire.

Benson had a dream of being in bed with an unexpected lover:

> I am having sex with Ellie, a woman I lived with a few years ago. At first the sex is very hot, but before long I grow bored. I am just incredibly bored with her even though she has a fantastic body. I suddenly ask myself, "What am I doing in bed with her?" This is crazy.
>
> *"In Bed With Ellie"*

In our interview I asked Benson:

INTERVIEWER: What is Ellie like?

BENSON: She was a lovely, sexy, sweet, kind woman who took good care of me. But she was also not very bright. We did not share similar educational backgrounds, had few interests in common, and she was not very clever. We broke up because I decided I wanted a brighter, more interesting woman.

I: So she is lovely, sexy, and sweet, and took good care of you, but not very bright or clever, and you didn't share the same interests. Remind you of anyone?

B: I hate to admit it, but when you put it that way, she reminds me of my new girlfriend. I guess I'm falling for that same sweetness and caretaking.

I: Have you been with other women like that?

B: I suppose all of my long-term girlfriends have been like that. My relationships with more intelligent women never last long. I seem to pick either extremely nurturing or extremely nonnurturing and somewhat tough women.

I: What is the very first relationship in which you were with a sweet, not very bright, woman like Ellie?

B: My mother. Oh God. This sounds just too trite. But it is true. How come I never saw the obvious before? So the question is, do I really want that old comfortable type of relationship, or will I ever be able to find and enjoy living with a woman who is both nurturing and interesting? I know they exist, but I just never seem to find one.

Benson was stuck in a rut. To break out he would have to give up some of his demands for extreme amounts of nurturing, which few career women could offer him, then he would have to learn to look for, be attracted to, and get along with women who were more stimulating while still being supportive and nurturing enough for him. These patterns are difficult to change; it takes time and determination.

David had been divorced for a couple of years and was just beginning to think about getting out and meeting new women when he had the following dream three nights in a row.

I see my father in a country setting, perhaps gardening in Georgia, where we used to live. He may be urinating. He looks over one shoulder like a deer with a so-what, disdainful, frowning attitude. Then I feel a woman's nipple brush across my face from the left eye to my nose. (This is so vivid; I still feel it when I awaken). I can't see her face. At first I feel pleasured by the dream but, the second and third night I dream it, I am aware of feeling smothered and held down in addition to the pleasure.

"Pleasure-Pain Nipple"

David's father, like the deer, had always been disdainful of him, and this had not helped his self-esteem. Low self-esteem seemed to be one problem he faced in reentering the singles' scene. But what the dream surprised him with was the realization that while he loved the nurture of a woman (he saw the nipple both as a source of nurture and of erotic excitement), he also feared being smothered by it. David's mother and his former wife were sexy, nurturing women, but they were also smothering women who fussed over him much too much for his comfort. David concluded that his fear of being smothered and held down by a woman was the major reason he had for so long avoided dating again.

I have worked with so very many women whose dreams confront them with the surprising and often unwanted insight that the nature of their current relationships is highly determined by their early relationship to their fathers that I could fill several books with their moving stories. These women are all very bright and usually well read in psychology. The dismay they feel in discovering that they have chosen men according to their unfulfilled needs and early imprinting on Daddy is outdone only by their surprise that this had actually happened to them, not just to other, less aware, women.

I have chosen two of Marianna's dreams because they eloquently express the force of what I have called Daddy's Curse, the spell under which most women live until they recognize their automatic, preprogrammed responses to men. Marianna is an artist of unusual intelligence whose father was a charismatic, extremely powerful captain of industry. At the time of the dream, she was living with a man named Dean who was insisting on a sexually open relationship. She described him as a brilliant, arrogant man who would not compromise ever and who suffered painful feelings of inferiority from a terrible childhood.

Marianna described the king in the following dream as a person with the ultimate power to decide the nature of her life. She bridged his strength and possessiveness to her father, who was so powerful in his career and at home. In the dream she plays the role of the queen, as to some extent she did in her family, her mother having been an alcoholic. Here is her first dream.

> The scene for the dream is the queen's richly tapestried bedroom—her haughty, sensual face—her silken robes.
>
> Why must the men who wait on the queen all be eunuchs? I wonder. Because they hold her in their arms while she makes love with the king, comes the answer. They must not be able to ravish her. But they do get aroused—and that is very erotic, she likes that—although difficult and frustrating for them, as they cannot act on their passion.
>
> And I wonder if a whole man could perhaps sneak in— No, his beard and his erection would give him away. But I think to myself that I will write the story so that he does— and I think the queen will fall in love with him—but the king may kill him.
>
> *The Queen's Eunuchs*

As we proceeded with the interview, Marianna bridged the king not only to her father but to her boyfriend, Dean, who was extraordinarily charismatic and whom she greatly admired. But as Marianna continued her description, we heard that Dean was also extremely egotistical and fundamentally insecure. He thought of himself as a sort of wise man who should naturally have several adoring, sexually available women in his life at any one time. Marianna, who was entranced by Dean's (and her father's) charisma, was also his prisoner. She was not free to be with a whole man. She was the obedient girl-queen-groupie to a very insecure king. Her next dream developed this theme:

The second dream is also of the queen. She seems to have it all. Sensual, in charge, but not really. She is not happy. The queen wakes up nude, in her tapestried bed, in the stone-walled bedroom. She is young, blond, with enormous breasts. She curls and stretches sensuously, running her hands over her body. Then she opens her eyes to find that one of her courtiers is sitting silently in the corner of the room, watching her. She sends him out.

This man is an important character. The queen is many hundreds of miles away from her own kingdom fighting a war. Things are not going well. She does not trust this man—is not sure he can be trusted—but she has to trust him, rely on him, because he is her right-hand man in this war, the most highly placed of her courtiers. She could not fight the war without him. He has all the essential strategic information—she feels uneasily that he, in fact, has more power than she does.

The queen is sending an urgent message—perhaps to the enemy? It is unclear. She is setting her royal seal in wax all over the parchment. She hands it to the courtier, not trusting him, having no choice. He bows and goes out. The queen fears that he is in league with the enemy and that he will read the plea for assistance.

The queen is outside the castle where the army is encamped. It is enormous, a skyscraper, looks like a towering apartment building of gray stone with little slitted windows as in a prison. It is on fire. Disaster! The troops are burning. Men are leaping out the windows for safety, falling to the ground. The army is being decimated.

A letter arrives from the enemy, Napoleon, laughing at her request for surrender or truce. He will press forward to engage her in battle. She must retreat. The courtier watches her read the letter. She has failed. All this fighting and death, for what? She is confused and frightened. Napoleon clearly realizes that he is stronger than she and has the power.

The army is retreating, they are going home. The queen is encamped in her silken tent. The courtier comes to her. He wants to make love. Passively, she consents. He begins touching her eagerly, and at first it is mildly erotic, then she loses all interest. He seems clumsy and crude. She cannot kiss him back. She realizes this is not what she wants to do, and she stops him.

"The Queen's War"

Marianna saw the queen as her erotic self, who only seemed to be in charge but who was really at the mercy of certain men in her life. The stone-walled bedroom seemed to her like a fortress that both protected and imprisoned her. She described the role of a courtier as that of waiting on the queen, and said that they are generally noble in their own right. She bridged the most highly placed courtier to her boyfriend, Dean. In the dream, the queen is far from her own kingdom, where she would be secure, just as Marianna felt somewhat uprooted in her current life situation. Her dream realization that her courtier held more power than she reflected the uncomfortable imbalance of power that existed between her and Dean, and she wondered if the prison-like windows were hinting that she felt somewhat a prisoner with Dean.

Then when she described Napoleon as a tremendously powerful general who had a huge ego and who tried to conquer the world, she realized that Napoleon perfectly characterized her father—and to a lesser extent Dean. Her personal power was indeed being decimated by her dependence on the boyfriend/courtier, and especially by the war she was waging against her father in her intense determination to live a counterculture life in stark contrast to her father's very conservative style. She had thought Dean would be part of her escape from her father's world, but via the dream she had begun to see that she had recreated some of the same dynamics of submission to her new-age boyfriend as she had experienced with her Napoleonic father. After she looses the war she sees the courtier as clumsy and crude, and this she describes as another side of Dean, which becomes clearer as she recognizes that Dean will not save her and that her battle is with her dad and the other Napoleons in her world. The courtier is no longer attractive to her.

As long as Marianna remains enthralled by the charisma of contemporary Napoleons, she will be their prisoner or captive, queen though she be. Her chances of finding a whole man in the same person of a powerful, arrogant, egotist are about as good as finding a whole man among the eunuchs. Her own power will be forfeit, and her lovers secretly insecure seekers after succor.

When a partner excessively uses sex as a remedial method of obtaining nurture and succor, or as an antianxiety treatment, both partners' dreams will vividly portray how this militates against healthy, mature, erotic I/Thou encounters. The last scene in Marianna's dream goes further to help her see her resentment at her relative powerlessness. But the entire dream shows her how she has cooperated to create such a situation in her life. This in-depth analysis of sexual relationships, including their historical roots, is what makes dreams so tremendously valuable in breaking Daddy's Curse—or Mother's Spell.

8

Sexual Nightmares: Abuse from Family and Therapists

Dear Dr. Delaney,

A friend of mine recently gave me "Dreams and the Recollection of Incest," your article in New Realities *Magazine. Since my recollection of incest began from a dream, I am availing myself of your invitation to write.*

The dream itself did not actually seem to refer to incest. I dreamed that I was looking at my tombstone, and it gave, as the dates of my birth and death, 1938–1983. I was actually born in 1950, and I dreamed the dream in 1989 (last June or July). I noted in the dream that 38 is 83 reversed, but in the dream I did not know the significance of those numbers.

I then dreamt that my sister (I have no sister in the physical world) was going to have an operation to cut her heart out. I saw her laid upon a slab draped in sheets, her chest opened, and a great, red, pulsating heart cut out.

Then, in my dream, an act labeled as "voodoo" was performed. I knew that if the act was successful, we could put my sister's heart back in her chest and that the chest would accept it, grow closed, and she would live. Moreover, she would have super powers.

That happened, and she rose off the slab. I then knew

that I was the one who had undergone that operation, and I now possessed the power not to be hurt.

End of dream. When I woke up, I was left with the powerful impression that something had happened to me when I was three, something so awful that my three-year-old self interpreted it as having her heart cut out. Something so awful that the little girl decided to have no real heart, to not feel anymore. (That, I think, is the super power referred to.)

I did not, however, know what the awful event was. I started wondering, however, and trying to reconstruct where I was and what had happened to me when I was three.

I actually managed to dredge up some incredibly early memories, some of which were very painful, but none for the appropriate time and place (I knew at that age my father was stationed in a foreign country and we were with him). I remembered something from when I was one and a half years old, but not this three-year-old event.

Then last August, one evening after AA I remembered. (I had been sober about two weeks when this occurred, and now realize all my drinking was simply so I could keep from remembering it.) I was talking to a woman at the AA meeting who mentioned that she had been sexually molested as a child.

Eyes opened somewhere in the back of my mind, a ghostly finger tapped me on the shoulder, and a voice seemed to say, "That's it, you know; the answer you've been looking for."

And then I remembered. Oh, not everything, not all at once, but I did know then that my father had molested me. Later I realized that the significance of the numbers 3 and 8 was that those were the ages between which my father abused me. My "sister" was a disassociated or split-off version of myself.

It isn't possible for me to confirm the fact of my abuse. Both of my parents are dead, and my brother says he knows nothing of it.

Interestingly, I have actually always had some memories of incest. But because I had completely forgotten any emotions attached to those events, I doubted that they were real memories. I had assumed (as an adult) that I was one of those women Freud talked about, who wanted sex with their fathers and so created these false memories out of wish fulfillment. The book The Courage to Heal *taught me that incest survivors not uncommonly do remember things that way, and that it was a true memory, not a fabrication. I think that realization validated my memories more than anything else.*

Charles L. Whitfield's book, Healing the Child Within, *has helped me recognize that I am someone who has been abused; I have all the personality stigmata of an abused child, as well as [those of] a child of an alcoholic (which my parents also were).*

I have gone into therapy with an incest survivors' counselor at the local Rape Crisis Center, and one day I hope to heal. I'm just at the stage of peeling off the layers of defenses that have hidden this from me for almost forty years, so can't say yet what I will do to resolve the trauma of the abuse, as you put it.

Thank you for letting me tell my story. Since the dream was an indirect one, I thought it might provide a slightly different angle for your study about discovering abuse via dreams.

Sincerely,
Lavonne

THIS CHAPTER IS ABOUT TRAGEDY AND SOMETIMES EXCRUCI-
ating pain. I have written it because there are so many adults who have been abused as children and do not yet know either what to do about it or that they have plenty of company among others who were abused and are still ashamed. I want to help those who were abused discover that their dreams can help them survive and flourish. I hope also to make available to psychotherapists guidelines for recognizing when their clients' dreams are dealing with incest and other abuse issues. If you

find this chapter disturbing, don't force yourself to read it all at once. Go on to other chapters and come back to this one when you feel ready.

A few years ago, I wrote a column in *New Realities Magazine* describing the various ways dreams can help a person discover and cope with a history of sexual abuse. I invited readers to send me their stories, and received letters (with permission to publish them) that filled me with sadness and anger for all the pain these women had suffered in secret (I received no letters from men who had been abused). Before their recall or recognition of the abuse, the women who wrote said that they had lived lives of anxiety, shame, and fear without knowing why. They typically doubted most of their perceptions and feelings, many had become alcoholics, and few had ever heard that their many nightmares might be trying to tell them something. All their letters described the symptoms, doubts, and fears my abused clients have told me. The types of dreams, and the waking problems with trust and intimacy, were the same. And the terrible fear that the woman was just imagining things or wishing for sex with Daddy was the same. Lavonne's letter eloquently expresses many of the problems and much of the pain experienced by survivors of incest.

Adults who have been sexually abused as children, but who have little or no memory of it, frequently discover or gradually recognize that they were abused after a nightmare or a series of nightmares helps them recognize their abuse. In fact, it may be that sexual nightmares are one of the most reliable if also one of the most regularly overlooked markers for sexual abuse even when the survivor has no conscious awareness of the trauma.

It is estimated that one in three or four women, and one in nine men, have been sexually abused in childhood. Exact figures are impossible to determine because the memories of abuse are often entirely repressed. When a survivor does remember, he or she may be very reluctant to tell anyone about it. Therapists often miss the signs due either to lack of experience or to the fact that the survivor has done such a good cover-up job for himself or herself and others. Some therapists miss the signs because, for whatever reason, perhaps even their own abuse, they are unable to deal with the issue.

I regularly see women who have been in therapy for years, unaware of earlier abuse, and come to me "just" to learn how to understand their dreams. Usually within one or two sessions, the abuse is portrayed in the dreams, and we begin the delicate process of looking at it. It is my passionate hope that psychotherapists will become better trained in dream work, because it can cut through the layers of fear and forgetfulness like nothing else I know. Furthermore, the dreamer can pace herself and not open up the box of her dark secrets too quickly by dreaming her own tailor-made route to recall and recovery.

Survivors of sexual abuse typically are more depressed, more anxious, and more prone to dissociation, somatization, and sexual dysfunction than are those who have not suffered sexual abuse.[1] Marion Cuddy and Kathryn Belicki at Brock University in Ontario, Canada, have found that victims of sexual abuse have more sleep disturbances and twice as many nightmares and repetitive nightmares as those unscathed by sexual or physical abuse in childhood.[2] Another study, by Susan Brown, found that women who had a history of incest had more misfortune in their dreams and that they were unique in confusing sex and aggression while dreaming.[3]

DREAMS THAT BLEND AGGRESSION WITH SEX

Brown believes that dream confusion of sex with aggression is a clear indicator that the female dreamer has experienced incest. I would not go quite that far, because I can think of a few instances in which women who apparently have not been abused have dreamt of aggression in sexual situations, and at least for a while, women who have been raped will make this association.[4] But my experience in working with the dreams of victims of sexual abuse confirms that sexual imagery that is confused or blended with images of aggression is very common in the dreams of abused women. And I do consider this blending to be a red flag suggesting possible sexual abuse. More than one of my clients has brought me a dream such as:

A man has caught me and put a gun up my vagina.

In one version of this dream, the man told the dreamer that if she resisted, or told anyone, he would shoot her head off by firing the gun that was inside her. The sexual dreams of abused men and women can get very ugly. Images of gaping bloody holes between legs, in chests, and where heads should be, of hateful violence and possessiveness and torture, reflect the searing emotional and sometimes physical pain sexually and physically abused children have suffered and continue to suffer as adults.

Dreams of being forced to have sex by people who threaten the dreamer with bodily harm if he or she resists are common, as is the desire on the part of the dreamer to protect or save a younger sibling who appears in the dream. Deborah dreamt:

A couple takes me into the back room of a restaurant. My sister is there tied to the bed. The man is planning to tie me up, too, and then rape us both. I am terrified and want to run. But I can't desert my sister, and he is too strong to overpower. Maybe if I go down willingly, he will spare my little sister.

"He Has Us Both"

The terror Deborah felt in this dream was so great that it led to her recall of incest with her father thirty years earlier. When she told her sister about the dream and the memories, her sister refused to talk to her. But later her sister confirmed that she had experienced similar nightmares and memories. Both had worried that they might be falsely accusing their father of incest, but after a few months of therapy, they decided to confront their parents and found solid confirmation of the abuse.

Before going any further, I would like to show you a dream that blends aggression with sexuality but does not seem related to childhood sexual abuse.

I am in my husband's and my bedroom with a man who pretends to be a photographer. But what he really does is invite women to the bedroom, have sex with them, then kill them. I am his assistant. He asks me to do this and that and I willingly, submissively comply with his requests. As we prepare for the next victim, I notice that he will somehow use the photograph he will take of her to blame the victim herself for her impending murder! I am *outraged*. Suddenly, I realize that *I* am to be his next victim. I know this because he is photographing me holding the casing of my husband's gun!

"Sex Then Murder"

Note that when the dreamer is threatened, she is not frightened but angry. Usually abuse survivors have a history of sexual nightmares in which they feel terrified, trapped, and helpless. It is only after they have begun to confront their abuse that they then recall being angry in their sexual dreams. Karina does not recall any abuse, nor does she have a history of sexual nightmares, nor does she suffer the common symptoms of abuse.

Karina understood this dream to be portraying the way she has felt sexually used by her husband. He has never been violent with her but neither has he been responsive to her requests for more sensual, passionate, and creative lovemaking. Karina said that her husband had killed her sexual interest by refusing to respond to her preferences and by angrily blaming her for spoiling their sex with her demands for foreplay lasting longer than ten minutes.

Dreams do not present such dramatic portrayals of problems unless they are terribly important. This dream helped Karina see the gravity of her situation and showed how she had played the perfect co-dependent by cooperating with her husband's love-'em-and-kill-'em scenario. By continuing to have unsatisfying sex with her husband, she perpetuated her problem. This dream opened Karina's eyes to her long-term pattern of submissive co-dependency and to her husband's sexual exploitation, but it did not lead to feelings of having ever been sexually abused earlier in life.

Not all dreams that mix sexuality with aggression are about childhood abuse, so be careful not to jump to conclusions and scare yourself before you explore the dream carefully. If the shoe doesn't fit, don't wear it. If you dream of sexual abuse, the feelings you experience in discussing the dream will usually indicate if you are touching on old, deep, and forgotten wounds of abuse. In any case, there is no need to draw any conclusions before you have worked with several or even many dreams that use imagery of abuse and until you have discussed with an experienced professional any feelings that trouble you.

DID IT REALLY HAPPEN, OR IS IT JUST A DREAM?

Many people are unable to get a parent or other relative or friend to confirm that suspected abuse actually occurred. This can be a source of much worry and doubt for the apparent victim, who doesn't want to falsely accuse a living alleged abuser and risk rejection by that person and perhaps the entire family. This rejection is a possible outcome whether or not the abuse is confirmed. You may have all the symptoms of an abused child (depression, distrust, low self-esteem, alcoholism, sex or drug addiction, suicidal thoughts, and so on), your family may fit the textbook description of an abusive family (nonnurturing, nonprotective, closed to the outside world, with a weak or absent mother and a controlling, mistrustful, suspicious father who uses physical power or the threat of it to get his way), yet you may never be able to recall the specifics of any abuse because they are buried too deep.[5] And there is the possibility that you may not have been abused even if your family seems to fit the profile of an abusive family.

Oddly, sex research specialists Masters, Johnson, and Kolodny believe that it is not always necessary to talk about past sexual abuse. They write in their latest edition of *Human Sexuality*:

Some people feel completely comfortable with a "forgive and forget" attitude and have no desire to talk about
(their incest) with anyone. Others who feel they were in
consensual, non-exploitative incest relationships may not
even see a need to forgive or forget, since they may view
the entire experience as a positive one.[6]

This position is incredible to me. I, myself, and my colleagues
with whom I have spoken have not seen any cases in which incest has not been exploitative of the abused child even if, on the
surface, the incest looked consensual. While sometimes the survivor can come to forgive the abuser, the very desire not to talk
about the abuse and the need to forget it are, in the opinion of all
the therapists I know, symptoms of denial, repression, and the
damage done by the abuse. Masters, Johnson, and Kolodny do,
of course, recognize that anyone suffering from "residual feelings of guilt, resentment, anger, or poor self-esteem that seem to
be linked to the incest experience" would do well to consult a
psychotherapist.[7] I would like to emphasize that very frequently
an individual may suffer from guilt, low self-esteem, and difficulty in maintaining healthy intimate relationships without
having any idea that these symptoms are derived in large part
from sexual abuse that may be partially or totally "forgotten."
Whether or not these symptoms appear to be linked to abuse,
they indicate the need for professional help from therapists who
understand that sometimes forgotten abuse is at their root.

Therapists have long understood that people who have suffered major traumas such as sexual abuse do better once they
can face the fact of the abuse and begin to cope with its fallout
from an adult, reality-based perspective. Denying and repress-
ing memories and feelings takes energy and requires various
forms of emotional armoring that can significantly limit an individual's emotional freedom, development, and health.

James Pennebaker and his colleagues at Southern Methodist
University in Dallas, Texas, have been conducting some fascinating research into the psychological and physiological effects
of disclosing traumas. Pennebaker and Joan Susman have found

that two groups who simply wrote anonymously about the feelings or about the facts and the feelings of the most upsetting and
traumatic events of their lives for fifteen minutes for four days
reaped psychological and physical benefits compared to control
groups who wrote about trivial events or about the facts but not
the feelings of their traumas.

The first two groups at first felt worse—they reported more
anxiety and depression each day after writing. This is a natural
result of emotional closet cleaning. When you start to clean out a
closet, you drag all your stored-up stuff out onto the floor and
your room looks worse than when you started. Then as you reor-
ganize the contents and discard useless things, you begin the
process of tidying up the room and creating a more functional
closet. And indeed, in the follow-up study conducted four
months later, the first two groups were happier, healthier, and
less anxious than the control groups, who seemed unaffected by
the experiment. Furthermore, six months after the experiment
the group that wrote about the facts and emotions related to
their traumas showed a significant drop in illness visits to the
health center compared to the other groups. [8]

Pennebaker and Susman conducted a second, similar study in
which they studied fifty undergraduates in two groups. The first
group wrote for twenty minutes for four consecutive days about
the facts and feelings of traumatic experiences, and the second,
control, group wrote for the same time about trivial experiences.
This time, blood tests were conducted before and six weeks after
the experiment. The researchers discovered that the group that
wrote about the traumas had improved immune system func-
tioning and that this group also visited the health center significantly less frequently than the control group, which wrote about
trivial events. [9]

Continuing their exploration into the health effects of hiding
or confiding traumatic events, Pennebaker and Susman sur-
veyed two hundred employees in a large corporation. They
found:

> Individuals who had experienced traumatic experiences
> in childhood *and* who had not confided these traumas to

others were significantly more likely to have contracted cancer, hypertension, ulcers, and even major bouts with influenza than were people either who had not had traumas or who had confided them. These effects held when controlling for social support and age, and recent traumatic experiences. [10]

Pennebaker points out that in confiding traumatic secrets, the brain itself may become more efficient in processing information. Traumatic experiences involve negative emotions that are processed in the right frontal areas of the brain. Conscious thought seems to be highly dependent on processing in the language areas of the brain normally found in the left temporal cortex. Extrapolating from recent studies on brain function, Pennebaker hypothesizes that by talking about traumatic events an individual may increase his or her previously inhibited linguistic organization of the event in the left temporal cortex and thus increase one's coherent and efficient processing of the painful memories. Pennebaker writes:

> When individuals are required to confront traumatic experiences, significant changes occur within the body. While talking or writing about traumas, compared with superficial topics, individuals evidence greater congruity in brain wave activity across the cerebral hemisphere, lower SCL (skin conductance levels, which are associated with perspiration on palms of hands and soles of feet), and improved immune function. These effects are most pronounced for high disclosers—that is, individuals who disclose extremely personal topics that they previously held back from telling others. [11]

Dreams that stir up feelings and memories of traumatic events may be the first signs a person recognizes that point to forgotten or repressed traumas. As such they provide valuable opportunities to begin discussing hidden traumatic secrets even if the first dreams and discussions are only about feelings that seem to come from nowhere. Later, as the dreamer becomes more open, the dreams become more explicit and help the dreamer to continue talking about and working on the traumatic issue.

If you suspect that you were abused as a child, I strongly urge you to find a good therapist and talk about your feelings. Then you might consider joining a group for incest survivors. Even when my clients have been too closed to work well with their therapist, or had an inexperienced therapist, attending a few group sessions has almost always settled the burning question: "Was I abused, or am I imagining it?" Seeing and hearing the stories of a number of women who have been abused helps you know rather quickly whether you feel like one of them, and how likely it is that you are a survivor yourself.

Attending a survivors' group helps to relieve guilt and improve self-esteem while helping each member realize that she is not alone in her misery or ostracized for her history. For some women, going to a group meeting provides their first feeling of being accepted, believed, and understood. Participation in a group will also act to counter the effects of being in treatment with a therapist who may not be good at dealing with incest issues. Some therapists are abuse victims themselves, and the ones who are still in denial about their own abuse may have trouble dealing effectively with your experience.

EXERCISE **8 - 1**
Make the Most of Your Day Notes

If writing about traumatic experiences over four days for only twenty minutes each day can bring such beneficial results, imagine how you could use your day notes in your dream journal to accomplish some of your personal work. If you have not already done so, try recording your day notes every day for at least one week. Remember to write down the facts and feelings of what you did and felt today. Then, when you feel ready, write about the facts and feelings of the worst thing that has ever happened to you. Do this for five minutes or for as long as twenty the first night. Then keep writing about your experiences a little on nights when you feel like exploring the issue further. Take your time. Closets do not need to be cleaned out by any deadline. If you find that you get very upset, look in the Resources section and Appendix to find suggestions on how to locate a good therapist.

ABUSE BACKLASH

Another disturbing phenomenon among therapists is what I call the incest backlash. It appears that some therapists have jumped on the incest bandwagon with more zeal than careful investigation, and have been carried away looking for supposed hidden incest to explain problems that have other origins. There have also been legal cases in which accusations of sexual abuse seem to have been motivated by financial and custody motives rather than by the truth. A number of therapists who are distressed at the bandwagon effect and the shady legal cases they have encountered sometimes express to me their anger at the false accusers in a way that I find troubling. Their tendency to see most vague memories as fantasy and wish seems as prejudiced as that of the therapist who treats every suspicion of abuse as a certain fact. A therapist who treats this issue as a political or gender issue may be incapable of dealing with the particulars of a given client's situation.

Sigmund Freud, who was the first to recognize that dreams could expose long-repressed incest memories, later took the position that these "memories" were only wish-fulfillment fantasies. The controversy still rages over whether this was a retreat due to Freud's inability or unwillingness to believe that such horrible things could have happened to his clients or to himself, whether he feared offending his referring colleagues who were fathers, or whether he had in fact discovered that some cases were only wish fulfillments and then simply overgeneralized. [12] However, now that the frequency and effects of abuse are better known and understood, few, if any, therapists would accept Freud's a priori assumption that such memories are only wishes.

In the Resources section of this book you will find listings of organizations that will help you locate a therapist and local support groups in case you wish to pursue any of your personal issues and take advantage of the assistance your community offers.

EXERCISE 8-2
Take One Tiny Step

Call one of the organizations listed in the Resources section under "Resources for Recovery from Sexual Abuse" on pages 261–62. Call for information only. Ask for brochures or a list of local support groups or of local therapists. If you ever want to use it you will already have it in hand. If you can't use the information, you may well have a friend who needs it.

CONFRONTATION

If you think you have been abused, get help. *After* you have explored the issue with a professional and developed a support system and confrontation strategy you will be in a much better position to take any further steps, such as confronting your abuser or other members of the family you think should have protected you from the abuser. Beki's letter vividly describes her discovery and her confrontation:

> *Dear Dr. Delaney,*
> *Your article prompts me to write you of my dream experiences. It's good to see I was in good company in my ignorance of my sexual molestation at ages 3–4. I didn't "discover" it until I was 32 years of age and that makes it unfathomable to most people. Just how could I "forget" my father abused me?*
> *At 32, I began having strong heart palpitations upon visits to my parents' home. On Christmas Day, I had a disagreement with my father and that evening my heart*

played Mexican jumping bean. I was irritable, cross, and just plain bitchy for months. My nights were plagued with what I referred to as "hate dreams." They usually involved myself and my mother. She would unjustly punish me for something I didn't do. (A very true-to-life experience. She is a manic-depressive and was/is out of control at times.) I would try to explain to my father "my side" in my dream, but he'd let her punish me. I'd wake crying hysterically and I'd feel hate—pure hate for my parents. I was always trying to be good and I'd get tripped up by circumstance, dream after dream.

I decided their controlling me had to stop, so I went to a counselor. I must have exuded abuse vibes because the first thing he asked me was if I'd ever been abused by my parents. I laughed sheepishly and answered, "No, I don't think so."

The counselor suggested I keep track of my dreams. "Write everything down as soon as you wake," he told me. I did. That very night I had the dream that told me my father molested me. The comprehension of the symbols (so simplistic, they're funny to me now) took me two weeks. By the time I returned to the counselor I had all the pieces together.

My dream: In my present-day kitchen at the counter. I was 3 or 4. I was frosting a cake with President Nixon. I was a child but not myself, maybe I was a boy. I said, "I'll give you a piece of my fraternity cake." Nixon wanted a piece badly, and said, "With frosting?" "Yes," I said. Some frosting from the bowl spilled on the counter from the knife. I took a small C-shaped crumb and dipped it in the spilled frosting. I thought he could have that but nothing from the cake. That would spoil the cake. Then, Nixon went into the living room and kept asking me for some cake. He kept asking if there was butter in the frosting. "Yes, there's butter," I answered. I woke up.

Here is the list of images I made that day in an attempt to analyze this dream. I had an idea it meant I was molested, but I didn't know who President Nixon represented.

Nixon = "tricky dick" who "broke into" Watergate, a cover-up, hypocrite, liar, and authority figure.

Cake = a "piece" = sexuality ("Have cake and eat it too").

White frosting = virginal ("frosting on the cake").

Frosting = sperm or semen.

C-shaped crumb = clitoris.

Fraternity = secret society for men, secrets and rituals, closed society with membership, initiation rites.

Butter = "stick" of butter, "pound" of butter. *Dad only likes butter frosting. Hates other kind.

My dream was eventually confirmed. In the end, my father admitted molesting me after a lot of angry denial. At first he accused me of lying, fabricating, etc. I was silent but resolved. I told him I didn't want to talk about it unless my counselor was there. He has admitted to molesting me, at first once, then to having done it on more than one occasion. My younger sister who lives in Los Angeles had accused him of molesting her. She is plagued by dreams of sexual abuse themes still. We've been to some family sessions with my counselor and my father sees another therapist. I'm sure our molestation was routine and he is blocking or lying. I was prepared never to accuse him of molesting me. My therapist felt he'd deny it and I'd pay the price. My younger sister actually did the accusing, and together we were finally able to get the truth. Actually, my mother hounded the truth out of my father. She kept asking him why we would make such accusations. Eventually he caved in.

My therapist/counselor has helped me deal with my molestation by my father. After my acceptance of the abuse I started having more dreams. They were centered more on me. My thoughts of sexuality. My fear of men. I

*After I realized Dad only liked butter cream frosting, I knew he was President Nixon.

realized I felt I had to have sex with any man who wanted it. I wondered why I froze up, even in a store, when a man just looked at me. In one dream, a carload of ugly, really ugly men were running me over. My response was to lie down and lift my legs into the air. (Smart!) I no longer feel that way. I can look a man in the face and know he may even be attracted to me but I'm in control. What a load off!

I'm still very angry. I joke to release it. I also dream a dream I had when I was 3 or 4. I am a boy—my counterpart. If I am a boy, my father won't molest me. He never bothered my brother, only the girls. This is based on what I remember to be a real escape for me. After this dream about a year ago, I really remembered "being a boy." It was a state of mind I entered to escape. I used it as a refuge. That explains why I am a boy in my frosting-the-cake dream. The fraternity comes to mind also.

I hope this has been of some value. It's been another therapeutic activity for me. My younger sister should really write you. She has some real beauties in the dream department. I hope they set her free someday.

Thank you for your work. I'm still in the healing process. It will take me some more time but I've come far. It's wonderful to know I'm not alone and there are people to turn to.

Sincerely,
Beki

Confrontations can be very satisfying and can relieve the survivor of many of her doubts about her abuse. But they are also very painful experiences. If family members angrily deny any possibility of abuse and if they then reject and blame you for suggesting such a thing, you will need plenty of support and familiarity with typical confrontation patterns. So if you want to confront your abuser, please get into therapy or at least a survivor's group first.

Common Elements in the Dreams
of Adults Abused as Children

The images described below, which I have found to be common in the dreams of my abused clients and in the dreams of survivors who have written me, are not necessarily certain markers of abuse. We must keep in mind that the same image can be used by different people in different ways that suggest different interpretations. As we have noted, dreams of having sex with your sibling may reveal how much like your sibling your spouse is. If the dream does not carry overtones of coercion, shame, or guilt, it is not very likely to be about incest. It is important to look at any image in its dream context as well as in the context of the dreamer's life.[13] What are the feelings evoked by the image, what do these feelings remind the dreamer of, and how do these feelings fit into the structure of the dreamer's dream and life experience?

Women's Dreams of Little Boys

Beki's story brings up another image I have often found in the dreams of abused women: that of being a little boy, or of seeing a little boy molested. Beki's interpretation mirrors how my clients have understood the boy to represent their way of defending against the dangers of being a girl, and of distancing themselves from the pain of girlhood when abuse is part of it. My clients have often described little boys as less at risk to be molested by Daddy and they have often said things like, "I used to believe, and still do, that if I had been a little boy I would not have been abused. I used to wish I were a boy because of that." Of course, plenty of boys are molested in childhood, but here we are discussing how my clients have judged the relative risks.

Abused or Neglected Little Animals

Women who tell me dreams of discovering little kittens or puppies who have been horribly abused or neglected become deeply moved when they describe their feelings about the little animals. They can then relatively easily recognize that they have felt like the burned, starved, frozen, or beaten little ones deep inside for a very long time. Sometimes the animals are little squirrels or deer. The animals are always defenseless and evoke not a few tears from the dreamer who reexperiences the dream. When we first work with these dreams, the dreamer is often unable to go further than to recognize the depth of her pain. The person responsible for the mistreatment is usually not indicated in the dream, and the dreamer is left to ponder whether it is she who has neglected the tender puppy within or if there is or has been some force in her life that led to this abuse or neglect. If the latter is the case, there are usually plenty of other dreams to signal it, as well as a number of symptoms in the dreamer's waking life. As the abused dreamer begins to let down some of her defenses, her dreams become less enigmatic. In the case of the abused little animals dreams, either the physical, emotional, or sexual abuser is hinted at or (in rare cases) identified, and the dreamer becomes more aware while dreaming that she is the abused little animal. Again, distinguishing actual abuse from feelings, fears, and dreams of abuse often takes time and plenty of cross-checking dreams, waking memories, suggestive symptoms, and family history.

Vampires

Although they can represent a variety of life-sucking threats, vampires frequently appear in the dreams of survivors of sexual abuse to portray incest or other molestation. Even in the dreams of women who have not been molested, the image of the dark vampire who forcefully draws his victims under his spell often depicts sexual conflicts. The horror a dreamer experiences when approached by a vampire is sometimes mixed with titillation, with the pleasure of submission and of renouncing all responsibility for whatever might happen. The dreamer usually knows that she must not give in to the vampire's power, and sometimes is aware of needing to protect younger dream characters from his destructive power. Dreams like this sometimes help the dreamer see that a new boyfriend is bad for her and that she must resist her sexual attraction and temptation to fall under his spell.

When vampire dreams turn bloody and violent, the likelihood that they are dealing with abuse issues increases. Dreams like the following usually lead the dreamer to bridge to more terrible memories of parental incest:

> A vampire came into the bathroom where I was getting dressed. He kissed me and suddenly my breast was in his teeth and he was sucking, sucking. All my blood was pouring out through my breast and I knew I was going to die unless I fought back. I tried to pull my breast loose but he was too strong. Finally, I let him have the nipple and cut my breast apart to get free.
>
> I staggered into the bedroom where my brother was asleep screaming for him to help me. He told me not to make such a fuss. The vampire laughed. I reached in the bureau and grabbed some garlic, which I stuffed into his mouth. He got weaker, but I feared I could not hold him off. I was screaming and screaming. . . .
>
> *"Attacked by a Vampire"*

Mother Spiders, Scorpions, and Beetles

I have heard and read relatively few incest dreams dreamt by men. In my two decades of practice I think I have heard only five or six. But from those I suspect that poisonous or smothering or otherwise repulsive (to the dreamer) insects may serve the function of vampires in women's dreams. In the male incest dreams I have worked with, an insect (often described as a mother insect) such as a black widow or a scorpion fills the dreamer with disgust and perhaps a bit of fear. Then the dreamer's mother appears and the dreamer is sexually aroused by her, but again feels disgusted at both his mother and himself. The mother may or may not be experienced as smothering in the dream. It is interesting to note that the men I've seen who have been abused by their mothers do not speak of terror, as do the women, but of disgust, of some fear and squeamishness, and sometimes of being infuriatingly smothered. I wonder what the dreams of men who were abused by their fathers are like. We hope to be able to collect many more dream examples from men abused as children and discover if this pattern is confirmed by larger numbers of dreamers.

Witnessing Abuse and Being Chased

The blending of sexual with aggressive and threatening imagery can take many forms. The sexual element may be manifest or explicit, such as the gun in the dreamer's vagina, seeing a little boy or girl being molested, or being chased by men or monsters against whom the dreamer has no defense.

Margo was in her late thirties when she dreamt:

> I am about to give a nice warm bath to a little girl, about three years old. She has been repeatedly molested by Mafia types who couldn't keep their hands off her. I seem to have rescued her. She asks me if she can keep her dress on during her bath. She has been so traumatized she wants to protect herself this way. How sad. I reassure her that she is safe now and that she can keep her dress on as long as she likes.
>
> *"Can I Keep My Dress On?"*

Margo immediately bridged the Mafia types to her husband, who often exclaims that he can't keep his hands off her even when she tells him that she feels molested by him. She then bridged the molestation to her feeling that she could not convince her husband to respect her boundaries in many areas of their lives—physical, emotional, and temporal. Not only did he caress her in public and private far more than she liked, he also made extreme demands on her time and emotional caretaking services. She cried and cried during our session, realizing that her feelings of vulnerability vis-à-vis her husband were very deep and very painful. She felt overwhelmed by his need to have things his way. Since Margo did not bridge to childhood feelings and does not think she has a history or current symptoms of abuse, we felt that this was an example of a dream that used child molestation as a metaphor. Margo's dream showed her that she felt like a molested child in her relationship with her husband.

Being chased in a dream is so common that probably everyone has had this type of dream to express something they were running away from and felt threatened by. I begin to suspect abuse when the dreamer has had the dream frequently and regularly since childhood, when the dreamer feels her terror and helplessness deeply, and/or when the single chaser is relatively much bigger than she. If, in the interview, the dreamer starts to bridge to feelings she had as a child with a family member, we can expect other dreams as well to lead us in the same direction of sexual and/or physical abuse.

You can't usually conclude that you have been abused on the basis of one dream. If you suspect abuse is reflected in your dreams, work on a series of dreams with a good analyst or therapist and see what patterns of dreaming, patterns of feelings about yourself and your history, and patterns of relationships emerge. These patterns will give you a clearer understanding and a more confident grasp of your situation.

Dreams of Sexually Intrusive Parents

As you can imagine, dreams in which the dreamer's father or mother or other family member is forcing sexual attentions upon the dreamer are likely indicators of abuse if the dreamer's descriptions of the dream feelings follow those lines. Early on in the recall process, men and women will tell me dreams in which Father or Mother insists upon looking under the dreamer's or a dream child's clothes to the dreamer's great discomfort. Or perhaps the mother will insist upon giving the male child a bath and linger too long soaping or drying his genitals, leaving the dreamer feeling used and coerced, not pampered.

In later stages, when recall is less threatening, the dreamer may remember dream scenes in which the parent or other family member actually engages in intercourse and other sexual activities with the dreamer. Not all dreams in which the dreamer is sexually engaged with a family member indicate sexual or other abuse. It may be that, if we all recalled most of our dreams, most people would remember at least one dream of having sex or of being in bed with a family member. If they are not colored by intense shame or fear, these dreams can mean a wide variety of things. As we have seen in chapter seven, some may reflect actual sexual interest in the dream figure or in someone else of whom the dream figure reminds the dreamer. For example, dreaming of having sex with your mother or sister may be your way of focusing on the characteristics (positive or negative) your current lover shares with the family member in the dream. The interpretation of any dream depends on the feelings and metaphoric bridges evoked by the imagery. Interview yourself carefully, or have a professional help you, and you will discover what your particular dream means for you.

Being Held Hostage or Prisoner

Dreams of being in prison are common in many nonabuse situations in which the dreamer's waking life includes no history of sexual or physical abuse. Dreams that do not identify a particular prisonkeeper and do not evoke feelings of terror but of restraint and frustration usually have to do with analogous situations the dreamer has created or is experiencing in her life. For example, she may have imprisoned herself by her inhibited, rigid habits of thinking or of acting. Or she may have created a marriage or career that feels like a prison. Even when the prison guard or kidnapper is portrayed as someone who caricaturizes the dreamer's spouse, the issue may well be a current emotional abuse of the co-dependent dreamer without reflecting childhood abuse.

However, when the emotions run to terror and pathetic helplessness, and when these feelings evoke feelings from childhood, abuse may be in the picture. At the age of seventeen, Willa had a dream she could not forget after twenty years.

I was held prisoner by an "evil scientist" who appeared as an older white man, short, and wearing a white lab coat. We were in a room that looked like a laboratory high up in a tower. He seemed to want to conduct some kind of painful experiment on me. My fear was immense. I tried to escape by flying out of the only window in the room. I did fly out, but he came after me and pulled me back inside.

"The Evil Scientist"

Twenty years after this dream, just before her father died, Willa started having her first abuse flashbacks. As happens to many women I have dealt with, these first came to her while driving a car. While driving, Willa started thinking about some knives her sister and she had found the day before while cleaning out her dying father's apartment. Whereas the day before she had felt vaguely squeamish about them, now she became almost hysterical, and as often happens to women in her situation, her body reacted strongly.

I started crying hard and my body started almost convulsing. I found myself saying over and over again, "Don't hurt me." I saw my father's very mean face and heard his voice say, "If you don't move, it won't hurt you." I was absolutely terrified. (Now I know why bees terrify me so. When someone says, "If you don't move, it won't hurt you," it triggers an anxiety attack.)

I now believe that my father used those knives against me, and that he also threatened me with a gun that he kept in his bedroom closet. I believe he was the mad scientist who conducted ritualized torture on me, using all manner of "tools," inserting them into my vagina and threatening to kill me. Flying out the window was my metaphor for escape via dissociation, and indeed I did develop a multiple personality disorder for a while.

As we see in this dream, flying dreams are not always pleasant; they are sometimes metaphors for escape mechanisms such as denial and dissociation. By dissociating, Willa was able to sort of disconnect herself from the pain she suffered. These things seemed to be happening to someone else while she, Willa, either looked on or spaced out. This is a mechanism that can help a person tolerate the apparently intolerable.

THERAPIST ABUSE

Willa and the other brave women who have dared to look their terrors in the face have a great need to establish supportive relationships with good therapists and recovery groups. Willa and too many other victims of abuse have had the misfortune to visit therapists who, in flagrant disregard of all professional (and human) standards and ethics, have sexually abused them by having sex with them or by disregarding appropriate verbal and emotional boundaries. While the therapeutic community has tried to weed out these rotten apples for years, there are still too many of them in the field.

The dreams of these women portray the therapist as an abuser, but are usually "overlooked" in therapy by the dreamer and therapist. Occasionally, patients who are being abused by the therapists they see on a weekly basis have dreams that include references to vampires, abusive family members, or malevolent people or animals that the dreamers encounter once a week. Such parallels as weekly abuse are not sure markers of therapeutic abuse, but they may indicate it. They may also indicate a dreamer's unexpressed feeling that he or she is being used or taken advantage of by the therapist for financial reasons. They may, on the other hand, reflect the dreamer's inordinate fear of anyone who resembles an abusive parent simply by being in the parental role of therapist, and so represent transference feelings.

In any case, these dreams are important and should be discussed with the therapist. A good therapist will nonjudgmentally, nondefensively elicit and listen to the feelings, descriptions, and bridges evoked by the dream interview and help the dreamer reflect upon them. For example, a good therapist will explore the dreamer's perception of him or her as a devil, and will modify the therapy accordingly if necessary. The appearance of such a dream may signal that it is time to consult another therapist for a second opinion. If you have any doubts or worries that your therapy is not going well, it is perfectly appropriate first to discuss your concerns with your therapist, and then to see another therapist for a few sessions to get another perspective. In doing this, you are not being disloyal or unkind to your therapist. You are taking responsibility to achieve the best therapeutic results possible. If your therapist is a good one, he or she wants the same thing for you. Professional standards and ethics require that your therapist cooperate with your wish to consult with someone else, and even to provide you with names of other therapists. Of course, if you feel that your therapist has transgressed the professional boundaries, you might want to locate another therapist on your own. (See the Resources section for suggestions on how to do this.) Remember, if it turns out that you are the one who has been overreacting, you are likely to realize it more quickly if you consult another therapist. You need not be embarrassed if you discover that you have overreacted. This is your therapy, you pay for the best services you can find, and any good therapist will understand your need to check things out.

There are some male and female therapists who take unforgivable advantage of their patients' vulnerability and inability to set firm boundaries. They rationalize having sex with their patients with lines like these, which were quoted to me by abused patients and by some abusing therapists: "By having sex with my patient, I was providing her with a healing experience"; or "By sexually caring for her [or him] I was able to provide my patient with a corrective reparenting experience." You have a dangerous therapist if he or she has ever said such things to you, or given you lines like, "Yes, it is incestual for us to have sex, but it is only by reexperiencing it that you can heal the wound" or "I really care about you. You attract me in spite of my efforts to resist. I think we should explore having sex together." Hearing such things from your therapist, and even engaging him or her sexually, may at first be very gratifying to you. But this is likely to be extremely damaging to you in the long run, and it will *not* help you resolve anything.

I can think of *no* situation that would excuse a therapist for saying even "I am attracted to your breasts" or "I wish I could make love to you." In the delicate therapeutic relationship, there is no therapeutic justification for the therapist to discuss his or her sexual feelings toward a patient with that patient. If a therapist is having difficulties with feelings toward a patient, he or she knows to go to another therapist for professional guidance and assistance. And of course, it is *never* all right for the therapist to touch a patient in any sexual way whatsoever. The result of such transgressions of therapeutic boundaries is to deepen the wound and increase the patient's distrust of the world. In an increasing number of states sexual contact between therapist and patient is a crime. If you are in such a therapeutic relationship, call one of the centers in the Resources section in this book for advice and a referral to a consulting therapist who will help you work out the problem with the total confidentiality you need.

Sexually abused women sometimes look for therapists with whom they can reenact destructive patterns. I have known of patients who insist that their new therapist continue the inappropriate sexual patterns established by earlier therapists. For example, a few women have felt rejected and quit therapy when their new therapists refused to feel their legs or breasts, watch them masturbate, or kiss them. Patients who are sexually seductive need therapists who respect clear therapeutic boundaries, who help the patient talk about and explore such feelings, but who refuse to help the patient act them out.

On the other end of the spectrum, several women have told me that they quit therapy when their therapists asked them to talk about their sexual history and their sexual feelings. It is difficult, if not impossible, to work out your emotional conflicts without examining your sexual life. As long as therapists keep their sexual desires and their hands to themselves—and by far the great majority do—one can benefit greatly from exploring sexual issues.

As always, be careful not to jump to conclusions about your dreams. You may sometimes dream of having pleasant, consensual, satisfying sex with your therapist after having made a good connection with him or her, or after having successfully worked together on a particular therapeutic issue. Norma had been abused by her older brother when she was a little girl. As a woman in her mid-thirties she was shopping for a therapist to work through her feelings about her abuse when she interviewed a male therapist to whom she felt an immediate and strong attraction. In her initial interview, the therapist seemed very experienced in treating abuse survivors and appeared to merit his high recommendation by others in the field. Norma was glad at last to have found a therapist who both understood her feelings and who seemed to have a method for treating her. However, she was concerned about her attraction to him. Before she made up her mind whether or not to choose him as her therapist, Norma incubated a dream about the matter. She dreamt:

> . . . The doctor was on the sofa in my apartment. I was going to sleep at the same time, but in my bed. Suddenly there was only my bed and the doctor was in it. I said, "Oh no. This means we are sleeping together in the same bed. We can't . . . and not only that but what if your wife comes back . . . this will look very bad." He said, "It's not like that. She won't be coming back." He came closer to me and asked if I wanted to see him as a doctor or as a lover. I would have lied and said as a doctor, but he put two fingers on the pulse of my neck to see if what I was about to say would be the truth. My pulse shot way up and I knew I wanted to make love.
>
> We suddenly looked at each other full of love and I knew that my prayers for a wonderful lover had been answered. He pulled himself on top of me, entered me, and I felt so completely free to have what I really wanted. I noticed that his nipples turned very small and dark and his penis was very small, but we didn't care because we were so in love.
>
> *"Doctor or Lover"*

In our interview Norma described the dream doctor as very attractive and noncoercive. He seemed genuinely interested in knowing the truth about her preference to see him as a doctor or as a lover. He implied that she had to make a choice and that he could not combine the two roles. Norma became aware of just how strong her attraction to the doctor was and that she really wanted him as a lover. Her dream work made it clear to her that she did not want to enter into therapy about sexual abuse and boundary issues with a man who even innocently elicited in her such intense sexual desires. Yes, these feelings could be seen as grist for the mill, but she decided that she had enough difficult material to work through and that she did not want to make the process any more difficult than necessary. The fact that her dream led her to notice that the doctor had a dark, diseased nipple and a very small penis told her that there would be trouble in paradise if she cared to look more closely. Norma decided to look for another therapist, and felt relieved not to have to try to manage her feelings in therapy with this apparently very good therapist who was not the right one for her at that time in her life.

THE REWARDS OF WORKING THROUGH ABUSE ISSUES

What makes it worth working through the excruciating pain of sexual abuse is that you will be able to reclaim your life and your pride, confidence, and freedom from fear. You will learn to break the cycle of abusive relationships and romances, and not necessarily always choose sexless, safe men as your refuge from the abusive ones you used to attract. You will have the chance to reclaim your sexuality and to choose if and with whom you want to share it. Pamela, who was abused by her uncle and father, describes how her repressed abuse determined the people in and quality of her life:

> As for my life, I have repeatedly engaged in relationships with men who were very much like my uncle in some

ways (hating women) and like my father in others (cowardly). I grew up with a desire to be good and please men—look nice, be nice, and be courageous—show no signs of vulnerability. I believed that if I were nice enough, no one would ever hurt me again, and if I were brave enough, I need never be ashamed or afraid. Boy, was I wrong on all counts.

Instead, I've lived an extremely narrow life in terms of freedom and expression. Good, nice, and brave. Very dry, indeed.

THE PHASES OF HEALING

Drs. Johanna King and Jacqueline Sheehan at California State University at Chico have described the phases abuse victims commonly pass through in therapy. [14] These phases are signaled by certain types of dreams that can help both the survivor and the therapist cope with the challenges of each stage. There is, of course, some overlapping of these phases, and the growth and insight process may be interrupted by waves of resistance at any phase. I have slightly modified and elaborated on King's and Sheehan's model with their blessings.

1. Initial Resistance

In this phase, the survivors may suspect, but do not want to know. They may not be able to remember dreams or may be unwilling to tell them. They may have dreams of refusing to hear what a friend or teacher tries to tell them:

> A good teacher wants me to attend a lecture on inbreeding. I say I can't bear to hear it. I leave and close the door behind me.

The therapy sessions may go very slowly, with the survivor remaining very tight and guarded even if seeming impatient for therapy to "work."

2. Discovery

Now come the dreams with increasingly clear suggestions of abuse. These usually include abuse of other people (not the dreamer) or animals, abused kittens and abused little girls or boys. Then the survivor may dream of watching or learning of the abuse of children of his or her gender, perpetrated by figures that remind the dreamer of one of her family members. Then may come dreams in which the dreamer clearly identifies herself as the victim and a particular family member(s) as the abuser(s). A dreamer may even cry out in the dream: "It's my father. My daddy did it."

Sometimes the survivor feels so much anxiety, grief, or shame in the early phases of discovery that she will stop therapy, or need to slow it down until she can tolerate the pain. It is important to adjust the pace and intensity of therapy to meet your present needs in the context of your life at any given time. Dreams in which the dreamer feels she is being pushed or is driving too fast can alert a therapist who knows how to work with dreams to this problem.

3. Assessing the Effects of Abuse

Part of the dreamer's coming to terms with abuse is recognizing how it has affected her entire life: her self-image, her self-esteem, her sense of trust, and her ability to enjoy herself and her relationships. Assessment dreams include scenes in which the dreamer sees herself or a contemporary who is crippled, injured, or limited physically or emotionally in some way that interferes with her enjoyment of life.

4. Insight and Growth

Progress in therapy and in rebuilding the survivor's sense of self will be reflected in dreams of new construction or reconstruction. Old bedrooms may be torn apart and rebuilt, transit systems improved, restaurants placed under new and trustworthy management. Forlorn little animals may begin to mature and become stronger, and self-image figures may become healthier and more secure.

5. Renegotiation of Boundaries and Mastery

As the dreamer continues to heal his or her wound, we see dreams of setting clearer and more confident boundaries:

> At some point in the dream, I make it very clear that I will not stay on the hotel's ground floor for security reasons. I ask that they give me a room higher up, and to my surprise they cooperate and give me a lovely room with a view and a very good lock on the door. I feel safe and happy.
>
> *"A Safe Room on Request"*

Dreams of mastery appear when solid progress has been made, even in a tiny area. The mastery they portray is often ahead of the dreamer's current level of mastery. These dreams act as congratulators, goal setters, and motivators.

SOPHIA'S DISCOVERY AND HER MASTERY

Sophia bridged the huge animal in the following dream to her sexuality and all the abuse issues surrounding it.

> I come into a living room. There are other people there. I sit on a couch and a big, huge, very black, shaggy, furry animal comes up to me. At first I think it's a big cat like a jaguar. But it could just as well be a big dog. It's huge.
>
> The beast comes up to me. Because I am sitting down, it is taller than I. In waking life, if a big cat's head is higher than yours, he assumes power and is likely to attack. I am absolutely breathless with fear as he comes up to the couch. His trainer is not here right now. She's out. I have to do this on my own. I have to manage this beast.
>
> The people in the living room are watching me, wonder-

ing what will happen. The big jaguar beast comes up, his head over me. I pet his head and bring his muzzle down. Kind of like playing, but also communicating. While doing this, I am so frightened I can barely function.

His fur is shaggy and thick and bulky. I realize I am wearing fur like his. Like big fur pants or a skirt. This fur I am wearing gives me authority or power or permission to deal with this jaguar beast. The fur somehow identifies me as being part of this beast and perhaps sharing in its strength.

He is huge and fierce, but he is responding to my feeble attempts to keep him under control and not attack me. He is almost purring. Almost playing. But still he is strong and overpowering. He turns and leaves the room. I am relieved.

"The Big Black Beast"

Sophia's ability to control her fear and at least tentatively deal with the big black beast of her sexual history was the beginning of a new era for her. She is beginning to be able to conceptualize the beast of sexuality as no longer terrifying but somewhat controllable and almost playful. Her sexual issues are still overpowering, but she feels now that she will survive them.

Sophia was able to dream "The Big Black Beast" only after she had battled her way through a lot of fear and pain. The next two dreams show both the horror of her recall and the hope of recovery. I hope they will embolden you to embark or continue on your journey if sexual abuse has been a part of your life.

I see a Mexican family sitting in Catholic church. Actually I see the father, a heavyset man, holding his little boy on his lap. The little boy is very young, like three or four. The little boy is squirming and fussing. I can see the father's penis. He is molesting the little boy. I am concerned and want to take action to stop this right now.

Now I see a little girl being molested by her father. She is squirming and moving around while he's doing something to her. She is very small, like a toddler or a three-year-old. Now she is standing back away from the scene. She says, "My father did it" or "My father molested me." At any rate, she's indicating her father did it, not just some man. It was her father. I am distressed and horrified. I keep thinking, "We must stop this!" This is all-important. I am consumed with the feeling that we must stop this above all else. In waking, I start to scream but nothing comes out. I make a big effort and scream harder and louder. I am trying to make this stop. I am moaning and making noises and wake myself up.

"Her Father Did It!"

Musing on this dream triggered Sophia's memory of complaining to her mother of a sore anus after visits to her gay father and his boyfriend's house. Later she remembered being in that house and being afraid to go near the bedroom. More memories followed. Sophia underwent weeks of high anxiety, but continued her therapy and dream work. After several months she had a very long dream, excerpts of which follow:

I am laughing and hanging out with some girlfriends. Then I notice it's hard to breathe. There is something unhealthy in the air. The air is gray, smoky, dirty. The church I was going to run to for cover is spewing out black smoke. It's all boarded up, but the pollution is coming out of the eaves, the cracks, everywhere. The church might almost blow up. It's churning out this filth.

And it's not going to stop. This is the end of the world. I think it's more than the church. It's not the church's fault. The filth and pollution are everywhere. It's affecting everyone. We are running for shelter. But shelter is just temporary. We cannot find anything to protect us from this. It's everywhere.

I am running. I realize I was outside a lot and got a lot of the pollution in me. Instead of being healthy, I realize I'm probably one of the sickest of the people around. My right shin is also starting to ache. I limp a little.

People are running everywhere. It's havoc. It's terrible.

My boyfriend, Stan and I have made a little cardboard shelter such as homeless people would have. We have to share it with some little Mexican boys. Even though Stan is there, they want to have sex with me. It's easy for me to fight them off, but they are angry and vengeful. If I rile them up too much, they might come back and kill me.

Sure enough, they come back. They are mad. They have a gun. I am afraid. As they get closer, I see the plastic insert in the opening of the gun that they make manufacturers put in toy guns so you can see right away they are not real guns.

The little boys come into the shack with their gun. It's an old-fashioned gun like Aaron Burr's. I ask to see the gun to admire it. I stroke it and make admiring comments that are clearly erotically tinged. Since it's not real and I'm not really threatened, I can play their game to try to soothe them to get them out of here.

But then Stan takes out a real gun and threatens the little boys. They run off. They'll never be back. I'm safe with Stan.

In the next scene after I let a mother know that she mustn't communicate directly just now with her daughter, I notice that my right leg is swelling up in width but shrinking in length. I notice I am still limping. I had not noticed the pain or how I had been making up for the leg's loss of mobility. I was just limping along. I realize it's cancer caused by the filth. I was too long out in the pollution. I am very afraid.

Everyone is still panicked and screaming and I become lucid and realize what a horrible dream this is. While dreaming the dream, I bridge it to the devastation and destruction to my world that remembering my abuse has brought. My world has ended. Things will not be the same because I remembered. Still lucid, I make the following deduction: Remembering is good for me. Maybe this destruction won't kill me after all. Maybe it's safe for me to be out of doors in this pollution. Maybe I won't die after all. . . .

Now I am in a movie. (Ta-da! What a change!) A big guy with long blond hair who looks like Gregg Allman is attracted to me. I am uneasy and distance myself. He's nice and all that, but I am very careful now to protect myself. He hasn't done anything wrong yet; I just want my space. I think the director talks to me about some action he wants in a scene. I guess I have a good part in the movie too.

"The End of the World"

Sophia wrote the following commentary:

I don't understand all of this dream, but I recognize the devastation of my world and no escape available. I have been limping along and need to recognize the extent of the damage. I don't really want to communicate directly with Mother at this time. The Gregg Allman figure I feel is my boyfriend, Stan. That is, a big guy in the sense of having a lot of credence with me, someone whose ideas could overpower me. I've been keeping my space lately and Stan has been wonderful. We're taking things very slowly.

This is what I've been going through. I feel very powerful at times, emotionally crushed at times, and very vulnerable. At the same time, I am more open with people I work with, not feeling threatened by their power. When people smile at me, I don't wonder what they want. I admire their smiles, their eyes, their spirits. If I feel like it, I smile back.

I am making incredible progress.

Sophia's progress is especially clear at several key points in the dream. She shows some mastery via insight when she realizes the guns are not real and that she need not feel threatened by them. When she dreams of Stan using a real gun to shoo away the little boys she gains mastery by employing an effective ally. She assesses the effects of her incest when she realizes that her leg cancer was caused by being out in the pollution for too long. Then she has a breakthrough and reassesses the possible effects of the filth; she thinks she might not die of it after all and that remembering is actually good for her! This new perspective seems to precipitate a new experience with a handsome male who does not act in a threatening way and whose attraction to her Sophia can handle. She ends the dream with hopes of getting a good part in the movie, which she interpreted as getting a good part in the rest of her life.

In the Resources section you will find books to read and centers to contact that will help survivors through recovery. You will also find resources for the treatment of sex addicts, those whose sexuality is out of control, as well as the name of a therapist who organizes support groups for husbands of incest victims.

9

How to Break Out of Limiting Patterns in Sexual Relationships and Clear the Way for Healthy Intimacy

MANY OF US ARE TRAPPED BY LIMITED, SOMETIMES DE-structive, patterns in our sexual lives. Some of us languish in life-less, lackluster sexual relationships in which one or both partners would just as soon forget about having sex except for some physical release a few times a month. Others of us feel trapped or bullied by our sexual partners, and still others feel frustrated that the love they share out of bed does not translate into steamy, erotic encounters at least now and then. How are we to break out of these patterns and make more enlightened romantic choices? How do we clear our minds and hearts of the debris of the past so that we can delight more and more in the joys of erotic and emotional intimacy?

SELF-EDUCATION

The first and simplest thing is to educate yourself about sexual-ity. Many men and women, some of my psychotherapist col-leagues included, haven't read a good book on the subject in years because they are too busy, have other priorities, or think they already know enough. People usually are far more inhibited and less educated about sex than they realize or admit.

If either you or your partner is reluctant to learn more about sex, you might find encouragement in this line from a friend of mine whose loving European husband knew that learning about sex is a lifelong exploration: "My husband has read every good book that has ever been published about sex in four languages. I have absolutely no complaints about my sexual life." The rich get richer. If you approach sexuality as a growing, changing, creative activity that will never be fully mastered, you will probably never be bored, in or out of bed.

EXERCISE 9-1

Read One or Two Books on Sex Every Year

Reading regularly about sex, one book every six months or so, keeps your sexual self limber; you regularly reassess your inhibitions and fears, and you refresh and inspire your sexual enthusiasm and creativity.

In the Resources section you will find a list of wonderful books and a list of the best sex education videos I have been able to locate. If you hesitate to buy a book on sex in a store, you can always telephone a bookstore to order one and pay with a credit card. If you wish to economize, don't forget that public and university libraries often carry a good selection of books on sexuality. After reading one or two books, you will probably be much more comfortable about your program of self-education. Unless you educate yourself about the basic facts about sexuality, you will likely feel more awkward dealing with sexuality and carry unnecessary and inhibiting misconceptions. This will make the more difficult work on your sexual conflicts far more daunting than need be.

IDENTIFY YOUR PATTERNS

You can learn a great deal about your self-image and your patterns in relationships from the history of your sexual relationships. What kinds of relationships have you been in, and how did you see yourself in each one? If you put this review in writing, it will be astoundingly more effective than if you just run it through your mind.

EXERCISE 9-2
Review the History of Your Sexual Relationships

Make a list of every major lover you have had or have especially longed for; going back to your list, describe briefly the main dynamics of each relationship. For example, did you and your partner play any of the complementary roles we discussed in chapter seven, such as rescuer/rescuee or substance abuser/co-dependent placator? Did you play the part of the scolding or the comforting adult to a partner who acted like a dependent child? Was your relationship based on co-dependency, sibling rivalry, fusion, mutual support, one-sided support, domination and submission, or endless struggles for power?

Were you co-adventurers, co-survivors, or family and business partners? Was one of you an intimacy beggar and the other a distance taker? By recognizing the roles you played, you will sharpen your ability to recognize similar patterns in your current relationships and to choose whether or not you want to continue them or change them. By bringing your adult perspective to bear on patterns of relating that may have originated in childhood and that you may have perpetuated into adulthood, you give yourself the opportunity to make adult choices based upon adult reflections and realities.

List the strong and weak points of each relationship. How did a given relationship satisfy and how did it frustrate your needs? Did you appreciate the emotional or financial security your partner offered? Did you find your lover to be emotionally insensitive, or overly sensitive and needy? Include your early hopes and pleasures, as well as your postmortem assessments. For example, did a lover who seemed to be supportive and thoughtful of your wishes turn out to be a master manipulator who only wanted to spend a summer with you? With the advantage of hindsight, what should you have noticed sooner and what would you have done differently? As you become familiar with this information, think about how you can use it to benefit your current and future relationships. The roles played and the dynamics that powered your relationships may have varied within any one, and may have been different in different relationships. But, if you are like most of us, you have probably repeated a limited number of patterns and will be able to identify them if you look carefully. I would suggest that you use a marker pen to highlight the patterns that occur in more than half of the relationships you described; then you can decide whether or not you want to continue these patterns.

EXERCISE 9-3
Become a Family Biographer

Write out a brief personality sketch of your mother, father, and of each of your siblings. Do the same for anyone else who was a major figure in your childhood, such as a grandparent or aunt or uncle. List their personality traits using adjectives that best describe each one's most distinctive qualities and faults. Describe the major ways you related to each one as you were growing up. How did you feel with X? Did you get what you needed, or did you hunger for approval and love that was denied? Were your adult caretakers kind, involved, distant, absent, smothering, incompetent? Do any of these personality types or the ways you related to them sound familiar? Note in your journal any parallels you notice. Writing a brief biography of key people in your life almost always yields surprising and welcome results. By doing this you will find a new understanding of and empathy for the person you write about. And you will increase your descriptive skills, which are so important in good dream work.

EXERCISE 9-4

Recognize Your Parents' Patterns

Now describe, as best you can, the emotional patterns in your parents' relationship and what you know or imagine to have been the characteristics of their sexual lives. Were they openly affectionate with each other, or was one distant while the other seemed to beg for attention? Was one constantly blaming and criticizing and the other placating? Have you re-created similar patterns in your sexual relationships? Describing in writing the parallels you notice will not only help you remember otherwise fleeting insights but will help you to continue to look more deeply and extend your powers of discovery and insight.

LOOK FOR THE MODELS UPON WHICH YOU MAY HAVE BASED YOUR OWN PATTERNS

We inherit more than our genes from our parents. We have all, to some extent, modeled our adult sexual relationships on, or in reaction against, the relationships we as children had with our caretakers and the relationships they had between themselves. Adults don't usually try to get blood from a stone unless they thought as children that Mother or Father Stone just might give blood if treated in some perfect way. If you tried unsuccessfully to get love and approval from a parent who was distant, perfectionistic, and critical, you will have an almost irresistible tendency to pick a similar type for a partner and from whom you will try, against all logic, to get love and approval. If you grew up with a controlling, smothering, but loving mother, you may repeatedly discover that the men or women you are serious about are also smothering and controlling. Why? Because you were imprinted to believe that this is love—maddening perhaps, but the real thing. If your parents bickered constantly, you will likely create a similar relationship—or go to ridiculous lengths to avoid your parents' fate.

By now, having looked at your dreams and written or thought

about these exercises, you have probably identified some of the sources of formerly perplexing relationship tangles you have repeatedly engaged in. Write down the parallels you have found between your adult and your childhood relationships, and think about them for a few days. Watch what you dream in response.

EXERCISE 9-5

Incubate a Dream on Breaking Negative Patterns

When you feel ready, try to incubate a dream asking for help in recognizing and breaking negative patterns. Try questions like, "Why do I keep falling for unavailable men?" or "What keeps me from being turned on by partners who would be good to and for me?" or "What limiting patterns am I reenacting in my current relationship?"

If your childhood was particularly painful, or if these exercises evoke too much anxiety, start by asking yourself milder questions, such as, "What would be a good first step in preparing myself to deal with my family issues?" or "What would be a good next step in improving my romantic relationships?" If you would like help in your investigation, make an appointment with a therapist who will be able to guide you through your explorations.

CONSIDER YOUR OPTIONS

Incubating your dreams can help enormously when you find yourself having difficulty acting on insights gained in your dreams and through autobiographical and biographical reviews. Les had been hoping to salvage a relationship with Betty for over a year. Betty had told Les it was over, although she periodically gave him hope that he still had a chance with her. Even though she had another boyfriend, Les could not let go. He told Betty to take her time, he would be patient while she worked things out in her heart. Les's self-study, which included working with his dreams, had pointed to the unloved but ever-faithful suitor role he had played more than once in his life. One night he incubated a dream, asking "What should I do regarding Betty?" He dreamt:

> Muhammad Ali is standing at a curb next to a limousine. He is waiting for Ella to come out of the front door of the house behind him. The people in the house like Ali a lot. He stands there, waiting patiently. A pure, God-like voice comes from behind me. It is filled with great wisdom, strength, and certainty. The voice says that "Everyone knows that Ella will not come out the door. But Ali waits. She is no longer there, but the great warrior waits. Ella is dead!"
>
> Everyone knows, but the champ waits. He stands strong, but Ella is dead. Boom! This is crushing, humiliating, and humbling. Ali has lost this bout. Alas, even the great warrior Ali, who has fought and won so many bouts, has to concede that Ella is dead. He had to accept it.
>
> *"Ella is Dead"*

Les did not at first understand the dream, but he suspected that he was not going to like its message. Our interview proceeded as follows:

INTERVIEWER: Who is Muhammad Ali? And what is he like?
LES: He is the greatest fighter who ever lived. He had the strength to say what he believed, and was a super boxer. Ali lost three championships and I've had and lost three important relationships in my life. And I'm a fighter, and willing to say what I believe. And like Ali, I can't believe that Betty will not come back to me.
I: What is Ella like?
L: She's a woman I used to know in Oklahoma. Now she's a writer in her seventies in Arizona. She is a kind, thoughtful woman who likes me.
I: Does this kind, thoughtful woman who likes you remind you of anyone?

L: Sure, Betty was like that when we were going together. I guess I've got to accept it, don't I? The part of Betty that was good to me is dead, she's never coming back.

Les was sad after this dream interview, but he understood that the first thing he had to do was to accept that no matter how loving and strong he was, Betty would not return to him. A few weeks later, Les dreamt that he saw Betty again and discovered that she was only twenty-two years old instead of her actual age of thirty-eight. This dream helped Les see that Betty, whom he tended to idealize, was really quite immature for her age. Not only did these dreams help Les let go of his addiction to Betty, they helped free him to look for more satisfying romantic choices. Les was getting tired of his Muhammad Ali hero role and of loving where there was no hope. Sometimes a sad dream can be remarkably liberating.

MAKING CHOICES

Dreams don't make your choices for you. They can, however, reveal unconscious motivations and show you what you are really up to (how you are acting destructively or how you are stuck). When you look at your situation with more honesty and objectivity, you usually have a good idea of where to start doing things differently. If you don't act on your insights, your dreams will continue to portray you in your stuck position. If you start to make positive movement, they will cheer you on, reinforce you, and indicate the next step along the way to solving your problem or to improving your situation. If you move in a self-destructive direction regarding a problem, your dreams will hang in there with you and continue to offer you warning signs and reminders of the trouble you are creating for yourself. If you simply remain stuck, your dreams will repeat similar themes over and over until you make movement or eventually come to the end of your life, dreaming the same dreams. It will always be left up to your waking mind to make the daily choices that determine the quality of your life, including your sexual life.

Hilary dreamt of being telephoned by a needy fellow who reminded her of her long-term boyfriend and of their exceedingly co-dependent relationship. Earlier dreams had pinpointed the major repetitive patterns that made her attachment to this guy so very constrictingly strong. In this dream, for the first time, waking or sleeping, she told him, "You are sick and weak, and I don't want you." The clarity of her dream response was an emotional breakthrough, but one that Hilary had to find the courage to act on.

Norma, a lawyer who had been married for six years to a depressed husband, had a series of dreams over many months in which she never quite managed to take off on her airplane flight to some interesting destination. In some dreams, she would get lost on her way to the airport, or miss the flight because she had waited too long to pack, or she would be just too afraid of flying. Interspersed with these dreams were others like the one in which she boarded a flight, felt reassured of its safety, but then disembarked, went shopping for antiques, and missed the plane. In others, she would practice flying in safe areas like her office or take a little girl and teach her how to fly in little spurts on her bike. As you might guess, Norma bridged flying to letting herself live more freely, with more risk but with much more excitement. She reluctantly realized that in order for her to fly in life she would have to leave her husband.

One night she dreamt of a scam exhibit of a bird at a fair. The bird was displayed as being domesticated and willing to stay on a pole rather than fly away. But Norma discovered that the bird was a kiwi, and kiwis don't fly. So she concluded that lack of flight in this case, and in her case, was no great sign of loyalty. It was more due to fear of taking action.

She also dreamt the classic "I Wish I Had That" dream:

> A group is leaving for London. I go to pack but wait too long and miss the flight. I'm half glad, half sad. Then I'm asleep in a mildewed room with my husband. I see a romantic couple outside admiring their happy reflection in my window. I feel very sad not to have their joy.
>
> *"Afraid to Go, Afraid to Stay"*

Norma worked very hard to face the facts of her life and of her relationship. Eventually, she decided to leave her husband. After she did that, she started having dreams of flying in which she flew with great delight. In her waking life she had attained a new level of freedom and the courage to take risks that paralleled her delight in her dream flight.

SELF-ESTEEM AND SEXUALITY

In the final analysis, your relationships reflect your self-image. You will almost always pick a partner, and form a relationship, that reflects your sense of yourself. If you see yourself as a rescuer, you will find a mate who needs to be rescued. If you believe you are a strong, worthy, interesting person, you will probably not be attracted to someone who needs to put you down or abuse you. If you are strong and do not have the codependent need to be a rescuer, you will not need to attract people who need to lean on your strength, but will be more likely to choose friends who are themselves strong and confident. In your sexual relationships you are subject to the same rule that self-image is destiny. Your body image will affect your sexual relations. How you think your body looks and what pleasures you think it deserves will determine a good part of the quality of your sexual life. If you believe that it is shameful to masturbate, or to know what kinds of fantasies and touching give you pleasure, how can you let your partner know what pleases you? What kind of man will want to play a guessing game that embarrasses you and to which you may not even have the answers? If you want a better sexual life, you will have no choice but to improve your self-esteem and body esteem.

Low self-esteem can manifest itself in many ways. Usually those who suffer from it consider their low opinion of themselves not an opinion at all but a fact. Do you say things to yourself like "Why would anyone with a lot on the ball be interested in me?" Or "I'm just not a very attractive [sexy, interesting, or worthwhile] person"? If you do, the first thing you should do is try to consider the possibility that these views of yourself may result from attitudes rather than from fact. Improving self-esteem requires careful self-observation and plenty of concentrated effort in exploring the various ways in which you put yourself down and fail to appreciate yourself. It also usually helps to investigate the sources of these habits and how you and your life events have reinforced them over the years. If your father constantly criticized you when you were a child and told you that you couldn't do anything right, that you would never amount to anything, the chances are that you will have adopted some of his opinions as your own. With the help of a good therapist, or perhaps through your own reflection, you may one day realize that your dad's opinion was a reflection of his own problems, not of your worth.

A critical attitude toward your body can wreak havoc with your ability to enjoy sex. You may criticize your body and be ashamed of it because you are extremely out of shape, or because you have focused on some characteristic that you consider to be an imperfection, or because you are ashamed of the very fact that it is a sexual body. Again, it will help if you look to see when these attitudes took shape. When did the child you once were begin to distrust and dislike his or her own body? What were the influences? Abusive or critical adults? Religious or social judgments and prohibitions? Has an illness affected your body? Or did you survive with your body image intact until the fashion magazines got their perfect-anorexic fangs into you? In our culture women are generally far more perfectionistic and critical about their bodies than men, and they have a lot more work to do before they can break out of their old habits of thinking and devaluing themselves than do most men.

Psychotherapy can be very helpful in helping you to reconsider and improve your self-esteem and body image. Reading good books can also help to get you started. I would suggest John Bradshaw's *Homecoming* and *Healing the Shame that Binds,* and Lonnie Barbach's *For Yourself* and *For Each Other.* Your dreams will help you work out the conflicts that keep you locked in limiting views of yourself, and they will chronicle and applaud your achievements as you go along. Gathering up the initiative to actively read about sex will speed your process of developing a more mature, less conflicted, sexuality and make it easier to work with your sexual dreams.

Dreams of Improving Self-Esteem

Sophia, some of whose dreams we have discussed in earlier pages, is a corporate manager, a former member of a rock band, and a member of one of the weekly dream study groups at the Dream Center. She has been using both her dreams and psychotherapy to confront childhood sexual abuse and its effects on her life. She told us two dreams within the same month that reflected the stunning progress she was making in learning to respect and assert herself as well in appreciating the important emotional support she received from her boyfriend. The second dream also portrays work yet to be accomplished.

I am having adventures in New York City. Sophisticated, grown-up, adult fun. I meet Sal Trilling. She is a woman in a band . . . We are attracted to each other. I feel a lot of love for her. She is leaving to go on tour with her band. I am hugging her, kissing her. I will miss her while she's gone.

Now I am with (my live-in partner) Stan. He knows about Sal and doesn't mind. I have a boyfriend. I have a girlfriend. It's no big thing. He is encouraging me to express that other side of myself, just as in waking life.

We are going around town, still looking for apartments, other places to live. Even though we are moving our things into the new place, we are still looking for a place that's right for us. Somehow there is no contradiction.

Not only that, but we're also going to the old places where I used to live and finding old stuff of mine and taking it to the new place. I'm finding stuff all the time and moving it in. I'm afraid Stan will get impatient. My stuff will be all over the apartment. The apartment might get crowded. We just keep moving more stuff in. But he doesn't get impatient. Maybe he's wondering when and where it will all stop, but he doesn't tell me I can't bring any more stuff in. And the apartment is not too crowded. It seems like there's always enough room for the next piece of furniture.

We go out looking at places. We are going back to apartments to have closer looks, inspect them, talk to the landlords. We come across an old place where I used to live . . . I'm feeling sad and wistful for that time in my life when I lived in Houston alone for the first time in my life. We found some of my stuff still there.

Now I am back at the NYC place, the grown-up place of adult concerns. It's a nighttime place, like bars and hangouts. People talking and eating and meeting for appointments. A young woman named Pia is now my girlfriend. She is more concerned with having a good time, money, material concerns, sex, status, drugs, and partying.

I am supposed to meet Pia. I love her. We had had a hot affair in the past. But as she comes in, she screams, "Darling!" and rushes to greet another woman. Stan sees this and tries to protect me from being hurt by her behavior. Pia leaves with her new date and I evidently didn't see anything or feel hurt. (From my vantage point as observer in the dream, I saw everything that went on. But as Sophia down there on the dance floor waiting for the woman, I didn't see it, so I wasn't hurt. Neither was I hurt in the role of observer from up high looking at the big picture.)

I am disappointed I don't find my date. But I have other things to be concerned about, too. I have things to do.

"Sex Dream With Woman"

In her journal, Sophia wrote the following interpretation:

The first woman I'm in love with, Sal, is very positive and wonderful. I love her dearly. The second woman, Pia, is very shallow and self-destructive. Even so, I am attracted to her, too. I remember at this time in waking life, I had been telling Stan about the old days when I would do drugs and run around and be wild. I feel this dream is about who I am now and who I used to be. Besides being willing to help me reclaim the important parts of my past, Stan protects me (as he does in the dream) from this old, wild part of myself. He is not enticed, nor is he fooled, by that self-serving, shallow self.

In the next dream we see Sophia successfully ridding herself of an undesirable roommate (her former, destructively wild, self), only to find herself trading sex for attention as her dream takes up another big challenge to growth: her tenacious feeling that she must trade submission for love and attention.

> I have a female roommate who is not very nice. I come home one day and find her taking my car out of the driveway. I tell her this is not all right and she can't do that. She says Hugo told her the use of my car was included in her rent. I tell her it's not and he did not have my permission to do that. I have her pack and move out immediately. No fuss!
>
> Then I go through the area of the house she had been renting. Wow! What a beautiful, shiny, huge, clean bedroom! I am amazed she had control over such a wonderful place. I'm thinking that instead of renting this out to another roommate, I'd like to keep it for myself. Wow.
>
> Now Rod Stewart has come into the scene. He is sex-mad, used to having whatever he damn well wants. He doesn't have to be concerned about the partner he's with. He can get whatever he wants at any time. I like him and I like being with him, but the sex we are now having scares me. He's doing such weird things and I find myself in such weird positions, I don't know which way is up. I ask him to slow down. I'm not sure I can deal with this. He gets disgusted and stops. I am afraid he will leave now. I really like him and want to be with him. But if I don't let him do what he wants, he withholds affection.
>
> He really is charming and bright and I like his company. I am willingly having sex with him. That is, I'm having it so I can be with him. I love him.
>
> *"Loves Lies Bleeding"*

In the first scene of the dream, Sophia reclaims for herself space in the apartment, or, as she said, she is reclaiming the positive parts of her personality that she had allowed to be inhabited by an aspect of herself that she did not like. The second scene shows Sophia, who has indeed made good progress in her inner growth, being confronted with an old interpersonal conflict. Here are the informal self-interview notes Sophia made in her journal:

> I woke up with the song "Love Lies Bleeding in My Hand" by Elton John. If I know of a song lyric that fits my dream, I subconsciously slip it in at the end when I wake up. It underlines the message of the emotions. It helps me remember the main feelings. It's not unusual for me to wake up with songs.
>
> In my previous choice of boyfriends, I see I have tried to re-create my father in various ways: alcoholics, gay like my father, rock star types who are sexually abusive or simply uncommunicative about sex. Rick was the last of the line. Coincidentally, my father's name was Richard and he was called Rick by his sister.
>
> Rod Stewart is a rock star. Rock stars do nothing on a person-to-person level to deserve the attention they receive from women. They are extremely demanding. They have no motivation to work on a relationship. If a girlfriend or groupie is too demanding ("I want a monogamous relationship" or "I wish you'd pay more attention to me"), the rock star can just dispose of her and get another one. Women are all around waiting for the rock star to pay attention to them. I used to like rock stars but now I don't. I want someone who wants me as much as I want him. I don't feel I should have to compete daily for the loyalty and attention of someone. I want someone who is willing to work on a relationship. I want someone willing to communicate his needs, questions, dreams, and desires.
>
> Rod Stewart in my dream is absolutely desirable. I love him with such a softness and longing. It's not sexual. The

sex is there because he wants it. I have to participate if I want to be with him. His company, his attention, his conversation, his laughter is what I want.

In the dream when the sex is going on, I am numb and quiet. I am trying to just let it happen. But at one point it's just too much. I can't breathe. I'm in such an unusual position, I feel like I'm upside-down. I have no idea where the floor is. I am totally disoriented. I have to make it stop. When I do, Rod Stewart gets mad. He is fed up with my limitations. I relent. All right. Do it. Just don't leave me.

The last sentence of the dream, "I love him," doesn't convey the full emotional breadth of what I felt. I loved him completely. I would do *anything* to be with him. My love consumed me. I loved him regardless of the ugly things he did to me. Those things had nothing to do with how I felt about him. I do not remember anything about Rod Stewart's emotions for me in the dream. In fact, the only emotion he displayed was disgust when I asked him to stop having sex with me.

Sophia has changed some of the destructive patterns of her past and has created a mutually supportive relationship with Stan. But she still has work to do. Her fear that she must do whatever is asked of her in order to maintain her love supply is still alive within her and will seriously threaten her ability to assert herself in her relationships if she doesn't keep working on it. Because of her valiant self-explorations, she has built up her strength and been able to counter these tendencies so far by choosing a partner who is self-confident enough that he does not need to dominate her. Yet at times Sophia still needs to distance herself from Stan because she fears that she could easily fall into her own submission trap. A more satisfying intimacy will be possible for Sophia after she has gained more confidence in her self-worth and in her ability to feel safe within the emotional boundaries she sets to fit her needs for safety.

Incubate a Dream on Your Self-esteem

When you are ready, you might try asking for a dream in response to questions like these:

- What is the major impediment to my having high self-esteem?
- What is the best first step I could take to improve my self-esteem?
- What are my best qualities?
- What keeps me from appreciating my best qualities?

CLEARING AWAY BLOCKS TO HEALTHY INTIMACY

How much intimacy do you want? How much familiarity, openness, affection? Does intimacy feel like a trap to you? As you become intimate with someone, at what point do you begin to feel uncomfortable? Are you unable to maintain your sense of independence and autonomy within an intimate relationship? If you want the bliss of sexual and interpersonal intimacy but find that it eludes you, your dreams can help you find out how you may be sabotaging your goals.

If you have been unable to establish a relationship for a long time, or if you have trouble maintaining one, you may find yourself saying, "There just aren't enough good women [or men] to go around." While this just may be true in some situations, the greater likelihood is that you are doing one or more of the following things to sabotage yourself:

1. Avoiding intimacy out of your own (perhaps previously reasonable) fears.
2. Compulsively picking just the sort of people who, just because they are the type they are, will be unable to give you the kind of love you want. This happens all the time

when, for example, we keep choosing partners who are like our cold, distant fathers when what we want is the love and warmth that our cold, distant fathers were unable to give us.

3. Cooperating with your partner to neglect the active involvement it takes to maintain a vibrant, loving relationship. It takes two to keep a relationship alive and interesting over the long run. Often both partners take a relationship for granted and one day wake to find there is no more life in it.

We have looked at dreams that focus on problems 1 and 2. You will probably already have several in your journal that will assist you in dealing with these major blocks. The third problem is perhaps as deadly, but it is much less complicated. The most memorable dream I have ever heard on neglect is one of Christina's, a woman who had recently separated from her husband of twenty years:

A wise and confident voice said very clearly, "Both you and your husband are guilty of having been slum landlords in your marriage." The voice emphasized that we were *both* guilty and responsible.

"Slum Landlords"

Christina described slum landlords as people who inexcusably fail to keep up their buildings and leave people to live in increasingly run-down, sometimes unlivable, conditions. She had a strong contempt for slum landlords, and was deeply impressed that she and her husband had been that neglectful of the sexual and other relational problems that had arisen between them through the years. The dream helped her stop blaming her husband and recognize how she, too, had swept the dragons under the rug. It helped Christina decide to enter couples therapy and try to rehabilitate their marriage.

EXERCISE 9-7

Incubate a Dream
About the Dragon in Your Relationship

If you are in a relationship you hope will endure, you can use your dreams to find and slay your dragons before they burn your house down. Why not incubate a dream tonight about the problems you have in relationships? Here are a few incubation questions to get you thinking about the particular question you might want to ask yourself:

- Why do I keep picking partners who are _____?
- What keeps me from enjoying my sexuality [my partner, etc.] as much as I might?
- What am I afraid of?
- How can I feel safe in a relationship?
- Why do I have so little interest in sex with _____?
- Why do I tend to feel _____ when I am in bed with _____?
- Why do I have trouble keeping an erection with _____? (Need I say that if this is a consistent problem, you should also check with a doctor to see if there is a medical answer?)
- What is my major sexual hang-up, and what can I do about it?
- What can I do to improve my sexual relationship?
- What can I do to maintain or revive my relationship?

The Italians and the French have a wonderful saying, *La notte porta consiglio*, or *La nuit porte conseille*. Which mean "Night brings good counsel."

PART THREE

CREATIVE PASSIONS

10

How Is Creativity
Related to Your Sexuality?

THERE ARE MANY DEFINITIONS OF CREATIVITY, BUT IN THIS chapter let us think of creativity as being the expression of originality of thought, which can manifest itself in myriad ways including problem solving, the generation of new ideas and applications, and the production of original objects, stories, reports, designs, movements, music, and events. We are all creative. Every night when we dream, we produce carefully crafted dramas and comedies. Daily life requires that we find creative solutions to problems at work and at home. Really good sex demands creativity on the part of both partners. Some of us seem to have easier access to creative energies than others. And there are usually different periods in our lives when we are more or less alive and creative.

HISTORICAL PERSPECTIVES

For millennia, various cultural traditions have taught that sexual energy is the enemy of creativity. While it is true that certain Hindu and Buddhist traditions accept sex as a source of pleasure and even see it as a possible path to spiritual enlightenment, these teachings have coexisted with more dominant teachings within the same traditions that teach that sexual energy should be redirected to higher creative and spiritual goals. These teachings are based on the assumption that there is only a limited amount of life energy in one person and that this energy can be vitiated or even polluted by directing it into sexual directions. If one aspires to holiness and higher consciousness, sexuality must be prohibited or severely limited. Some ancient Egyptian, Pacific Island, and other tribal cultures provided alternative perspectives to this view, but they have not had a strong influence on our Western traditions.

Judaism condemned incest, adultery, and homosexual acts, but the Song of Songs in the Old Testament portrayed sexuality as a pleasurable and creative force not limited to purposes of procreation. In contrast to traditional Christian views, which hold that sexual relations even between a husband and a wife are primarily for the purpose of procreation, sexuality within marriage has always been seen as a source of pleasure for both partners in the Jewish tradition, which did not distinguish physical from spiritual love. Thus, while Judaism condemned certain forms of sexuality such as adultery, incest, and homosexuality, sexuality itself is seen as a healthy and desirable part of living.

Christianity identified sex with original sin and borrowed some Jewish sexual restrictions on incest, adultery, and homosexuality. Christianity also adopted the ancient Greek classification of females as sexually valuable primarily for their ability to bear children. Saint Paul added the idea that wives were also sexually useful in saving men from worse sins by providing them a place to vent their "base" sexual energies. By the fourth century, Saint Augustine firmly set the course of the Church regarding sexual matters. He condemned sexual stimulation as sinful and condoned only marital sex capable of producing offspring. This dark view of sexuality and the treatment of women as property led to the chastity belts of the Medieval period, the keys to which were often kept by the husbands. But even in this period, the highly restrictive and negative official attitude toward sexuality expressed in church and civil law was often punctuated by both blatant and secret illicit sex in upper-class and clerical settings.

The Renaissance reintroduced humanist values and brought a

slight loosening of sexual strictures as the classical Greek appreciation of humanism and the human form found expression in the arts and the relations between men and women in the artistic and the upper classes. This liberalization might have been more pronounced had not a massive epidemic of syphilis been ravaging Europe at the same time. With the Reformation, Protestants such as Martin Luther and John Calvin reclassified sexuality as not inherently sinful, even if they stopped far short of calling it joyous and healthy. Except for a brief period of increased sexual tolerance in England and France in the 1700s, sex continued to be described as sinful and often deleterious to health by the Puritans in the 1700s in the American colonies and later by the prudish Victorians. [1]

Sigmund Freud, more than anyone before him, underlined the natural, vital importance of sexuality across the life span of human beings. He also explored the dynamic connection between sexuality and creativity. Freud described creativity as a sublimated (diverted or redirected) expression of libidinal sexual urges into socially acceptable and redeeming forms such as painting, music, writing, and scientific endeavors. In so doing, he echoed in psychological language earlier religious beliefs that sexuality was a baser form of energy needing transformation into higher forms. In contrast to the religious goal of closer union or harmony with God or the universe, Freud saw the goal of this sublimation as the reduction of intrapsychic (inner) tension and the greater harmony of the individual with his society. If not sublimated, libidinal energy would manifest itself in prohibited sexual and aggressive behaviors such as murder, patricide, incest, and adultery, which weaken the fabric of society.

The psychiatrist Carl Jung viewed psychic energy or libido as an essential life force that could be channeled into a variety of directions, only one being sexuality. Jung proposed that introverting sexual libido (turning the sexual impulse inward), rather than expressing it outwardly in excessive sexuality, creates an inner concentration of psychic energy that is likely to result in the formation of symbols of spirituality and creativity in the unconscious that "give rise to psychic fantasy and reflection." [2] Jung believed that symbols arising from the unconscious provided an individual with imagery (psychic fantasy) that could precipitate insightful reflection on conscious and unconscious levels.

Jung's belief in the desirability of reserving some sexual libido for spiritual and creative experience is similar to Freud's idea of sublimation: both saw sexual expression as somewhat dead-ended. Both saw sexuality as taking energy away from rather than as supporting or encouraging creative expression. However, Jung's notion of creativity as a natural expression of psychic energy, not a redirected and distorted expression of sexual energy, yields a significantly different perspective. Jungian analyst and author John Beebe says, "For Jung, creativity was not so much a sublimation of libido that would otherwise surely have been sexual, as a culturally significant, individual concentration of energy. This energy might just as naturally be channelled into a creative, spiritual, and introverted direction as into a procreative, instinctual, and extroverted one."[3]

THE SEXUALITY/CREATIVITY LINK

Sexuality and creativity do not seem to be closely linked in some people. In others the connection is a vibrant one. I have been unable to locate any systematic research on the sexual lives of creative people. But there is no end of anecdotal examples of artists, such as Leonardo da Vinci and Liszt, who had very active sexual lives. Picasso had a wife forty years his junior when he was ninety. William Blake, Lord Byron, Keats, and Shelley championed free love in the nineteenth century. Henry Miller, George Sand, and Anaïs Nin associated exuberant sexual lives with feeling alive and creative. But then there are those artists whose sexual lives were severely limited by their time, place, and/or personality. In this group we might count most female Western artists, including the Brontë sisters, the reclusive spinsters Christina Rossetti and Emily Dickinson, and the invalid Elizabeth Barrett Browning, whose possessive father kept her prisoner until she escaped with Robert at the age of forty. Poet John Milton, who described intercourse with his wife as a "brutish congress" of "two carcasses chained unnaturally together," and painter Vincent van Gogh, whose emotional torments dominated his life, are vivid examples of artistic expression flourishing side by side with sexual inhibition and conflict.

In raising the question of how creativity and sexuality are related, we are exploring a relationship in which the latter element especially has a history of regularly being feared, condemned, furtively and guiltily enjoyed, or chained and hidden in the basement. That denial of the natural, healthy expression of sexuality is still with us is evidenced by the dreadfully inadequate sexual education for our children in many if not most of today's countries. Other symptoms of this denial can be seen in our own often dark, touchy, ill-informed sexual attitudes and our frequently underdeveloped sexual skills.

Examples of how creative people live their sexual lives can give us only a limited idea of how creativity is related to sexuality. Most artists have lived in societies in which the subject of sexuality carries a social and religious taboo. Add to this the fact that sexual taboos are vastly different for each sex, and that women are often disparaged as the source of men's temptation and as vessels for their physical relief. Traditionally women have rarely been seen as robustly desirous sexual beings whose sexuality is a sign of strength and vitality. Even if women had shared the sexual liberties men have enjoyed throughout history, we would still be faced with the fact that many creative women never became famous or developed their own abilities because they have been too busy as mothers and wives.

Today, we have effective contraception, women are gaining a more equal status legally and socially, education about sexual matters is improving, sexual superstitions are receding, and many of us in the industrialized nations have the luxury of more free time to pursue self-development and sexual creativity.

How can we make the most of our present-day opportunities in these areas? Many people feel that they are more creative when they are not in an actively sexual relationship. When asked why, some say they need to budget their energy and spend most of it on their creative endeavor. Most of the people who have told me this are women who go on to explain that they would otherwise lose themselves in their sexual relationships. They tend to stop marching to their own creative drummers and fall into step with their lovers' parades. Less often than men do women find a sexual partner who can provide good sex *and* practical and emotional support for their creative endeavors. When they are intensely sexually involved, many women have trouble maintaining the separate time and space boundaries that protect their creativity. As psychoanalyst Jessica Benjamin argues, until women become more aware of their own desires, both sexual and otherwise, they will tend to experience entering into a sexual relationship as an act of surrender and self-denial. [4] In focusing on a partner's desires, a woman falls into a submissive role that discourages both the awareness of and the ability to express her own creative worldview. I believe that this is not a question of a *sexual* energy drain but rather an interpersonal problem that drains both time and energy in general. We should also remember that relationships themselves can be considered creative projects that generally require work, time, and sometimes plenty of energy. Depending upon its nature and quality, a relationship can be an example of a creative endeavor or a siphon of creative energy.

A number of men have told me that being single is detrimental to their creativity because they then spend so much of their time looking for and courting women. These men explain that having an established relationship frees them to get on with their other creative work. The main relationship provides the man with security, stability, and support. If it does not provide enough interesting sex, other limited relationships can act as supplements without necessarily disrupting the basic equilibrium.

Many of us have noticed that when we leave or lose a lover, get divorced, or experience a personal tragedy, it sometimes precipitates greater creativity as we bury ourselves in our work and have little or no sexual desire. At such times, the need to flee from painful feelings can funnel enormous energy into a creative endeavor. In these situations, it is not the creative exertion but the tragedy and pain that usually diminish sexual desire. Another way of responding to almost unbearable pain is to give expression to those feelings in a variety of artistic forms such as poems, stories, paintings, or the creation of organizations dedicated to memorializing the loss or to combatting the illness or behavior that precipitated it. Here we have a situation in which the need to cope with pain, not the lack of sexuality, leads to an upsurge in creativity.

A few women and many men have told me that when the creative juices flow, so do their sexual juices. Or vice versa. Individuals who have experienced sexual awakenings and/or a significant reduction in sexual inhibitions sometimes describe equally exciting openings in their creative energy.

EXERCISE 10-1

Describe Your Creative High Points

When do you feel most creative? When are you most *productively* creative? Can you think of periods in your life when you have been *joyously* creative? When has the work of preparation and actualization of your creative project felt almost magically driven and accomplished by your enthusiasm?

- In your journal briefly describe the creative high points of your life—when you intensively studied something new or when you created things like paintings, poems, programs, beautiful interiors, clothes, or business ventures.
- How old were you and what was going on in your life at the time of each creative episode?
- What was going on at work, in your major relationships, and in your sexual relationships and development?

Take your time. At first you might think that you have little to write, but just reread these questions and start with a few short responses. Like little fragments of largely forgotten dreams, your responses will unfold upon gentle reflection.

MODERN RESEARCH

The seductive hypothesis that decreased inhibition and increased openness in one part of your life lead to greater openness in other aspects is not easy to investigate. Most people still prefer to keep the details of their sexual lives secret, and the task of accurately measuring sexual and creative satisfaction is a complicated one.

Researchers, even in the 1990s, must wear kid gloves in the conduct and reporting of experiments for fear of offending their funding sources and the public. A bold experiment conducted by Russell Eisenman at Temple University looked at the effects of two procedures on the sexual behavior of eighty college men and women.[5] Working on the principle that creative people are generally more open to new experiences, Eisenman used two methods of increasing openness and creativity to see if either or both would result in greater openness regarding sexual behavior on the part of the students. One method successfully increased creativity (as measured on standardized tests) by encouraging a reduction of rigid, authoritarian attitudes through group modeling and pressure. The second method was aimed at increasing openness to sexuality through fantasy. It consisted of telling students that sexual fantasies have a healthy effect on sexual development, reading them a model fantasy, and then asking the subjects to write down as many sexual fantasies as they could think of in a period of twenty minutes. One week after having participated in either, both, or neither of these two exercises, students were asked to fill out reports on their sexual behavior in the last week.

The results were impressive. Both the fantasy exercise and the reduction of rigid authoritarian attitudes procedure resulted in increased sexual behavior. Eisenman hypothesized that both procedures led the students to internalize, at least temporarily, the beliefs in greater openness implied by creativity or fantasy, and that this resulted in behavioral change. Since it is probable that the students all carried some degree of closedness or inhibition regarding sexuality, it is not difficult to imagine that increased creativity and openness could be generalized and affect inhibitions and rigidities in this area as well.[6]

Over the normal person's life span, the roles of sexuality and of creativity, as well as the interactions between them, are bound to vary greatly. Sexual, intellectual, and creative maturation follow their own paths. Due to physiological changes and to social and interpersonal circumstances, our sexuality may at times overwhelm us—and at other times recede into the background of our lives. So, too, our creativity will fluctuate in response to our intellectual, creative, social, and interpersonal environment. My proposition is twofold: that a healthier, more open sexuality would enrich our creativity; and that we can use our dreams to encourage a mutual enrichment of our creative and sexual lives.

Many writers have explored the rich contribution that dreaming has made to the creative output of people throughout history.[7] Ingrid Sladeczek and George Domino at the University of Arizona found that creative subjects fall asleep more quickly and solve more problems through their dreams than do less creative subjects.[8] Two decades of working with my clients' dreams has led me to believe that personal creativity has to do with self-expression, which is more likely to be exuberant if the individual's sexuality is not tied up in knots (highly conflicted). Yes, I have seen clients who are remarkably creative in creating interesting home environments or effective projects at work whose sexual lives are highly inhibited. But I have also seen some of these same people use their dreams to work through their sexual conflicts and arrive at new levels of creative expression that make their earlier achievements pale in comparison. And most important of all, they feel happier, less burdened by inhibition, and more satisfied with their sexual and creative lives.

EXERCISE 10-2

Describe How Your Creativity Might Be Linked to Your Sexuality

If we use our dreams to heal sexual wounds and to liberate ourselves from rigid and unduly restrictive inhibitions, would we

find that we have easier access to our creativity both while waking and while dreaming? If we resolve sexual conflict and establish a satisfying sexual relationship, would we find our creativity
to be increased and/or more joyous?

What do you think? If you are sexually inhibited and unfulfilled, does this inhibition carry over into your attitude toward
taking creative risks and discovering new things? Do you avoid
intense sexual relationships because you tend to lose yourself in
almost any relationship with a lover? Explore your responses by
writing about them in your journal. If you would like to use your
dreams to live a fuller sexual and creative life, turn to the next
chapter.

CHAPTER

11

Enlisting Your Dreams to Uncork the Bottle and Let the Genie Out

Y OU MAY BE ONE OF THOSE PEOPLE WHOSE CREATIVE GENIE is hindered by the same distrust of your own feelings and desires that inhibits your sexual expression. If your attitudes regarding sexuality lead you to be fearful of intimacy, ashamed of your body and of your desires, or rigidly dominant or submissive in your relationships, it may well be that changing those attitudes would do more than brighten and enliven your sexuality. Learning to trust and feel safe in your sexual interaction surely would improve your self-confidence and your openness to your inner promptings, many of which are creative in nature. In feeling more accepting of yourself, more alive, more daring, you are bound also to be more open to your creative urges.

EXERCISE **11-1**

Target Your Dreams on Your Creativity/Sexuality Link

If in working with the last chapter you have decided that you would like to take action, why not incubate a dream by asking "How is my creativity linked to my sexuality?" or "In what ways do I needlessly inhibit myself sexually and creatively?" You could, of course, target your dreams on just your sexuality or just your creativity on a given night with good results. However, if you specifically aim at understanding the interactions between the two, your dreams will help you to work on two important life issues at one time.

Your dreams will help you get a good look at how you have formed your beliefs about sexuality and creativity based upon earlier experiences and current perspectives and pressures. If you find you hold limiting or self-defeating attitudes such as "I can't open myself to intense sexual pleasure and get my work done, too" or "If I am sexually active I won't have time for the higher things in life," you can incubate dreams asking what is at the root of your black-and-white thinking.

You can also ask for dreams on questions such as "What is keeping me from being more creative?" or "What changes could I make in my sexual attitudes that would enrich both my sexuality and my creativity?"

You may prefer to tackle one issue at a time and simply bene- fit as you go along from the mutually enhancing aspects of your exploration of your creative and erotic lives. Dream incubation questions such as "Why can't I get going on my project?" and "What keeps me from having a fulfilling sexual life?" may sur- prise you with dream responses dealing with attitudes that affect both or even all aspects of your life.

Gwendolyn, at twenty-seven, was a brilliant woman whose writing career had not yet taken off. She was also in a relation- ship with a man she had met in high school, her first and only lover. One night her lover, Ken, treated her to wonderful cunni- lingus, but Gwendolyn resisted intercourse for reasons she sus- pected were excuses. That night she incubated a dream by asking "Why don't I get full satisfaction from intercourse?" Here is the dream she triggered:

> I am on a very advanced spaceship, with Ken. They are going to give us a demo flight. We take off, slowly at first. I am afraid they will go too fast, go all the way to the moon, while we are still outside on the deck. Ken assures me that they won't, but then they start to. Then we are inside, in a

huge room, watching the stars spin by the window—I am very dizzy—then we start to slow down. The captain tells us we have gone around the moon, but we didn't go to the dark side, because we must be careful of the Spanish, who somehow control part of it. I laugh to myself, thinking that when this science-fiction novel was written the author didn't know that, in fact, it is the Russians, not the Spanish, who are our major enemies/competitors. (There is something ludicrous about the idea of it being the Spanish.)

Then we go off again, spinning in the opposite direction. I am feeling dizzy and a little sick—nothing serious, but I ask Ken if there isn't somewhere on the ship, some room with some sort of force field so that you don't feel dizzy, so that the stars don't look like they're going by so fast. We ask the captain and he says yes, but he's not sure it works anymore. He looks sad, regretful, and tells us that we can go to Multipod.

Then we are entering a locked room, through two doors. The first opens with a key, the second with a little button that you push with your finger, hidden in the center of the doorknob. I am glad we know this secret button. We enter the room. The captain has gone. We are the only ones on the ship and we must figure out how to work this room, which is actually a giant computer, or the whole mission will fail and we will crash.

The light switch doesn't work. I sit down on the floor and feel it humming, feel a rush of power. I ask Ken if he feels it but he says no. I say maybe he has to find the right spot. The ship is still flying and I don't feel sick but we still can't communicate with Multipod (the computer) to give it orders. Multipod is starting to go out of control (this part is sort of fuzzy). It wants to communicate, but it doesn't understand when we call out commands, say "Hello," etc.

There is the sense it has been abandoned for generations and is desperate. It is losing control of the ship. Then suddenly I try something—I call out "I love you"—call it out over and over. Ken looks startled and says "I forgot you could say that to a machine." Then I suddenly notice the telephone by the door—this is the way to talk to the computer! I pick it up and say "Hello?" There is some garble, the machine continues to speak nonsense, then slows down, pauses, and says "Hello?" back to me. I say, "We don't understand how to work you. Can you tell us what commands to give?" It says that for beginners it would recommend starting with one basic phrase—then begins telling me a phrase in a foreign language that sounds like French. Phonetically, the phrase begins "Aloose nevyay"— it stresses that it's not "aloose yay-yay"—then the alarm goes off and I wake up.

"Space Flight"

Gwendolyn interviewed herself in writing, which is a very effective way to study your dreams on your own. Here is her self-interview:

Interview/interpretation: what I've figured out so far:
The "very advanced spaceship" is my body/mind. The flight represents sex, and also on a larger level my whole life, creativity, etc. I don't want to "go all the way" to the moon on the first flight, and they tell me I won't, but then we do. This feels like the way I jumped into sex, intercourse, with no preparation, no years of slow making out or extended foreplay. In my recollection of the dream I am not clear whether it is Ken or someone else on the spaceship (some part of myself) who is responsible for this decision. Similarly, in waking life, it was both of us who were responsible for it. The flight could be exciting and beautiful—the stars spin by the window—but it makes me dizzy and nauseous because I am not ready for it.

Now comes a part of the dream I am not clear about—The business of the dark side of the moon being Spanish.

What is the moon? The moon is a beautiful, shimmering place very far away and dangerous, hard to get to. I think this trip represents sex to me—also because when I've had really good sex, I often express it to myself as having "been to another planet."

What is the dark side of the moon? It is very mysterious, hidden, magical, feminine—also frightening and maybe dangerous, because who knows what is there.

What are the Spanish like? They are very sensuous, romantic, artistic; also lazy and kind of impractical.

The Russians? Cold, competitive, calculating, intellectual, brilliant. The cold war. [Gwendolyn's dream occurred before the big thaw.]

Who is the captain? He is in charge, but doesn't really know the full picture—he didn't write this story. Later in the dream, he disappears. He's sort of a relic from an earlier era (my father?) but when the dream starts he is still flying the ship.

So: We seemed to travel to the moon, but in actuality we cut ourselves off from an important part of it—the mysterious, feminine, unknown side. There is a part of myself that I haven't let sex reach into, which I have been afraid to open up to and explore, and it is somehow at the core of the sexual experience. I have been afraid to because I have been afraid of the Spanish—the sensuous, artistic, creative part of myself; maybe partly afraid of it because I associate it with being lazy, impractical, and incompetent. But really, whoever wrote that story line for me didn't have all the information. The real danger for me is the cold, intellectual, defensive, on-guard aspect of myself. That is what has really been keeping me from going all the way around the moon. The captain—my ego?—has bought into the story, and is still flying the ship. Fortunately he is becoming less important . . . So, we go spinning off again. I am feeling dizzy and sick, and want to find some safe room on the ship which has some sort of force field that will protect me. The captain says there is one, sort of, but he isn't even sure this safe room—Multipod—works anymore—it has been so long since I used this part of myself.

Why is it called Multipod? *Multi* means many, lots, multiple. What is a pod? It is a protective shell that keeps seeds safe until they are ready to sprout. Interesting (I had no idea I would give that description before I wrote it!). I have erected multiple protective layers to keep certain fragile parts of myself, full of potential, from being destroyed. So keeping this part of myself shut down originally served a protective function. Unfortunately I sealed these seeds off from myself, as well. I did this so young I'd forgotten all about it, don't even know if these parts of myself still function.

But hurray! In the dream Ken and I actually get into the room. In order to do this we go through two doors—one opened with a key (intercourse), the other with a concealed "little button that you push with your finger" (clitoral stimulation). I am glad we know the secret of this little button—I sure am! (Clitoral stimulation is an important part of this process, and I shouldn't downplay its importance.)

Now we are on our own. The room is a giant computer (associations with "multivac," an Isaac Asimov computer) and the whole floor is humming with power—power specifically for me. We must learn how to work this room—I must access this core creative, sexual part of myself or the whole mission will fail. Oh, the sorrow this part of me feels at having been ignored and neglected! It is almost crazy with grief and frustration but doesn't know how to communicate. I have shut it off for so long. It is desperate and since it really is at the heart of running the ship the ship is going to crash. This creative part of me is the CENTRAL part of who I am. I call out commands to it but it doesn't understand.

Then I try saying "I love you." Reaching out with love to this shut-off, frightened part of myself. Ken jumps, startled—I think in this case he represents the part of ME that had forgotten I could do this and when I reach out with love, the tool for communication suddenly becomes obvious—a telephone, which was there all along.

Why did a telephone work when just talking didn't? How is a telephone different from just talking to someone? A telephone is something you use when someone is a long way away. A telephone is for talking one to one—it is focused and specific, not diffuse, like a line in rather than a mike on a tape deck. Also telephones, for me in dreams, tend to symbolize communication—the importance of talking and communicating. So the telephone represents the importance of speaking about this, directly and specifically.

I ask the being how to communicate with it, and it begins to tell me.

What do those words mean? Phonetically, "Aloose nevyay," although in the dream I think of it as something in French—like it might be spelled "allieuse nevier" or "alleus nevier"—I studied French in high school but I don't remember any words like that. Maybe the idea is that this part of me speaks a DIFFERENT LANGUAGE. I have to learn to talk its language.

Then the alarm goes off.

I don't really understand what this walled-off part of me is saying, and we are interrupted, but the sense is that the process has begun, we have made contact, and now we will be all right.

The dream relates to something else I've been thinking a lot about. I am tired of living in my rational, intellectual, surface consciousness. I want to go deeper, deeper, access the enormous mysterious depths—I want to be mystical, magical, intuitive, not rational and linear and analytic. That's one of the reasons I haven't been writing in my journal—it seems like—words! words! words! I've felt trapped in the skin of my consciousness—I've felt trapped in endless wandering aimless mind chatter, mental gymnastics, cut off from the experience of mystery and mystical union that I keep READING about, THINKING about, and not EXPERIENCING. I want so much to experience it, to live there, and I can't even seem to touch it for a second.

My new identity—the witch, the moon, the water. Magic. Creativity. NOT the scholar, the brilliant dry analytic . . . not the ascetic—but with all the union with the absolute that the ascetic yogi can achieve.

Gwendolyn was delighted with the results of her interview. Had she not taken the time to write it out, this complex dream would have been very hard to work on alone. You will notice that Gwendolyn felt she was able to bridge a number of the elements in her dream without first writing out a description. This can lead to premature and inaccurate bridges if one is not careful to verify that the dream image fits the interpretation well and that all the bridges fall into a coherent whole by the end of the dream work.

THE SERIOUS ROLE OF HAVING FUN

As you work through the conflicts that block your greater sexual and creative flowering, keep an eye open for an often over-looked source of fulfillment, that of having fun. Your dreams will from time to time remind you of the healing and inspiring importance of playfulness. You may dream of flying with grand abandon, of clowning with your lover, or of any other scene of just plain fun. Take these dreams as seriously as you take any others. They will give you a boost, perhaps open your eyes to sources of happy energy that will help you through the darker, more painful aspects of your life.

The week after Simone with some embarrassment had bought and secretively experimented with a vibrator, she dreamt:

I had just had a fantastic orgasm with my new vibrator in my vagina. Now, standing up, I pull it out of myself, hold it up to show it. It looks like a turkey drumstick. I announce to whoever might care to hear that these things are wonderful, and very practical. I say that, like turkey, they are good for your health and can play an important role in any good diet. The whole scene struck me as very funny, and I was amazed at my lack of embarrassment or even self-consciousness.

"Turkey Vibrator"

Simone found that she told some of her close friends about the dream and discovered that she was not the only one who used a vibrator. In fact, discussing the humor of the dream helped Simone begin talking about sex in a much easier and more useful way both with her girlfriends and with her boyfriend.

Talking about slightly embarrassing sexual dreams, such as the ones in which a parent wanders into your room while you are having sex, can also introduce a sense of humor into your discussion of sexual feelings. This can go a long way in reducing awkwardness and anxiety for both you and your partner.

By the way, since most people will say that a sense of fun is a big help in encouraging creative sex and creative work, you might consider working on having more fun while you are awake. Why not decide to do something that is fun every day? Even if you only take five minutes to listen to music you love, sing a song, or take a walk, you might find yourself more fun to be with. If you put more energy into developing your enjoyment of pleasure, such as taking luxurious baths or massages or dressing up with your partner for a delivered pizza dinner, the rewards might flow into your sexual life and your creative initiative. Sex manuals (a few good ones are listed in the reference section) are filled with suggestions for fun and dramatic surprises one partner can offer the other. Whether you experiment with simple or elaborate surprises doesn't matter. What counts is that you take an active role in avoiding the paralyzing force of habit that keeps you stuck in dull and noncreative patterns of thinking and acting. As Sam Keen wrote in *The Passionate Life: Stages of Loving:* "Play of the senses or the imagination, is the magic, the grace, the elixir without which roles become habits, personality becomes a facade, character becomes character-armor, culture becomes a prison."[1]

THE PASSION OF BEAUTY

Risk-taking, daring excursions into untried emotional and sexual self-explorations and interpersonal intimacies, challenges us to grow and can reward us with dramatically heightened sensory, emotional, and spiritual awareness. These are the rewards of slogging through the emotional swamps of our past and finding new, more mature, modes of perception, reaction, interaction. This is the path of blood, sweat, and tears that all of us travel from time to time in our journey to a fuller, freer adult life. But it is not the only road available. We can travel part of the way on another path, that of beauty.

Plato wrote that one "should begin in youth to visit beautiful forms" and learn to contemplate beauty in one form until able to see the beauty in all forms, institutions, and sciences. Then one should continue to contemplate beauty until able to see divine, immutable beauty. Plato taught that the joyous communion with this beauty would grant any mortal capable of it a measure of immortality.[2] Psychologists have not yet fully appreciated the potentially motivating role of beauty in the dreams and waking life of human beings.[3] If pain is the stick that goads us to face up to our unresolved fears and conflicts, beauty can be the carrot that lures us to let go of the past and embrace a more loving, open, joyous present.

Some people find beauty in a garden, a human face or form, a building, music, or a generous act. Where do you see beauty? When do you experience it? Let's not be picky about the kind of beauty or its immutability or divinity, but be open to its many forms.

EXERCISE 11-2
Recapture a Moment of Beauty

Look at your life and identify some of your experiences of beauty. Describe them in your journal, if you are keeping one. If you can't think of a particular instance at the moment, take a few minutes to play a recording of the most beautiful piece of music you own. Then describe how you felt listening to it.

When we abandon ourselves to beauty, we let go of fear, anger, resentment, and distractions. Anything that can get us to do that certainly has potential for increasing our creativity and our sexual fulfillment. By making it a point to frequently immerse ourselves in whatever we know as beauty, we can reinforce states of being that are conducive to openness, grace, and delight of all kinds. If you link some of your daily contemplations of beauty to your sexuality, you will be more likely to notice their creative effects on your erotic life and imagination.

So much of what we hear and see about sex is either dreadfully clinical and practical or simply vulgar. Our associations to sexuality often lack the lyrical, the magical, the beauteous. Many women even think of their own genitalia as ugly or gross, of the sexual act as messy and icky. Imagine how different things would be if we had grown up seeing beautiful images of sexuality in photographs and paintings that were not thought of as obscene or pornographic. How many museums of fine art display paintings of explicit sexual acts?

What might you do to build more positive and beautiful associations into your images and feelings of sexuality? Margo Anand's spectacular book, *The Art of Sexual Ecstasy,* suggests that we dance for our lovers, create lovely environments, that we play beautiful music when we engage in pleasuring each other. By taking the time to bring the beauty of poetry, song, or lovely visual and sensory experiences into lovemaking, we bring the power of beauty to bear on our outdated but not-yet-outgrown inhibitions and fears. Some people drink wine to embolden them to risk being open and intimate, but you can achieve far more ecstatic states by sipping beauty. This draft's intoxication will heighten rather than diminish your sexual, verbal, and perceptive powers, and you will suffer no hangovers from your nights of splendor.

Nicholas is a choral singer who late in life discovered a passion for Italian lyric opera. He began to use opera as a tonic when he felt down or uninspired in daily life. Then, one night, he decided to introduce his girlfriend to the joys of one of his favorite operas by cooking an Italian dinner for her during which he told her the story of the opera and played her carefully selected excerpts. She was swept up by the music and the voices. When Nicholas later made love to her throughout her first hearing of the whole opera, the beauty of the music suffused their beings and magically heightened their shared experience.

DREAMS OF CREATIVE AND SEXUAL PASSION

My clients who are artists or who surround themselves daily with art or music seem to report more dreams of beauty than do those who do not recognize or attend to their minimum daily requirements for aesthetic experiences. (Yes, I do believe that for optimal well-being we do have an MDR for both vitamins *and* beauty.) Even when the artist or art lover is suffering conflict and pain, dreams of beauty now and then grace the interior landscape. And even many of their unpleasant dreams include images of compelling beauty. Here is an amazing dream in which Victoria, a musician, used the image of a pleasurable sexual encounter with her extraordinarily creative brother to evoke a thundering delight in her own creativity and her sexuality. Victoria had this dream after a week-long intensive master class in piano and just before she was to begin a performance tour. She described this as "the monumental dream of my life. The first in which I remember becoming fully orgasmic." I shall place in parentheses key descriptions from her interpretation that will help you understand as you read along.

> I am to meet my brother, Michael (a creative genius I have envied and struggled with, my creative self) and Dad (strict, rigid) at some airport. I'm riding a train, uncertain about how to handle a hamper full of stuff that I'm dragging around with me (my old emotional baggage of resentments and jealousy of my brother, of my artistic insecurities in the face of my dad). In the dream I realize that I should just leave this stuff behind.
> Suddenly I am in the narrow hallway of my birth home's second floor. I walk into Michael's room and there is Ben (sweet, supportive, playful, but not sexually attractive husband), celebrating the completion of his dissertation. Michael's bed is a table upon which are arranged many

flowers, vases with flowers. It is an altar to beauty in its many stages. One vase has blooms closed, opening, opened, dropping. Another, irises on a gladiolilike stalk—color of pastel purple/blue (Michael knows a lot about beauty and creation).

There are also deep and light pink flowers arranged on the table. It takes several sightings for me to notice that large, scoop-petals are arranged around some centrally located object. Then I notice the clutter on the floor—bags and books and empty/full makeup containers and clothes and dust jackets—all of this is a sharp contrast to the ordered and disordered beauty on the table, where each element is surrounded by clear space. (The clutter of my life that leads me to vege out rather than to design and create.)

Internally, I chastise myself for forgetting to send Ben flowers for his big day of finishing his dissertation. I decide to come up with some offering. I riffle through my bag for the something I must surely have purchased for him. I find instead my pretty new rose-color quartz makeup containers and a book which arrests my attention. (My creative life is much more important to me now than my marriage.)

I think the book is the *Unseen Real*, although the dust cover says something else. (Like the book, I am about the black goddess and the reclaiming of the senses, even if my facade has camouflaged my reality.) I settle down into my armchair to read until I'm interrupted by someone's return. For a moment I am confused as to whether it is Ben or Michael. I was expecting Ben, but it is Michael, decked out in new clothes, safari style.

The colors are all greens: leather coat, khaki shirt, dark pants. He is jaunty, strutting. He walks around the table to give me a closer look at his duds. I question this drastic change in his style from quiet to explorer, very, very sexy and outdoorsy. (My own style is changing in the same directions.)

"I've been dressing like this," he says. "Check it out."

I notice that his shoes, while of the same style, are different colors—one beige, one dark brown, both sandals that go to mid-calf. (He's a free spirit, doesn't care to match.) His leather coat has fringes on the arms. He is also wearing a green, fringed mask, skull tight (mystery, fearless, he is in tune with life cycles and instinct). He asks me if I like his look.

As he moves closer to me, teasing me, arousing me sexually, a voice inside says over and over, "I don't like it, I don't like it," in reply to his questions about the effect on me of his behavior and appearance. My body, however, rocks in the chair, knees up, convulses as one tickled, though Michael, the green man, is not touching me. I am giggling. As I notice my physical reactions, a softer, less insistent voice, says, "I like it".

Green man has left. Ma, Dad, others make noise entering. I am intoxicated and frantic to clean up Michael's room. Ma has come upstairs to see what I'm doing. I rush out of the room to greet her, am obviously in an altered state. Feel myself talking loud as if in attempt to "be normal" through this atmosphere of headiness surrounding me. (In the last year, I've begun to worry less about seeming normal, I want to be free to be really different.)

I meet Ma mid-stairs, turn her around, talk to Dad. They introduce me to a white man with droopy eyes who is working with a company I don't trust. (Mainstream dull guy, parents' status quo type they would like for me.)

It's as though each word and movement echoes out into an atmosphere particular to me and that it takes extra effort to penetrate that atmosphere to communicate with folks not in it. Ma follows me upstairs, is about to follow me into Michael's room when he returns and sidetracks her. He explains the strangeness—which she detects as she looks sideways at me—as a result of a creative project nearing completion. He is cheerful and effective. He is both with and without the dense, water/air-like ambience in which I float. The atmosphere has both light and weight, as if its substance redefines myself as moving and living beyond my body. Mamma never gets closer to me than this extended self, senses it as a boundary she cannot penetrate. (This atmosphere about me has protected me from Mom's intrusions, but it's sad that she can't really know this passionate, creative part of me.)

Michael leads me into his room, where the table of beauty is now his bed and he guides me to the edge of it, in front of his full-length mirror, and says, "Let's finish you." He then proceeds to drink the melting between my thighs. So skillfully. Tongue and tooth and lip sucking, extracting, lengthening.

Without awareness of the transition, I go outside to a garden for climax. I am naked, making my way down stone stairs. It is night. The stairs and garden in the dream house are those of some gothic castle. It is indigo night.

Ma and Dad are arguing inside the castle. Ma says "Just because you were a dropped birth (meaning abandoned, unwanted) you're angry at the world." Or perhaps Dad says, "Just because I was a dropped birth you hold this against me." That past, the past. (All that anger, it's their life, not mine.)

I crouch in the dirt right below the stairs. Masturbate. Or do I? Something maintains a constant, ecstasy-producing attention on my clit and vulva. My flower is so close to the earth, both in color and distance, that it is difficult to distinguish the two. Voices to the left and behind me chant, "Ecstasy, ecstasy, ecstasy," both in gratitude and announcement.

Here, I flash in and out of dream and real time, trying to determine if I am actually masturbating. This split of attention subsides as I surrender to the orgasmic throbbing and liquid of the moment. This is completion. I awaken to my own, low murmurings of satisfaction and know for the first time that my fingers were securely folded under my ear during the entire dream. I give gratitude to ecstasy for the visitation, and I dedicate the opening to continuing creative flowering.

"The Great Dream"

Victoria's dream marked a turning point in her life. She was letting go of her need to be "normal" and win approval from her parents. She was beginning to identify with her creative brother rather than envy him, and his stimulation was creative and affirming. Victoria felt the dream to be simultaneously a creative and a sexual opening to beauty and freedom. The value of such a dream grows with time as the dreamer recalls it, savors the feelings, and uses the imagery to inspire her and to keep focused on her goals.

Victoria's dream was precipitated by her psychological and artistic growth, not by movement in her sexual life. She was very happy to remain married to her husband, and felt she simply needed to shift some of her energies to her career. Nicholas, on the other hand, had one of the most moving dreams of beauty, sexuality, and creativity as he was entering into a new sexual relationship with Sylvie, who had ignited in him the desire to live passionately and to rejoice flamboyantly. Early in the relationship Nicholas dreamed:

I am on Mt. Olympus or in Valhalla—somewhere in the clouds as close as mortals can come to the immortals. The winds are sweeping clouds above and below. I am unbelievably exhilarated. This reminds me of my feelings with Sylvie. The spaciousness, the freshness, and the drama of the scene make me feel brave, light, and intensely, passionately alive.

I am here to take my vow. I approach an altar of clouds. The gods are gathered somewhere in the wind and the mists. The most thrilling, beautiful music I've ever loved is permeating this elegant ceremony. I call to the gods my courageous oath: "I swear never again to turn away from the life of passion." I realize as I do this that such a promise is rarely kept by mortals, and that I will at times find it terrifyingly painful to honor my vow. But the alternative, that of living in quiet safety, appears to me to be no longer worth living. This aliveness is too beautiful, too fitting, too right to ever abandon again. I awake wondering if I will be able to keep my vow.

"I Swear"

Nicholas was not able to live every minute of his life according to his courageous oath, but he did refuse to give up the struggle by falling back into his former life as a man too interested in security and calm to really test himself and taste the excitement of a more daring life. Five years after this dream he still talks of it as the most important of his sexual, personal, and professional life. He says it acts as a beacon when he is making choices and setting goals, and that it helps him to counterbalance his timid, self-restricting tendencies with the vision of his dream.

UNCORK THE BOTTLE AND LET THE GENIE OUT

Careful dream work can help liberate us from the fears, inhibitions, and outworn attitudes and traditions that keep us from living a passionate life. Dreams are powerful tools in working through conflicted parental and current intimate relationships because they show us how we unwittingly re-create or overcompensate for unhealthy patterns we first learned in childhood. We can use our dreams to identify and understand the dynamics of problems that keep us stuck in these repetitive patterns. Then we have the possibility of dreaming our way into new ways of seeing and being in the world. Taken together, the fruits of good dream work offer each of us the chance to unwrap ourselves and to embrace each other and life passionately.

Dreams challenge us to grow out of our fears, out of our constricting inherited parental and social attitudes, and step into a more exciting, surprising life. A life in which we can dare to feel deeply and be less afraid to cry or jump for joy. A life in which we can courageously confront inhibitions that keep us from feeling intensely the fullness of our experience of love and of loneliness, of enthusiasm and of disappointment. How many times have we refused to let ourselves dance with glee in the hope that we might win a certain sweetheart, or job, or prize, or for fear that we might later experience disappointment?

While we dream, we nudge, bludgeon, cajole, and seduce ourselves to dare to live intensely, to risk intimacy when the situation is right, to march to our own drummers, to say yes to life rather than no, or maybe, or someday.

EXERCISE **11-3**

Find Your Free Spirits

Look through your dreams for images of free spirits. How do they fare in your dreams? Are you ever one yourself? Sometimes images of free spirits come in the forms of birds or other lovely, wild, or endangered animals. Sometimes the free spirits show up as people you know and admire in waking life. Like Michael in Victoria's dream, such images can inspire you to live more expressively and creatively.

If the free spirits in your dreams are hidden, threatened, or imprisoned, set yourself to their liberation. Do you have dreams of being in jail? Of beautiful animals shut up in a constricting zoo? Are there parts of yourself like these animals that you lock up and deny their natural freedom and place? You can use your dreams to find out the causes and the remedies of their imprisonment. Then if you are willing to risk criticism from conformists, the loss of security in a safe but dead relationship or job, and the possibility of failure if you attempt new things, you have a chance to live a thrilling life with intensity and passion denied to those who live safely and tamely in the zoo.

A P P E N D I X   1

Sexual Dreams
Questionnaire

IN ORDER TO FIND MORE ANSWERS TO THE MANY STILL-unanswered questions about sexual dreaming, we need the help of people who are willing to be open in disclosing (anonymously, of course) information that is very personal. We simply do not yet have enough information to answer basic questions about sexual dreaming. Do people have more explicitly sexual dreams when they are sexually active or inactive? How do people react to their sexual dreams? What sexual dreams do men and women dream most often? How is creativity related to sexuality and to sexual dreams?

For example, are changing sexual attitudes reflected in an individual's dreams? The two major studies on this question came up with conflicting answers. Hall and Domhoff and their colleagues compared the dreams collected from undergraduates in 1950 and 1980 and found that the intervening thirty years, which included the feminist movement and the sexual revolution, had made little change in the content of the students' dreams. Furthermore, they found that the differences between men and women's dreams, including the findings that men dream more frequently of having or witnessing a sexual encounter, have remained unaltered. [1]

Meanwhile, Milton Kramer and his colleagues analyzed the dreams of eleven men and eleven women undergraduates that

they collected from the dreamers as they slept in a sleep laboratory. Kramer found that compared to the undergraduate home
dreams collected and analyzed by Hall in 1950, his dreamers
showed significant differences. Whereas Hall's male dreamers
reported more aggression and misfortune to self or others,
Kramer's male dreamers were not significantly different from
his female dreamers in these categories. Whereas Hall's female
dreamers were more likely to report a dream and had more social interactions in their dreams, Kramer's men and women
showed no significant differences on either scale. Kramer's
study confirmed differences found by Hall (men had more male,
single, and strange characters; more auditory activity, full containers, old-age references, large sizes, and curved and crooked
references—women had more cognitive activity and more
strong intensity or emotionality), but suggested that the changes
he found may reflect effects of the sexual revolution. Women
and men may now be equally concerned about assertiveness issues and about fears of misfortune or failure. Concerns about
relationships with others may now be equally important to both
sexes. [2]

Domhoff points out that dreams collected in laboratory settings tend to be more guarded compared to home dreams,
which are recorded in private, at home. [3] While this fact interferes with a direct comparison of the 1950 home dreams collected by Hall and the 1980 laboratory dreams collected by
Kramer, could it suffice to explain the important differences in
the two findings? Could it be that college students are not the
best indicators of social and attitudinal changes? For example,
would the dreams of older, more sexually experienced, working
men and women more likely reflect societal changes regarding
sex differences and attitudes toward sexuality? One could easily
argue that undergraduate life has changed less than has life at
work, in the home, and in society for most men and women. A
study by Monique Lortie-Lussier and her colleagues showed
that the dreams of working mothers differed from those of
homemakers, and suggests that changing social roles do indeed
influence what we dream about. [4] Clearly we need more data in
the form of many more dreams and more research before we

can know if and how changes in our social world affect our dream lives.

Do people who are more sexually active in waking life dream more often about sex than people who are less active or abstinent? We just don't have enough information to know.[5] It could be that people who are more comfortable thinking and talking about sex or whose work deals with sex, such as sex therapists, adult movie makers, sex toy designers, and others, are more likely to use sexual images as metaphors for a wide variety of nonsexual concerns when they dream. Thus, their use of sexual dream imagery may have less to do with their waking sexual thoughts and activities than would be the case if sex played a more narrow role in their lives.

It may be that people dream more explicitly sexual dreams when they are more conflicted about sex and when they are more focused on that conflict. In a study of the dreams of 123 undergraduates, Paul Robbins and his colleagues found that students who were more anxious had more manifest or explicit sexual content in their dreams than did the less anxious students.[6] Stanislaw Dulko studied the patterns of sexual behavior of two groups of 23 female-to-male and 14 male-to-female transsexuals. Both groups reported more dreams with erotic content than did two control groups of nontranssexuals, even though the intensity of sexual drive of the transsexuals did not differ from that of the control groups.[7] Would we see a similar result if we compared the dreams of a group of people attending a workshop on sexual relations to a group attending a workshop on house repair?

Psychotherapists have expressed clinical impressions about these and other questions based on more or less experience with sexual dreams, but we need to hear from many people like you who are willing to take the time and the effort to openly answer some rather direct questions before we can confidently answer most of them.

The questionnaire below contains some of the questions asked by Domhoff, while others expand the scope of the search for information on sexual dreams.

Whether or not you decide to participate in our survey by

mailing this questionnaire to us, you will most likely learn useful things about your sexual dreams by writing out your answers to the following questions. I suggest that you carefully number each of your responses and write them out on full-sized, lined paper or type them out, so that you will have as much space as you need and end up with a more legible record that will begin your journal of sexual dreams that you can expand over the coming months.

THE DELANEY & FLOWERS
DREAM CENTER SURVEY
ON SEXUAL DREAMS

1. Sex _____
2. Age _____
3. Occupation _____
4. Have you ever been in psychotherapy? If so, for how long? _____
5. Have you ever participated in a psychological growth program?
6. Have you ever kept a dream journal? _____
7. If so, for how long? _____ months _____ years
8. When did you last reread your dream journal?
   _____ never _____ months ago _____ years ago
9. About how many dreams did you review? _____
10. Over what length of time did these dreams occur?
    _____
11. Have you ever had sexual dreams that were entirely free of complications or conflict or any discomfort? If yes, would you describe one?
12. Do you usually write these entirely pleasurable dreams in your journal if you are keeping one at the time of the dream?
    never _____ rarely _____ usually _____ almost always
13. Frequency of sexual dreams in which the manifest im-

agery is explicitly sexual or there are erotic feelings or
overtones within the dream (please answer 1–7).

1	2	3	4	5	6	7
never	not in the last year	1–4 times in last year	5–10 times in last year	approx. 1/month	2–4 times /month	more than 1/week

14. Frequency of sexual dreams in which there is no mani-
     fest imagery or erotic feeling overtones, but in which
     there were images or actions you interpret as sexual
     (please answer 1–7).

1	2	3	4	5	6	7
never	not in the last year	1–4 times in last year	5–10 times in last year	approx. 1/month	2–4 times /month	more than 1/week

15. List some of the apparently nonsexual images or dream
     actions you have interpreted as sexual in past dreams.
16. Would you please write down or photocopy from your
     journal the last sexual dream (with sexual imagery and/
     or sexual feelings) that you can remember?
17. Could you please write down your favorite sexual
     dream?
18. Do you think this favorite dream means anything? If so,
     what?
19. List the themes of other pleasant sexual dreams.
20. Would you please write down or photocopy your most
     uncomfortable sexual dream?
21. Do you think it means anything? If so, what?
22. List the themes of other uncomfortable sexual dreams.
23. Have you ever dreamt of having sex with other family
     members? Which ones?
24. How do you feel about such dreams, and how do you
     interpret them?
25. Have you ever dreamt of being raped? Describe the
     dream(s).
26. Do you remember ever dreaming of having sex with
     someone of the same sex if you are heterosexual, or of
     the opposite sex if you are homosexual?
27. Have you ever dreamt of coercing someone to have sex
     with you? Describe.
28. When do you think you have the most sexual dreams—

when you are sexually active, or inactive, or under other conditions?

29. Frequency of nocturnal orgasms in the last year _____

30. Could you please write down any dreams that you can remember that precipitated a nocturnal orgasm.

31. What is your sexual orientation?

32. How would you characterize your current attitude toward sexuality? Very conservative, somewhat conservative, moderate, somewhat liberal, or very liberal?

33. Frequency of sexual intimacy in the last year (times per week, per month, or per year).

34. Frequency of masturbatory activity (times per week, per month, or per year).

35. Marital status: Single, married, divorced, widowed, currently living with a significant other, currently involved with a significant other.

36. Have you ever learned a new sexual technique or expanded your sexual knowledge via your dreams? Please explain.

37. Have you ever learned anything about your sexuality from your dreams? If so, what?

38. Have you ever told a sexual dream to your partner? To anyone?

39. What differences, if any, do you see between your sexual dreams and your sexual fantasies?

40. Do you think your sexual dreams have changed since you were twenty? If so, how?

41. Have you kept a dream journal that you would like to share for the purposes of this research? If so, please write Dr. Loma Flowers or me at our center.

COMMENTS: Feel free to write any other comments you would like to make.

If you would like to take part in our survey, return your answers to us at:

The Delaney & Flowers Dream and Consultation Center
337 Spruce Street, San Francisco, CA 94118
Or call:

415-587-3424

If you would like to receive information about the center and an update on our progress with the study, send us a double-stamped, self-addressed business envelope (a DSASE) separate from your response in order to preserve your anonymity. If you have friends interested in dreams, or are a member of a dream study group, we would be delighted if you would consider inviting them to take part in the survey as well.

How to Select a Dream Specialist, or a Sex Therapist, or a General Therapist

Choosing a Dream Specialist

Many psychologists, psychiatrists, and counselors have little or no training in working with dreams. Some people who have no letters after their names, who may be poets or engineers, have learned to be very effective dream analysts. So, you can't count on graduate degrees or a reputation as a master therapist to guide you to a good dream specialist. Your best bet is to read a few books on dreams and then ask friends, therapists, or your favorite authors for referrals. Next, telephone a few people you might like to work with and interview each one. In about five minutes you should be able to obtain responses to questions like these:

- Could you tell me what education and training you have had specifically in dream work?
- What is your theoretical background in dream work, and what methods do you use?
- How long have you been teaching dream work, and how many people have you worked with in group and individual settings?
- How many clients have you worked with for a year or longer?

The responses to these questions should help you identify practitioners whose perspectives, style, and experience suggest a good match with your needs.

Choosing a Sex Therapist

Masters, Johnson, and Kolodny suggest you first contact sex therapy centers that are affiliated with medical schools or hospitals. You might also contact the Masters & Johnson Institute or the Kinsey Institute, both of which are listed here under "Resources for Sexual Education and Sex Therapy." I would suggest that in doing so you ask very specific questions regarding the degree of training and experience your particular, assigned therapist would have. I certainly would not want to be treated by a resident who might be just beginning his or her training. Ideally, I would want a therapist with at least ten years of practice in the field. Do not be intimidated by clinic and hospital people who are unclear about exactly how much experience and exactly what training your potential therapist has gained. If you find the fees of the more experienced therapists too high, consider seeing such a therapist less frequently and tape-recording your sessions so that you can get the most out of them. I would rather send someone I love to an experienced therapist once a month than once a week to a novice whose supervision by a senior therapist may or may not be very thorough.

You could also call your local psychological association or medical society for references. Many authors in the field have private practices, and you might want to contact one whose work you like. The AASECT (listed here under "Resources for Sexual Education and Sex Therapy") will provide you with a list of sex educators, counselors, and therapists in your area. Then interview your potential therapist by telephone with direct questions about his or her degrees, certification, methods, experience, and fees. When you have narrowed the field down to two or three you might want to schedule brief twenty-five-minute appointments with each before deciding which one you would like to work with.

Choosing a General Therapist

If you would like to work on relationship problems, or if you want to work on abuse issues, find a good therapist by asking your friends, family doctor, or local psychological associations or medical societies for referrals. If you have been abused by a therapist in the past and/or worry about the possibility of being abused this time, tell your prospective therapist about your concerns and be sure he or she states clearly that sexual intimacies between you and the therapist will be completely off-limits in your work together.

In a brief telephone interview, ask for specific answers to your questions about the therapist's training, experience, fees, and methods. Consider seeing two or three therapists for brief sessions before deciding which one you want to work with. This financial investment is usually well worth it.

NOTES

INTRODUCTION

1. These dreamers have all given me permission to write about their dreams, and I have given each an alias.

CHAPTER 1

1. Calvin S. Hall and Robert L. Van de Castle, *The Content Analysis of Dreams* (New York: Appleton-Century-Crofts, 1966). A follow-up study that compared the dream content of undergraduates thirty years later to that collected by Hall and Van de Castle also found that the men reported more manifest sexual imagery than did the women: Calvin S. Hall, G. William Domhoff, Kenneth A. Blick, and Kathryn E. Weesner, "The Dreams of College Men and Women in 1950 and 1980: A Comparison of Dream Contents and Sex Differences," *Sleep* 5 (2) 1982, pp. 188–94. As in the earlier study, the dream reports were handed in to male instructors (personal communication with W. Domhoff).

2. Ross B. Kremsdorf, Lucy J. Palladino, Douglas D. Polenz, and Barbara J. Anista, "Effects of the Sex of Both Interviewer and Subject on Reported Manifest Dream Content," *Journal of Consulting and Clinical Psychology* 1978, vol. 46, no. 5, pp. 1166–67.

3. Paul R. Robbins, Roland H. Tank, and Faraneh Houshi, "Anxiety and Dream Symbolism," *Journal of Personality* 53:1, March 1985, pp. 17–22.

4. These dreams include those of my clients as well as those recorded by 140 people who, while attending lectures on dreaming, filled out questionnaires asking them to describe their favorite and most uncomfortable sexual dreams. The 110 women who completed my "lecture audience" questionnaire ranged in age from twenty-five to seventy, with most being in their thirties and forties. Almost all were heterosexual. About 90 percent worked outside the home for a living. They belonged to singles clubs, professional associations, business and community groups, and came to hear a talk on problem solving in dreams, using dreams for creativity and insight, or on sexual dreams. They filled out the questionnaires in fifteen minutes before the lectures.

5. Dr. Domhoff, author of *The Mystique of Dreams,* has recently collected information on the sexual dreams of 273 undergraduate students, 172 of which were female. He has generously loaned me the completed questionnaires so I could include some of the material in this book. The dreams of the Santa Cruz undergraduates who are twenty to thirty years younger than most of my clients and lecture attendees nevertheless seem to follow a number of similar patterns.

6. Loma Flowers, M.D., has suggested the term *forechores.* Chores first, play after!

7. June M. Reinisch with Ruth Beasley, *The Kinsey Institute New Report on Sex: What You Must Know to be Sexually Literate* (New York: St. Martin's Press, 1990), pp. 88–91.

CHAPTER 2

1. In Domhoff's survey, several women and men wrote notes saying that it would be better to have respondents fill out the questionnaires in a more private setting. I am sure that many of the respondents to my lecture audience questionnaire suffered similar discomfort, which limited their responsiveness. Nevertheless, Domhoff's male dreamers provided a number of detailed dreams when asked to describe their last erotic dream and the most striking or memorable erotic dream they could recall.

2. It may be that such dreams are withheld or forgotten by men, who find them embarrassing. Or it may be that they simply do not often occur in a culture that produces men who do not require scenarios of coercion to liberate them from sexual inhibitions.

3. William H. Masters, Virginia E. Johnson, and Robert C. Kolodny, *Human Sexuality,* 4th ed. (New York: HarperCollins, 1992), p. 347.

4. J. Allan Hobson, *The Dreaming Brain* (New York: Basic Books, 1988), pp. 294–95.

5. Martin Cole, "Socio-sexual Characteristics of Men with Sexual Problems," *Sexual and Marital Therapy,* vol. 1, no. 1, 1986, p. 100.

6. June M. Reinisch with Ruth Beasley, *The Kinsey Institute New Report on Sex: What You Must Know to be Sexually Literate* (New York: St. Martin's Press, 1990), pp. 88–91.

7. A. Estin Comarr, Jeffery M. Cressy, and Michael Letch, "Sleep Dreams of Sex Among Traumatic Paraplegics and Quadriplegics," *Sexuality and Disability,* vol. 6, no. 1, Spring 1983, pp. 25–29. See also, John Money, "Phantom Orgasm in Paraplegics," *Medical Aspects of Human Sexuality,* vol. 4, 1970, pp. 90–97.

8. Masters, Johnson, Kolodny, *Human Sexuality,* p. 196.

9. Calvin Hall and Robert L. Van de Castle, *The Content Analysis of Dreams* (New York: Appleton-Century-Crofts, 1966).

10. David G. Schwartz, Lissa N. Weinstein, and Arthur M. Arkin, "Qualitative Aspects of Sleep Mentation," in *The Mind in Sleep: Psychology and Psychophysiology,* ed. Arthur M. Arkin, John S. Antrobus, and Steven J. Ellman (Hillsdale, N.J.: Lawrence Erlbaum Associates, Publishers, 1978), p. 175.

CHAPTER 3

1. Ross Campbell and Robert Hoffman, "Variables Affecting Frequency of Dream Recall," unpublished.

2. Raymond F. Martinetti, "Sex Differences in Dream Recall and Components of Imaginal Life," *Journal of Perceptual and Motor Skills,* Oct. 1989, vol. 69 (2), pp. 643–49.

3. Paul R. Robbins and Roland H. Tanck, "Interest in Dreams and Dream Recall," *Journal of Perceptual and Motor Skills,* Feb. 1988, vol. 66 (1), pp. 291–94.

4. Carl P. Browman, Rosalind D. Cartwright, "The Influence of Evening Activity and Psychological State on Dream Life," *Journal of Psychiatric Treatment and Evaluation,* 1982, vol. 4 (3), pp. 307–11. In L. J. G. Gooren, "Human Male Sexual Functions Do Not Require Aromatization of Testosterone: A Study Using Tamoxifen, Testolactone, and Dihydrotestosterone," *Archives of Sexual Behavior,* vol. 14, no. 6, 1985, pp. 539–48, L. Gooren, an endocrinologist in the Netherlands, has reported: "Administration of dihydrotestosterone to eugonadal men led to a transient increase of nocturnal sexual dreams and erec-

tions and irritability, waning after 3–4 weeks of dihydrotestosterone administration." While there may exist a variety of drugs that increase the frequency and/or the recall of sexual dreams, the induction of erotic dreams via chemicals is not a route we shall explore here.

CHAPTER 4

1. Similar versions of this cue card have been published in: Gayle Delaney, *Living Your Dreams* (New York: Harper Collins, 1979, 1981, 1988); and in Gayle Delaney, *Breakthrough Dreaming: How to Tap the Power of Your 24-Hour Mind* (New York: Bantam Books, 1991).

CHAPTER 5

1. Alexander N. Leavy and Joseph Weissberg, "The Role of Dreams in Sex Therapy," *Journal of Sex and Marital Therapy*, vol. 5, no. 4, Winter 1979, p. 335.
2. You will find extensive directions for incubating dreams and many examples in: Gayle Delaney, *Living Your Dreams* (New York: Harper Collins, 1988).

CHAPTER 6

1. Jessica Benjamin, *The Bonds of Love: Psychoanalysis, Feminism, and the Problem of Domination* (New York: Pantheon Books, 1988), p. 53.
2. Ibid., p. 126.
3. Ibid., p. 29.

CHAPTER 7

1. For a good introduction to the varieties of co-dependency, see Melody Beattie, *Codependent No More* (San Francisco: Harper & Row, 1987).
2. Alexander N. Leavy and Joseph Weissberg, "The Role of Dreams in Sex Therapy," *Journal of Sex and Marital Therapy*, vol. 5, no. 4, Winter 1979: pp. 334–39.
3. Ibid., p. 337. For a brief literature review and a discussion of a psychoanalytically oriented approach to the use of dreams in couples ther-

apy, see Richard A. Perlmutter and Raymond Babineau, "The Use of Dreams in Couples Therapy," *Psychiatry*, vol. 26, February 1983, pp. 66–72.

4. William Masters, Virginia E. Johnson, and Robert C. Kolodny, *Human Sexuality*, 4th ed. (New York: HarperCollins, 1992), p. 347.

5. Martin Blinder, *Choosing Lovers*, (Macomb, Ill.: Glenbridge, 1989).

CHAPTER 8

1. Mavis Tsai and Nathanial Wagner, "Women Who Were Sexually Molested as Children," *Medical Aspects of Human Sexuality* 12 (August 1979):55–56; and Joseph Briere and Martin Runtz, "Symtomatology Associated with Childhood Sexual Victimization in a Non-Clinical Adult Sample," *Child Abuse and Neglect* 1988, vol. 12, no. 1, pp. 51–59.

2. Marion A. Cuddy and Kathryn Belicki, "Nightmare Frequency and Related Sleep Disturbance as Indicators of a History of Sexual Abuse," *Dreaming*, vol. 2, no. 1, 1992, pp. 15–22.

3. Susan Rachael Brown, *The Dreams of Women Molested as Children*, doctoral dissertation, The Wright Institute, 1988. Order number DA 8904699, Dissertation Abstracts International, vol. 49, no. 12, June 1989.

4. Johanna King, personal communication.

5. Jill Blake-White and Christine Madeline Kline, "Treating the Dissociative Process in Adult Victims of Childhood Incest," *Social Casework: The Journal of Contemporary Social Work*, September 1985, pp. 394–402.

6. William H. Masters, Virginia E. Johnson, and Robert Kolodny, *Human Sexuality*, 4th ed. (New York: HarperCollins, 1992), p. 462.

7. Ibid.

8. James W. Pennebaker and Joan R. Susman, "Disclosure of Traumas and Psychosomatic Processes," *Social Science Medicine*, vol. 26, no. 3, (1988), pp. 327–32.

9. Ibid.

10. James W. Pennebaker, "Confession, Inhibition, and Disease," in *Advances in Experimental Social Psychology*, vol. 22 (New York: Academic Press, 1989), pp. 222–23.

11. Ibid., p. 229.

12. Elaine Westerlund, "Freud on Sexual Trauma: An Historical Re-

view of Seduction and Betrayal," *Psychology of Women Quarterly* 10 (1986), pp. 297–310.

13. For example, I worked with a bulimic patient who dreamt of vomiting and offered descriptions and bridges to rageful feelings of disgust that her father might have abused her. Another paired bulimic and incestual images in her dreams. Both were using their dreams to look at the link between their incest and their bulimia. A nonbulimic patient, or one who had not been abused, could use similar images in different dream contexts and surround them with different feelings. See also: Harold L. Levitan, "Implications of Certain Dreams Reported by Patients in a Bulimic Phase of Anorexia Nervosa" *Canadian Journal of Psychiatry*, vol. 26, June 1981, pp. 228–31.

14. Johanna King and Jacqueline Sheehan, "Dreamwork: A Therapeutic Modality for the Treatment of Incest Survivors," workshop presented at the Organization of Counseling Center Directors in Higher Education, 1991. (Unpublished).

CHAPTER 10

1. William H. Masters, Virginia E. Johnson, and Robert C. Kolodny, *Human Sexuality*, 4th ed. (New York: HarperCollins, 1992), pp. 8–12.

2. James Hillman, "On Psychological Creativity," in *The Myth of Analysis* (Evanston, Ill.: Northwestern University Press, 1972), p. 65.

3. John Beebe, San Francisco analyst, editor of *The Jung Library Journal*, coeditor of *The Journal of Analytical Psychology*, and author of *Integrity and Depth* (College Station, Texas: Texas A & M University Press, 1992); personal communication. For an interesting discussion of the relation of sexuality to creativity that is beyond the scope of this chapter, see: David W. Allen, *The Fear of Looking* (Charlottesville: University of Virginia Press, 1974), chapter 6, "Some Comments on Scopophilia and Exhibitionism in Creativity."

4. Benjamin, *The Bonds of Love*, p. 89.

5. Russell Eisenman, "Sexual Behavior as Related to Sex Fantasies and Experimental Manipulation of Authoritarianism and Creativity," *Journal of Personality and Social Psychology* (1982), vol. 43, no. 4, pp. 853–60.

6. Psychotherapists have noted that certain illnesses, such as depression, can short-circuit both creativity and sexuality. Some therapists believe that certain childhood sexual traumas can lead to forms of sublimation and transformation of emotional pain and frustration that re-

sult in increased creative drives. In this chapter, however, I would like to keep our focus on the less often discussed, broader range of sexuality and creativity that does not emphasize the roles of sexual and creative disorders.

7. Roy Dreistadt, "An Analysis of How Dreams Are Used in Creative Behavior," *Psychology*, vol. 8, no. 1, February 1971, pp. 24–50; and Delaney, *Living Your Dreams*, pp. 139–55.

8. Ingrid Sladeczek and George Domino, "Creativity, Sleep, and Primary Process Thinking in Dreams," *Journal of Creative Behavior* (1985), vol. 19 (1), pp. 38–46.

CHAPTER 11

1. Sam Keen, *The Passionate Life: Stages of Loving* (San Francisco: Harper & Row, 1983), pp. 45–46.

2. Plato, *Symposium* 211, 212.

3. Sigmund Freud wrote briefly about the seeking of happiness through the enjoyment of beauty, which "produces a particular, mildly intoxicating kind of sensation." He noted that although civilization could not do without it, there is no evident use or necessity for it. He wrote that the science of aesthetics was unable to give an explanation of the nature or origin of beauty, and that "Unfortunately, psychoanalysis, too has less to say about beauty than about most things. Its derivation from the realms of sexual sensation is all that seems certain; the love of beauty is a perfect example of a feeling with an inhibited aim. Beauty and attraction are first of all the attributes of a sexual object" (Sigmund Freud, Civilization and Its Discontents, in *Great Books of the Western World*, ed. Robert M. Hutchins, vol. 54, [Chicago: Encyclopedia Britannica, 1952], p. 775).

APPENDIX ONE

1. Calvin S. Hall, G. William Domhoff, Kenneth A. Blick, and Kathryn E. Weesner, "The Dreams of College Men and Women in 1950 and 1980: A Comparison of Dream Content and Sex Differences," *Sleep*, 5(2): 188–94.

2. Milton Kramer, Lois Kinney, and Martin Scharf, "Sex Differences in Dreams," *The Psychiatric Journal of the University of Ottawa*, vol. 8, no. 1, March 1983, pp. 1–4.

3. Bill Domhoff, "Home Dreams Versus Laboratory Dreams," in

Dream Psychology and the New Biology of Dreaming, ed. Milton Kramer (Springfield Ill.: Charles C. Thomas, 1969).

4. Monique Lortie-Lussier, Christine Schwab, and Joseph De Konick, "Working Mothers Versus Homemakers: Do Dreams Reflect the Changing Roles of Women?" *Sex Roles* (1985) vol. 12, nos. 9/10, pp. 1009–1021.

5. If we really want to know what affects the frequency, quality, and other aspects of sexual dreaming, we will have to conduct studies that include talking to the dreamers about their dream feelings and descriptions, rather than depending solely on written dream reports. Studies such as Paul R. Robbins and Roland H. Tanck, "Sexual Gratification and Sexual Symbolism in Dreams," *Bulletin of the Menninger Clinic,* January 1980, vol. 44 (1), pp. 49–58, define as sexual any clearly elongated object, such as tree trunks, neckties, and overcoats, or containers such as boxes, ovens, ships, or tables. Steps, escalators, walking up or down, climbing, or being run over were interpreted as representations of the sexual act. Today, it would be difficult, if not impossible, to persuade many nonpsychoanalytically oriented researchers that such interpretations would likely be warranted in the majority of cases. The sexual definition of any dream image that is not manifestly sexual must be reconsidered in the light of modern thought on dreaming interpretation, and preferably in light of the dreamer's descriptions and bridges.

6. Paul R. Robbins, Roland H. Tanck, and Farzaneh Houshi, "Anxiety and Dream Symbolism," *Journal of Personality,* (March 1985), 53:1, pp. 17–22.

7. Stanislaw Dulko, "Sexual Activity and Temperament in Polish Transsexuals," *Archives of Sexual Behavior* (1989), vol. 17, no. 2, pp. 163–71.

RESOURCES

RECOMMENDED BOOKS, TAPES, AND RESOURCE CENTERS

Resources for Dream Study and Consultation

The Delaney & Flowers Dream and Consultation Center
337 Spruce Street, San Francisco, CA 94118
(telephone: 415-587-3424)

Loma Flowers, M.D., and I founded our center in 1981 to train people in problem solving and the development of new ideas through the practical understanding of dreams. In addition to private individual and pair consultations for dream work and psychotherapy, we conduct programs to teach proficiency in dream incubation and dream interpretation for work alone or with the dreams of others.

Our classes and programs are designed for individuals and groups at beginner through professional levels, and are taught both in San Francisco and around the world in English, French, and Italian. Brief intensive programs lasting from a few days to several months are offered to out-of-town and foreign students at all levels throughout the year. Some individual consultation and training sessions, as well as some supervision sessions, can be conducted by telephone.

Both amateurs and professionals may enter our Diploma Program, which trains and certifies students who want to gain a high level of skill in working with the Dream Interview method of interpretation. Send us a double stamped, self-addressed envelope if you would like to receive our program brochures.

The Association for the Study of Dreams
P.O. Box 1600, Vienna VA 22183

Founded in 1982, ASD is the first international association of its kind to provide a forum to amateurs and professionals for the interdisciplinary study of sleep and dreams. Membership is open to all and provides a quality journal, a quarterly newsletter, and discounted registration to annual five-day conferences. Dr. Loma K. Flowers was the first chairman of the board, and Dr. Gayle Delaney is the founding president of the association. Please send a self-addressed, stamped envelope to receive more information.

Dream Tools Kit and Audiocassettes: The Dream Companion
To order call: 1-800-DREAMS-1

I have created *The Dream Companion: A Tool Kit for Dream Interpreters* to provide you with immediate practical and specific instructions on what to say and do when you are actually working with a dream of your own or with a friend's dream. *The Companion* has audiocassette instruction on how to work with dreams, discussions on a variety of special dream topics, and guidelines on how to use the other tools in the kit. The tools include nightly, weekly, and monthly dream analysis sheets, as well as quarterly and annual dream review guides that will help you spot important patterns in your dreams and in your waking life. Most importantly, *The Companion* gives you actual cue cards that you can hold in your hands as you work with a dream. Dream image cards list the basic questions you need to ask about a given dream element (there are cards for people, animals, settings, actions, etc.). Other cards list the key interview questions for common dreams, and others describe the basic steps of the interview procedure. Having these cards at hand while working alone or with a dream partner has made it much easier and quicker for my students to interpret their dreams. To order *The Dream Companion* call 1-800-DREAMS-1 and please write me at the Dream Center with any comments you have on the kit after you have used it for awhile. Your feedback will help me make this the most efficient and powerful dream tool possible.

Videotape: Bring Me a Dream

Drs. Flowers and Delaney discuss and demonstrate the interpretation and incubation of dreams for specific problem solving. For more information write the Delaney & Flowers Dream Center.

Recommended Books on Dreaming

ANTROBUS, JOHN S., ARKIN, ARTHUR M.; and ELLMAN, STEVEN J., eds. *The Mind in Sleep: Psychology and Psychophysiology.* Hillsdale, N.J.: Lawrence Erlbaum Associates, Publishers, 1978.

BONIME, WALTER. *The Clinical Use of Dreams.* New York: Da Capo Press, 1982.

CARTWRIGHT, ROSALIND DYMOND. *A Primer on Sleep and Dreaming.* Reading, Mass.: Addison-Wesley Publishing Company, 1978.

CARTWRIGHT, ROSALIND DYMOND, and LYNNE LAMBERG. *Crisis and Dreaming: Using Your Dreams to Solve Your Problems.* New York: HarperCollins, 1992.

DELANEY, GAYLE. *New Directions in Dream Interpretation.* Albany, N.Y.: State University of New York Press, 1993.

———. *Breakthrough Dreaming: How to Tap the Power of Your 24-Hour Mind.* New York: Bantam Books, 1991.

———. *Living Your Dreams.* New York: HarperCollins, Publishers, Inc., 1988.

GARFIELD, PATRICIA. *Pathway to Ecstasy: The Way of the Dream Mandala.* New York: Holt Reinhart and Winston, 1979.

HARARY, KEITH, and WEINTRAUB, PAMELA. *Lucid Dreams in 30 Days.* New York: St. Martin's Paperbacks, 1991.

HARTMANN, ERNEST. *The Nightmare: The Psychology and Biology of Terrifying Dreams.* New York: Basic Books, Inc., 1984.

HOBSON, J. ALLAN. *The Dreaming Brain.* New York: Basic Books, Inc., Publishers, 1988.

HUNT, HARRY T. *The Multiplicity of Dreams: Memory, Imagination and Consciousness.* New Haven, Conn.: Yale University Press, 1989.

KRIPPNER, STANLEY, ed. *Dreamtime and Dreamwork: Decoding the Language of the Night.* Los Angeles, Calif.: Jeremy P. Tarcher, Inc., 1990.

KRIPPNER, STANLEY, and DILLARD, JOSEPH. *Dreamworking: How to*

Use Your Dreams for Creative Problem-Solving. Buffalo, N.Y.: Bearly Limited, 1988.

MAYBRUCK, PATRICIA. *Romantic Dreams: How to Enhance Your Romantic Relationship by Understanding and Sharing Your Dreams.* New York: Pocket Books, 1991.

MOORCROFT, WILLIAM H. *Sleep, Dreaming, and Sleep Disorders.* New York: University Press of America, 1989.

MOFFITT, ALAN; DRAMER, MILTON; and HOFFMAN, ROBERT. *The Functions of Dreaming.* Albany, N.Y.: State University of New York Press, 1993.

NATTERSON, JOSEPH M., ed. *The Dream in Clinical Practice.* New York: Jason Aronson, Inc., 1980.

ULLMAN, MONTAGUE, AND ZIMMERMAN, NAN. *Working with Dreams.* New York: Delacorte Press, 1979.

Recommended Books on Relationships

BEATTIE, MELODY. *Codependent No More: How to Stop Controlling Others and Start Caring for Yourself.* New York: Harper & Row, Publishers, Inc., 1987.

BENJAMIN, JESSICA. *The Bonds of Love: Psychoanalysis, Feminism, and the Problem of Domination.* New York: Pantheon Books, 1988.

BLINDER, MARTIN, with Lynch, Carmen. *Choosing Lovers: Patterns of Romance: How You Select Partners in Intimacy, the Ways you Connect and Why You Break Apart.* Macomb, Ill.: Glenbridge Publishing Ltd., 1989.

COWAN, CONNELL, and KINDER, MELVYN. *Smart Women Foolish Choices: Finding the Right Men, Avoiding the Wrong Ones.* New York: Penguin Books USA Inc., 1985.

DELIS, DEAN C. *The Passion Paradox: Patterns of Love and Power in Intimate Relationships.* New York: Bantam Books, 1990.

FORWARD, SUSAN. *Men Who Hate Women and the Women Who Love Them: When Loving Hurts and You Don't Know Why.* New York: Bantam Books, 1986.

GILLIGAN, CAROL. *In a Different Voice: Psychological Theory and Women's Development.* Cambridge, Mass.: Harvard University Press, 1982.

HENDRICKS, GAY, and HENDRICKS, KATHLYN, Ph.D. *Conscious Lov-*

ing: The Journey to Co-Commitment. New York: Bantam Doubleday Dell Publishing Group, Inc., 1992.

HENDRIX, HARVILLE. *Getting the Love You Want: A Guide for Couples.* New York: Henry Holt and Company, Inc., 1988.

KAPLAN, LOUISE J. *Female Perversions: The Temptations of Emma Bovary.* New York: Bantam Doubleday Dell Publishing Group, Inc., 1991.

LAZARRE, JANE. *On Loving Men.* New York: Dial Press, 1980.

PAGLIA, CAMILLE. *Sexual Personae: Art and Decadence from Nefertiti to Emily Dickinson.* New Haven, Conn.: Yale University Press, 1990.

TANNEN, DEBORAH. *You Just Don't Understand.* New York: Morrow, 1990.

SCARF, MAGGIE. *Intimate Partners: Patterns in Love and Marriage.* New York: Random House, Inc., 1987.

Recommended Books on Sexuality

BARBACH, LONNIE. *For Yourself: The Fulfillment of Female Sexuality.* New York: Doubleday, 1975.

———, ed. *Erotic Interludes.* New York: Harper & Row, 1987.

———. *For Each Other: Sharing Sexual Intimacy.* New York: Penguin Books USA Inc., 1982.

———, and LEVINE, LINDA. *Shared Intimacies: Women's Sexual Experiences.* New York: Bantam Books, 1980.

CAFARO, DINO. *Sesso 2000: Il comportamento sessuale degli Italiani alle soglie del XXI secolo [Sex in the Year 2000: The Sexual Behavior of Italians on the Eve of the Twenty-first Century].* Rome: Editioni ASPER, 1992.

CARTER, STEVEN, and SOKOL, JULIA. *What Really Happens in Bed.* New York: Bantam Doubleday Dell Publishing Group, Inc., 1989.

HARARY, KEITH, and WEINTRAUB, PAMELA. *Inner Sex: The Erotic Fulfillment Program.* New York: St. Martin's Paperbacks, 1991.

MASTERTON, GRAHAM. *More Ways to Drive Your Man Wild in Bed.* New York: Penguin Books USA Inc., 1985.

———. *How to Drive Your Woman Wild in Bed.* New York: Penguin Books, 1987

REINISCH, JUNE M., with Beasley, Ruth. *The Kinsey Institute New Re-*

port on Sex: What You Must Know to Be Sexually Literate, edited by Debra Kent. New York: St. Martin's Press, 1990.

ST. CLARE, OLIVIA. *203 Ways to Drive a Man Wild in Bed.* New York: Harmony Books, 1993.

TANNAHILL, REAY. *Sex in History.* New York: Reay Tannahill, 1980.

WESTHEIMER, RUTH. *Dr. Ruth's Guide to Good Sex.* New York: Crown, 1986.

———. *The Art of Arousal.* New York: Abbeville, 1993.

Resources for Sexual Education and Sex Therapy

American Association of Sex Educators, Counselors, and Therapists (AASECT will provide the general public with a listing of sex educators, counselors, and therapists in their geographic area.)
435 North Michigan Street, Suite 1717, Chicago, IL 60611–4067
(telephone: 312-644-0828)

The Masters & Johnson Institute
24 South Kingshighway, St. Louis, MO 63108
(telephone: 314-361-2377)

The Kinsey Institute
313 Morrison Hall, Indiana University, Bloomington, IN 47405
(telephone: 812-855-7686)

National Self-Help Clearinghouse
33 West 42nd Street, New York, NY 10036
(telephone: 212-840-1259)

Videotapes on Sexuality

The Sexuality Library Catologue
1210 Valencia Street, San Francisco, CA 94110
(telephone: 415-550-7399, fax: 415-550-8495)

The Better Sex Video Series
The Townsend Institute, Dept. ZPB23
P.O. Box 5310, Lighthouse Point, FL 33074
(telephone: 800-888-1900)

Recommended Journals on Sexuality

Archives of Sexual Behavior
Plenum Publishing Company
233 Spring Street, New York, NY 10013

Journal of Sex Education & Therapy
435 North Michigan Avenue, Suite 1717, Chicago, IL 60611

Journal of Sex & Marital Therapy
Brunner/Mazel, Inc.
19 Union Square West, New York, NY 10002

Siecus Report
130 West 42nd Street, Suite 2500, New York, NY 10036

Resources for Recovery from Sexual Abuse

Adults Molested As Children United
P.O. Box 592, San Jose, CA 95108
(telephone: 408-280-5055)

Adult Survivors of Incest Program
2306 Taraval, Suite 102, San Francisco, CA 94116
(telephone: 415-661-8738)

Incest Survivors Anonymous
P.O. Box 5613, Long Beach, CA 90805
(telephone: 213-428-5599)

National Center on Child Abuse and Neglect
P.O. Box 1182, Washington, DC 20013
(telephone: 202-245-2858)

National Child Abuse Hotline (referral service)
(telephone: 800-422-4453)

National Resource Center on Child Sexual Abuse
106 Lincoln Street, Huntsville, AL 35801
(telephone: 800-543-7006)

Survivors of Incest Anonymous
P.O. Box 21817, Baltimore, MD 21222
(telephone: 410-433-2365)

Sex and Love Addicts Anonymous
P.O. Box 119, New Town Branch, Boston, MA 02258
(telephone: 617-332-1845)

Sex Addicts Anonymous
P.O. Box 3038, Minneapolis, MN 55403
(telephone: 612-871-1520

Scott Nelson
Workshops for Men Whose Partners Were Sexually Abused
Workshops for Couples in the Aftermath of Sexual Abuse
163 East Blithedale Avenue, Mill Valley, CA 94941
(telephone: 415-383-9254)

Voices in Action, Inc.
P.O. Box 148309, Chicago, IL 60614
(telephone: 312-327-1500)

Recommended Books on Abuse

ADAMS, CAREN, and FAY, JENNIFER. *No More Secrets: Protecting Your Child from Sexual Assault.* San Luis Obispo, Calif.: Impact Publishers, 1981.

ADAMS, CAREN; FAY, JENNIFER; and LOREEN-MARTIN, JAN. *No Is Not Enough: Helping Teenagers Avoid Sexual Assault.* San Luis Obispo, Calif.: Impact Publishers, 1984.

ADAMS, KENNETH M. *Silently Seduced: When Parents Make Their Children Partners, Understanding Covert Incest.* Deer Field Beach, Fla.: Health Communications, Inc., 1988.

BALDWIN, MARTHA. *Beyond Victim: You Can Overcome Childhood Abuse—Even Sexual Abuse.* Moore Haven, Fla.: Rainbow Books, 1988.

BASS, ELLEN, and DAVIS, LAURA. *The Courage to Heal: A Guide for Women Survivors of Child Sexual Abuse.* New York: Harper & Row, 1988.

BLUME, SUE E. *Secret Survivors.* New York: Wiley, 1989.

BRADSHAW, JOHN. *Healing the Shame that Binds.* Deer Field Beach, Fla.: Health Communications, Inc., 1988.

ENGEL, BEVERLY. *The Right to Innocence: Healing the Trauma of Childhood Sexual Abuse.* Los Angeles, Calif.: J. P. Tarcher, 1989.

FORWARD, SUSAN. *Toxic Parents.* New York: Bantam Books, 1989.

GANNON, PATRICK. *Soul Survivors: A New Beginning for Adults Abused as Children.* New York: Prentice-Hall, 1989.

LEW, MIKE. *Victims No Longer: Men Recovering from Incest and Other Sexual Child Abuse.* New York: Nevraumont Publishing, 1988.

MILLER, ALICE. *Thou Shalt Not Be Aware: Society's Betrayal of the Child.* New York: Penguin Books USA Inc., 1984.

————. *Breaking Down the Wall of Silence: The Liberating Experience of Facing Painful Truth.* New York: Dutton, 1991.

REIT, SEYMOUR. *Sibling Rivalry.* New York: Ballantine, 1988.

RUTTER, PETER. *Sex in the Forbidden Zone: When Men in Power— Therapists, Doctors, Clergy, Teachers, and Others—Betray Women's Trust.* Los Angeles, Calif.: Jeremy P. Tarcher, Inc., 1989.

A Newsletter on Abuse Issues

The Healing Woman
Edited by Margot Silk Forrest
P.O. Box 3038, Moss Beach, CA 94038
(telephone: 415-728-0339)

Audiotapes on Sexual Abuse

Bradshaw Cassettes
(a three-tape series on incest and sexual addiction)
P.O. Box 980547, Houston, TX 77098

Recovery Programs for Co-dependency, Alcoholism, etc.

Adult Children of Alcoholics World Service Organization
2522 West Sepulveda Boulevard, Suite 200, Torrance, CA 90505
(telephone: 213-534-1815)

Alanon Family Group Headquarters
P.O. Box 862, Midtown Station, New York, NY 10018
(telephone: 212-302-7240)

Alcoholics Anonymous General Service Office
P.O. Box 459, Grand Central Station, New York, NY 10163
(telephone: 212-686-1100)

Resources for Information on Safer Sex

Center for Disease Control (national)
(telephone: 800-342-AIDS)

San Francisco AIDS Foundation
P.O. Box 6182, San Francisco, CA 94101-6182
(telephone: 415-863-AIDS)

National AIDS Hotline
(telephone: 800-342-AIDS)

National AIDS Information Clearinghouse
(telephone: 800-458-5231)

Northern California AIDS Information
(telephone: 800-FOR-AIDS)

STD (Sexually Transmitted Diseases) National Hotline
(telephone: 800-227-8922)

INDEX

ABOUT THE AUTHOR

DR. GAYLE DELANEY was educated at Princeton and earned her doctorate in clinical psychology from Union Graduate School in Cincinnati, Ohio. She is currently the director of the Delaney and Flowers Dream and Consultation Center. She is the author of *The Hidden Language of Dreams, Living Your Dreams,* and *Breakthrough Dreaming,* and she contributes regularly to psychology and health magazines. Dr. Delaney lives in San Francisco.